Elegant New York

BY JOHN TAURANAC
PHOTOGRAPHED
BY CHRISTOPHER LITTLE

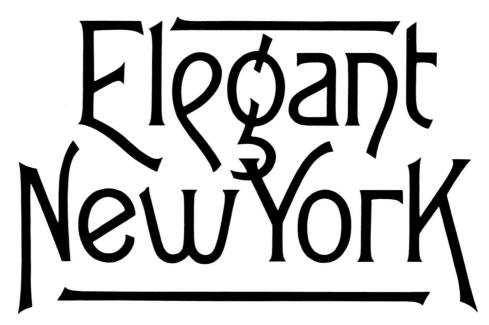

Elegant New York

THE BUILDERS
AND THE BUILDINGS
1885-1915

ABBEVILLE PRESS · PUBLISHERS
NEW YORK · LONDON · PARIS

For Jane

Editor: Walton Rawls
Art Director: James Wageman
Designer: Amy Lamb
Copyeditor: Don Goddard
Production Manager: Dana Cole
Production Editor: Robin James

Frontispiece:
For the front of the United States Custom House, sculptor Daniel Chester French created the statue of *America* with the face of the idealized American woman—neo-classical in her Greco-Roman features, slightly wistful but far-seeing, gentle though definitely unapproachable.

Library of Congress Cataloging-in-Publication Data

Tauranac, John, 1939–
  Elegant New York.

  Bibliography: p.
  Includes index.
    1. Eclecticism in architecture—New York (N.Y.)
2. Architecture, Victorian—New York (N.Y.)   3. Architecture, Edwardian—New York (N.Y.)   4. New York (N.Y.)—Buildings, structures, etc.   I. Little, Christopher.   II. Title
NA735.N5T38   1985   720'.9747'1   85-15728
ISBN 0-89659-458-0

First edition
10 9 8 7 6 5 4 3 2

Contents

Introduction

The money that created America's Age of Elegance, which only lasted from the 1880s until the coming of World War I, flowed from the Industrial Revolution and belonged to the new industrial aristocracy. It was a time of great family fortunes and of consumption that was on a grand scale and as conspicuous as possible. The few who had it unabashedly flaunted it, and one of the great places to flaunt it was New York City.

The period's architects and their clients were responsible for the city's first great wave of residential, cultural, corporate, and municipal palaces, and they laid the groundwork for the modern city that we know today. The age needed trained architects, and by the 1880s, the Massachusetts Institute of Technology and Columbia College were producing them. At the same time, the influence of the Ecole des Beaux-Arts in Paris was becoming widespread. A rebirth of grandiose academic classicism resulted in the "American Renaissance," which manifested itself in neo-Italian Renaissance palazzi and neo-Loire Valley chateaux, while adherents of the City Beautiful Movement saw to it that neoclassical statuary dotted the cityscape. During the period, new building techniques were making skyscrapers possible and ideas on city planning were being translated into zoning laws whose influence is still being felt.

Much of the city was built, directly or indirectly, by the same tightly knit power elite that was shaping and building the nation's wealth. Morgan, Vanderbilt, Astor, Carnegie, and Pulitzer are names that appear time and again. Less known but nonetheless important are the names of many businessmen who succeeded, like the Fuller Company's Harry S. Black; and even some who failed, like Peter Banner, who went bankrupt before he could finish his dream apartment house.

It was an era when nothing came cheap, and complaints about the cost of living were as loud then as they are now. At the turn of the twentieth century, when the average unskilled laborer was earning $460 a year, or less than nine dollars a week, a four-room tenement apartment in an immigrant neighborhood rented for fifteen dollars a month. The city was said to be no place to live for the "average" worker who was trying to support a family on $1,000 to $3,000 a year. Monthly rents for a small, middle-class apartment in a decent but unfashionable neighborhood hovered around $600 a year for a four-room apartment. The rents at the first-class Belnord Apartments on

Broadway at 86th Street began at $2,100 a year, or about $175 a month. To many New Yorkers who did not consider themselves poor but who nevertheless believed that they should be able to afford sunlight, comfort, and tasteful surroundings with a modicum of luxury, those rents were a staggeringly high price to pay. Ominous predictions were made that there would soon be few New Yorkers who could afford to live anywhere in the city except the very rich—and even they complained. After all, William H. Vanderbilt had only paid $400,000 for a whole Fifth Avenue blockfront between 51st and 52nd streets in 1879, and thirty years later that sum might only buy a few lots on Upper Fifth.

The definition of money and what it could buy was in a state of flux. A millionaire was no longer viewed as someone who had a million dollars but someone whose annual income was a million dollars. Even some houses were built on speculation for half a million dollars. Mrs. Mary J. Kingsland, for instance, bought the building at 1026 Fifth Avenue in 1906 for $510,000, the highest price ever paid for a speculatively built house in the history of the city. A few months later, George C. Clark paid $540,000 for the neighboring six-story, forty foot-wide, white marble townhouse at 1027 Fifth. If the purchasers' names mean little today,

they meant equally little then. A generation before, as the *New York Times* commented, there was probably only one house in the city that had cost so much, and that belonged to department store magnate A. T. Stewart. "Whoever could have afforded such a dwelling must have been one of the half dozen richest men in New York," said the newspaper. "He would have been so conspicuously rich that everybody would have known about his fortune, and how it was acquired," and the *Times* marveled that these two presumable multi-millionaires were not even known to the general reader before they appeared in connection with the sales. A British visitor observed that "to live in New York," meaning Manhattan, "it is well to take the precaution of being a millionaire."

Millionaires, aspirant millionaires, and speculators built a city that still largely survives, despite all that has happened since the Age of Elegance. Some buildings are gone because they outlived their usefulness, others because of the very real-estate values they helped to create. Some of what remains is the subject of this book, with each chapter constructed around neighborhoods and begun with either a building that has been torn down or otherwise mutilated or with a building that was planned but never built at all.

1. *Architect Ernest Flagg held up his Beaux-Arts design for the Singer Building as a model for showing that a big building could be a good neighbor. Few speculators were willing to build freestanding towers at a sacrifice of rental space.*

1

Corporate New York

T he businessmen's stronghold at the turn of the century was Lower Manhattan, where by 1908 there was factory space for 237,000 workers and office space for another 130,000. Only one percent of the land was undeveloped, and that, no doubt, was the glint in a speculator's eye. This great concentration of commerce could not have taken place without the advent of the technological advances that resulted in skyscrapers, which, constructed with steel rather than iron frames, rose higher than had ever been dreamed.

To build the average fifteen-story skyscraper on a 50-by-100-foot plot required about 4,000 barrels of cement, 1,250,000 bricks, and 1,000 tons of steel. The construction of the biggest buildings required as many as 1,400 workers, with scores of bosses. Besides the architect, there were engineers for weights, wind pressures, and superstructures, for brickwork, terra cotta, and plumbing. The Architectural League of New York considered skyscrapers an expression of genius in American architecture, a brilliant solution to highly complex conditions achieved with consummate rationality and individuality.

Skyscrapers were erected as corporate headquarters or as speculative ventures. Sites were expensive to acquire and skyscrapers expensive to build, so financiers, syndicates, and mortgagers were usually involved. But expense did not slow down the pace of new construction in Lower Manhattan. In the spring of 1906, for instance, plans were consummated for the construction of fifteen tall office buildings, which would add about 2,500,000 square feet to the real-estate market. The face of the city was changing so rapidly that there was little pattern to it, with a great tower here and another there, each usurping the light and air of its neighbor.

The question arose as to whether some voluntary plan could be worked out or whether legislation would be required to limit the height of buildings so that they would not crowd one another out. Architect Francis H. Kimball believed that only under a despot with the imperial authority of a Napoleon III could all buildings be harmonized in design and height. In any case, decisions about design and height were not the architect's to make but the property owner's, and many of them simply could not afford to build skyscrapers. Since New York land values were based on the potential of vertical spaces, the idea of limiting the height of buildings also produced some understandable objections. Architect Ernest Flagg pointed out that to set a low limit would not only greatly reduce available floor space for the future and interfere with the city's growth, it would also bring about a shrinkage of values. A limit would also discriminate unjustly against owners who had not already built in favor of those who had.

It was Flagg who determined that something had to be done, and in 1908 he set down the basis for the city's first zoning law, which was to be enacted in 1916. He imagined a city of towers rising from setbacks, with the base of a building no taller than one-and-a-half times the width of the street it faced. On one quarter of the plot, the developer would be allowed to build a tower as high as he wanted, provided the tower was set back from the building line and that all sides were treated architecturally. Neighboring property owners could sell their rights to adjoining towers, so light and air were protected or compensated. As a bonus, the street wall would assume the appearance of order and sobriety that comes with a uniform height and a continuous cornice line.

Flagg had graduated from the Ecole des Beaux-Arts in Paris, where the focus was on the classical elements and such disciplines as city planning. By 1907, he had designed two buildings for the Singer Sewing Machine Company. But before the second building was even finished, the company—realizing that, more than mere office space, corporate headquarters could also be a corporate symbol and provide free advertising for its products—announced that it was in the skyscraper game for all the marbles.

Large sites in the financial district were becoming increasingly difficult to assemble, but Singer had quietly expanded its site on the northwest corner of Broadway and Liberty Street until it owned a 133-foot frontage on Broadway as well as the neighboring Bourne Building on Liberty Street. The company's plan was to use the frames of the existing buildings, make them a uniform fourteen stories high, then erect a sixty-five-foot square tower with a facade of ornamental brick and limestone that would straddle the buildings from a set back and rise to a height of forty-seven stories. The Singer Tower building would rise 612 feet, 200 feet higher than the Park Row building, which was then the world's tallest. It would be second in height only to the Eiffel Tower. Its 412,820 square feet of floor space was the equivalent of 9.5 acres, or twenty-eight ordinary city blocks. And its announced cost was an unbelievably low $1.5 million—the lobby alone, with its bronze elevator doors and handrails and marble staircase and marble-clad piers and glass-domed vaults, seemed to have had that much lavished on it.

The building was a tourist attraction before the steelwork was thirty-seven stories high, and VIPs like Prince Wilhelm of Sweden were taken to the top to view the panorama. When comparisons were made to show the height or length of something, such as the *Lusitania*, for instance, it would often be stacked up against the Singer Building. But not all the press was good. The site was described as too

exiguous, and Singer was advised either to shorten the building or buy more land. Flagg was confident, however, that the building did not usurp the rights of others, since the tower 'depends on its own land for its light. It casts a shadow, to be sure, but it seriously interferes with the light of no surrounding property. It presents a finished facade to all points of view. It adds to the picturesqueness of the skyline of the city, and its bulk rises well back of the street facade." In short, it did the things that Flagg believed a skyscraper should do, and it set the standard around which the city should rally. "It is certain," said Flagg, "that the city cannot be built up solidly with high buildings of the kind we now have unless we are to live in darkness." And just as Kimball had pointed out, there would always be some high and some low buildings; it was the nature of things.

Chamber of Commerce, State of New York

65 Liberty Street, at Liberty Place
1902
BUILDER: The Chamber of Commerce of the State of New York
ARCHITECT: James B. Baker

The new building for the Chamber of Commerce was a case in point. The Chamber had been around since 1768, when the state was still a province and the city was perched on the edge of a wilderness. The Chamber's revolutionary goal was to wring from the British "such laws. . . . as may be found necessary for the benefit of trade in general." The founders were not seeking commercial hegemony, they just wanted trade with Pennsylvania.

By the end of the nineteenth century, New York was the nation's most powerful city, the "empire city," and the Chamber's goals were being realized in vast profits for its members, many of whom could trace their ancestry in the portraits on the Chamber's walls. John Jacob Astor IV could find his father, William Astor, and his father's father, William Backhouse Astor, and his grandfather's father and founder of the dynasty, the first John Jacob Astor. Likewise, Cornelius Vanderbilt II could find William H. Vanderbilt and Commodore Cornelius Vanderbilt.

In 1900, Morris K. Jessup, a retired banker and the president of the American Museum of Natural History, was the Chamber's president. The three vice-presidents were perhaps the city's wealthiest and most powerful individuals—J. Pierpont Morgan, John D. Rockefeller, and Andrew Carnegie. When the Chamber spoke as a body in resolution or protest, local and national functionaries listened.

The Chamber had occupied temporary offices in any number of merchants exchanges and office buildings, but

2

with no permanent roof over its head, it was New York's longest established floating power game. As early as 1865, Chamber President Abiel A. Low had tried to get a building commensurate with the organization's prestige. In 1897, President Alexander Orr was still at it, trying to raise $1 million for a new building (Orr's scheme included a banking room on the first floor whose rental would defray maintenance).

By 1900, the Chamber had received pledges totaling $960,000, and in December a news story leaked the imminent purchase of a 116-by-66-foot site on Pine Street for $300,000. A month later came the announcement that the Chamber had bought the plot on the northwest corner of Liberty Street and Liberty Place, with a 63-foot frontage and a 91-foot depth. Henry Morgenthau's Central Realty Bond & Trust Company had bought the property for $580,000, and was asking $750,000 for it, more than twice the price for about two-thirds the Pine Street plot. Morgenthau became a Chamber member at the same time and quickly learned that the Chamber's annual fifty-dollar dues were a good investment.

The Chamber's needs were modest—a few rooms for the offices, a library with writing desks, and an assembly hall that could accomodate large meetings and supply wall space to hang the great collection of portraits, which included works by Charles Willson Peale, Rembrandt Peale, Henry Inman, John Vanderlyn, and Asher B. Durand. But the members' needs were not modest. They spent nearly $1.5 million to create an appropriate symbol, a building that has all the trappings of a rich man's club, a Beaux-Arts extravaganza.

No steel girders were used. Instead, each marble stone from the quarries of Vermont's Senator Redfield Proctor was carefully cut and fitted as specified by architect James B. Baker. The banking room was trimmed with mahogany fittings and had a marble floor. The first-floor vestibule and

3

stairs for the Chamber's use were of Caen stone and marble. And the Great Hall on the second floor was indeed great. At 60 by 90 feet, it was spacious enough for the Chamber's regular meetings, and at 30 feet high, it provided enough wall space to hang the members' portraits. To cover the Great Hall's marble floor, W. & J. Sloane designed and furnished a hand-tufted Berlin rug that measured 38 by 60 feet and weighed 2,750 pounds. It was the largest rug ever imported, and required fifty men to move it. William Sloane, like architect Baker, had been a member since 1897.

To celebrate the opening of the new building in 1902, the Chamber held a banquet for 700 guests. Not even the Great Hall could accommodate the crowd, so the festivities were

2. Businessmen usually pointed with pride to the city's skyscrapers, but the Chamber of Commerce commissioned James Baker to build this lilliputian gem. In the Beaux-Arts tradition, statuary was an inherent part of the design, but the statues of DeWitt Clinton, Alexander Hamilton, and John Jay fell victim to decay.

3. Above the portraits of the city's burgher princes in the Chamber of Commerce's Great Hall is a back-lit glass ceiling set into neo-Renaissance plaster, each the perfect foil for the other and all splendid.

held at the Waldorf-Astoria. Seated with President Theodore Roosevelt were many notables, including Mayor Seth Low, son of the man who had first suggested a permanent home for the Chamber. The hit of the evening was a speech by Sir Albert Rollit, M. P., chairman of London's Chamber of Commerce and nicknamed the "Chauncey Depew of England." Rollit referred to the Chamber's previous home in the sixteen-story Mutual Life Insurance Building, the cast iron building the Chamber demolished to make way for its new home, and the fact that it had not moved to the Flatiron Building. "You have no longer a mansion in the skies. You have no iron flat or flat iron, but you have a beautiful building which recalls a startling change to my mind since I was last in New York 32 years ago. Then I had to go to the top of Trinity Church to see the tops of other buildings, and now I have to go on other buildings to see the top of Trinity." The new building was being lauded for its gentle scale in the midst of Lower Manhattan's Brobdingnagianism which, ironically, was one aspect of the city to which most business men pointed with pride.

The New York Stock Exchange

8 Broad Street, between Wall and Exchange Place
1903
BUILDER: The New York Stock Exchange
ARCHITECT: George B. Post

Looming large in the American consciousness is the New York Stock Exchange, for most of the world the symbol of fiercely competitive capitalism and great fortunes made and lost. The Exchange, which started in 1792, had occupied a T-shaped building on Broad Street since 1865, but by 1885, despite a recent enlargement, its 141-by-145-foot trading floor and the concomitant office space were not large enough.

The site of the Exchange was on one of the most highly esteemed and increasingly valuable blocks in the city. With very little hooplah, the Exchange made two important pur-

5

6

because it placed the Exchange in the role of a dowager of reduced circumstances forced to rent rooms, so architect George B. Post was asked to design a building for the exclusive use of the Exchange. It was to be a commercial palace in keeping with the prestige of the organization. Post gave it as many pretensions as a midblock site allowed, designing a neo-classical facade of Georgia Marble and filling the Broad Street facade with 52½-foot-high Corinthian columns, whose height made the building's proportions grander, statelier, less squat. Occupying the entire depth of the building was the 80-foot-high trading room, the "floor" where the bulls and bears could go at each other. The trading room's enormous windows were set behind the colonnade, with steel mullions supporting the panes of glass. To diffuse light, Post specified electrically operated vertical shades, and to keep out the chill, he specified double panes of glass in the windows and small heaters between them. Off the floor were lounging rooms, private consultation rooms, a barber shop, and baths, all served by a call system to be used when a broker's presence was required on the floor.

During construction, foundation contractor John F. O'Rourke encountered water at twelve feet and sand for another 38 feet before hitting bedrock. He did something, it was reported, that had never been done before. After sinking caissons, he built a continuous concrete dam around the site to keep out the water and sand that kept rising in the best Sisyphean manner as digging continued.

Opening day in 1903 saw the new New York Stock Exchange decorated with potted plants and cut flowers, with ladies invited to tour the usually all-male bastion. Speeches were given by Mayor Seth Low and Exchange President Rudolph Keppler, who had guided the construction of the building, and Trinity Church's Morgan Dix administered the consecration. Seated in the front row were banker J. Pierpont Morgan, financier Russell Sage, First National Bank President George F. Baker, Henry Morgenthau, president of the Central Realty Bond & Trust Company, and Morris K. Jessup, president of the Chamber of Commerce.

chases, buying the Union Building at 16-18 Broad Street for $85,000, or $212 a square foot in 1898, and the Swan Building at 8 Broad Street for $425,000 in 1899. Allowing for the irregularities of the plot, the price of the 29-by-100-foot Swan lot was $244 a square foot, almost $100 more a square foot than 20 Broad Street had sold for the year before. These prices had been exceeded only a few times in the upward spiral of downtown real estate, but the combined properties gave the exchange a 138-foot frontage on Broad Street and a 153-foot frontage on New Street, with the assemblage valued at $3.5 million.

The original plan was for an eight- or nine-story $1.5 million building, with the Exchange occupying the lower stories and renting out the upper floors to defray expenses. The scheme was judged unseemly, however,

4. Just as the pedimental figures in classical antiquity celebrated Greek ideals, those at the Stock Exchange celebrate the ideals of business. The heroes in J. Q. A. Ward and Paul W. Bartlett's *Integrity Protecting the Works of Man* are the workers, among whom is a pregnant fieldhand.

5. The heavily embellished neoclassical ceiling above the floor of the Stock Exchange is as grand as any in the city. The view is almost entirely obscured today by an unfortunate but necessary frame that supports electronic equipment.

6. The boardroom in the Stock Exchange has the appearance of a high court, a role it sometimes serves in the adjudication of internal business.

The United States Trust Company

37–43 Wall Street, between Broad and William Streets
1907
BUILDER: The Lands Purchase Company
ARCHITECT: Francis H. Kimball

William K. Aston was a speculator who patiently assembled properties and just as patiently waited until the time was ripe to sell them. In 1896, he bought the ten-story United States National Bank Building at 43 Wall Street for $805,000, which gave him a 31-foot frontage on Wall Street. It was just the toehold he wanted, since he already owned the property that abutted from Exchange Place, which made the entire plot Wall Street property with the added advantage of two fronts.

Land was becoming so valuable in the financial district that real-estate dealers were contending that a building of ordinary dimensions no longer paid, that the only way to get the money out of a property was to erect a tall building. The assumption in Aston's case was that a new building would be erected on Exchange Place to connect with the ten-story National Bank Building on Wall Street, but the tables were turned. Aston sold the entire site, with the Exchange Place property going to a corporation calling itself the Wall Street-Exchange Place Building Company, a hint of things to come. The new building of 1903 at 43 Exchange Place rose straight up for 26 stories, setting a new standard.

Three years later, plans for the Wall Street site that the *Tribune* said would "surpass in many respects anything yet seen in New York" were filed by architect Francis H. Kimball, whose client, the Lands Purchase Company, was controlled by the United States Trust Company. The Fuller Company, the construction firm that was fast becoming famous for the speed it built skyscrapers, erected the steel framing at the rate of about four stories a week. There was nothing higgledy-piggledy about the logistics. The parts were scheduled to arrive about 24 hours ahead of need; it was a matter of fitting them together according to mathematical nicety. A single error in delivery—a missing beam, a shortage of rivets—and the whole schedule for the 600 workers was thrown out of synchronization. Foundation work was to begin in August 1906, the steel work to be completed by the following January, and the brickwork by February, when the building would be ready for finishing. In October 1907, precisely on schedule and a bit more than a year after work began, the building inspector gave his okay. The 25-story building, with a heavily encrusted Beaux-Arts design in marble for the lower six floors and red brick with occasional marble trim for the rest, was 317 feet high and had risen on only a 61-foot frontage.

7

Aston knew that his purchase of the Wall Street site had established a new value for the assembled property, and the U.S. Trust Company took full advantage of it. The building was constructed back to back with the building on Exchange Place, and the floors were perfectly aligned, which gave credence to the name "Wall Street-Exchange" building. As the Wall Street building arose, the rear walls of the Exchange Place building were knocked through and the floors were connected to create rentable space of about 5,000 square feet per floor. A 25-story building had been built from street to street through the middle of the block.

7. According to speculators, land in the financial district was so valuable that the only way to realize a profit was to erect tall office buildings, even if it meant building them on narrow sites. In contrast with the hulking bulk of this twenty-five-story behemoth at 43 Wall Street, architect Francis Kimball designed one of the city's gentlest Beaux-Arts facades for the lower floors.

8

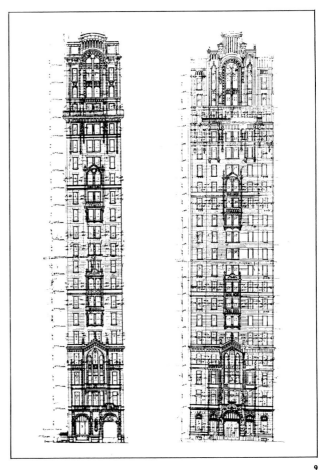

9

The Trinity and U.S. Realty Buildings

111 and 115 Broadway, at Thames Street
1905 and 1907
BUILDER: U.S. Realty Company
ARCHITECT: Francis H. Kimball

Harry S. Black, who took over the presidency of the George F. Fuller Construction Company upon the death of his father-in-law in 1900, dreamed of forming the largest real-estate company ever assembled. He already had Judge Samuel P. McConnell as his legal counsel, but he needed more power brokers, so he recruited a banker, James Stillman, president of First National City; a real-estate and trust manager, Henry Morgenthau, president of Central Realty and Trust Company; and a solid political connection, former Mayor Hugh J. Grant.

Considered ripe for development was the irregular piece of property where the five-story Trinity Building stood. The site had a 40-foot frontage on Broadway and extended 260 feet along Thames Street to Trinity Place. With Trinity

Churchyard to the south, the property was guaranteed light, while dark and narrow Thames Street to the north would provide air. On the block north stood the Boreel Building, which had a 101-foot frontage on Broadway and extended 145 feet west to Temple Street, which paralleled Broadway in those days. Black's goal was to buy all the property from Trinity Churchyard to Cedar Street between Broadway and Trinity Place and erect a pair of office buildings on equal sites. Since the sites were narrow, all offices would have outside exposures without having to resort to wasteful courtyards. It also meant closing Temple Street and shifting Thames Street.

8. In addition to 43 Wall Street, Kimball also designed the Trinity and U.S. Realty buildings, where he demonstrated how tall buildings could be constructed on narrow sites. The advantage here was that no office overlooked courts or airshafts.

9. The first plans for the Trinity and U.S. Realty buildings were neoclassical, but the U.S. Realty Company was struck by conscience and decided to design the buildings in harmony with their surroundings. The Gothic style was adopted in deference to neighboring Trinity Church.

Buying the major sites and working a deal with the city would have presented major financial and political hurdles for even the most practiced wheeler-dealer, but Black had a good start and some brute financial force on his side. In 1901, the Fuller Company bought the Boreel site for $2 million. A year later, the company bought the Trinity Building for $2.2 million.

In the meantime, the Fuller Company offered to donate to the city a nine-foot swath of property between Broadway and Trinity Place to allow Thames Street to be widened providing the city allowed the roadbed to be shifted, and the company offered what was described as a handsome settlement for Temple Street if the city would close it. The city acquiesced to the entire package, and Black's newly created U.S. Realty Company, with capitalization of about $60 million and the Fuller Company as a wholly owned subsidiary, was allowed to acquire a pair of 68-by-260-foot plots, sites that were big enough for a pair of 21-story office buildings.

Black would build on every inch of land and take the buildings about as high as they could technologically go. He estimated that about 70 percent of the aggregate area of the buildings' square footage could be rented, thanks to the inherently economical floor plans of the long narrow plots. At the market rate of three dollars a square foot, the annual rent rolls on the 495,000 square feet would come to about $1,485,000. With a total investment of about $12 million, Black would be in the black before taxes and maintenance in about nine years.

The preliminary designs were neoclassical, but the builders decided to follow the "community" plan and harmonize with the neo-Gothic of neighboring Trinity Church. Black did not skimp on construction. Light blue Indiana limestone was specified for all the facades except the Thames Street sides, which were faced in brick. The Broadway entrances were limestone and bronze, with vestibules of Siena marble. The main-floor corridors were a glittering array of marble, bronze, and gold leaf, enhanced by suffused artificial light and stained glass windows. To prevent the spread of fire from building to building across Thames Street, the facing windows were fitted with wire glass as well as copper sashes and frames. Interior fireproofing including hollow terra-cotta partitions and treated mahogany.

Typical of the Fuller Company, the construction went forward at a dizzying pace, and the whole job was finished within a year.

J. P. Morgan & Company

23 Wall Street, on the southeast corner of Broad
1913
BUILDER: J. P. Morgan & Company
ARCHITECTS: Trowbridge & Livingston

Harry S. Black's name might not have been synonymous with real estate, but J. Pierpont Morgan's certainly was with banking. And for good reason. Morgan was the bankers' banker, and his bank was not just any bank. It was instrumental in the formation of such giants as the United States Steel Corporation and the Northern Securities Company. If an individual had an account with J. P. Morgan & Company, the money was not there to pay household bills; the funds usually represented a surplus that was disposable for investing. The Morgan bank had about $200 million in deposit acccounts alone, and the bankers knew what was going on. The Pujo Committee's report on the "money trust" pointed out that of 341 directorships in corporations, no less than 72 were held by members of Morgan's firm in 1913.

After the Panic of 1907, however, Morgan himself began to weary of it all and to spend less time in New York tending to business and longer and longer periods in London or sailing the Mediterranean aboard his yacht. He remained interested, however, in acquiring the site on the southeast corner of Broad and Wall streets where his bank had stood since the days when it was Drexel, Morgan & Company. The Drexel corner at 23 Wall Street had set a New York City real-estate record when Philadelphia banker Anthony J. Drexel paid $348 a square foot for it in 1872, a price that was not topped until the sale of One Wall Street in 1905 at $559 a square foot. J. P. Morgan & Company

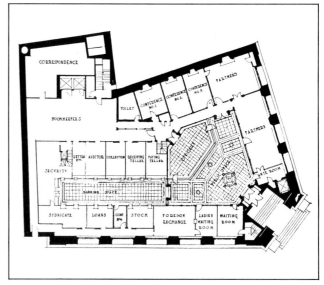

11

had occupied the Drexel site since the company's formation in 1894, but Morgan had never been able to tear down the old building and erect the kind of building that suited his personality. The Drexel estate spurned all offers and tenaciously hung onto the site. Then, in 1912, it inexplicably sold out to Morgan. The price was never revealed, but real-estate

10. The floor plan for J. P. Morgan's bank reveals a private staircase from the waiting room at the left of the entrance to Morgan's corner office on the second floor.

11. Banker Morgan had Trowbridge & Livingston design this diminutive building for his Wall Street site, Lower Manhattan's most highly valued corner. It was true to form for Morgan to want something small and fine.

analysts believed that Morgan only paid the assessed valuation of the property, or about $2.5 million for the 9,500 square feet. At $265 a square foot, he got a bargain. Bankers Trust had paid $675 a square foot for the site diagonally across the street in 1909, and Morgan's corner was more desirable.

Perhaps anticipating the sale of the Drexel plot, Morgan had taken an option on the 31st floor of the Bankers Trust Building in 1911. He stayed in this aerie high above the city during the time that the old Drexel Building was being torn down and his new building was rising.

The new building was typical Morgan. Real-estate dealers had assumed that a skyscraper had been planned for the site, but architects Trowbridge & Livingston were asked to design a four-story building, with the upper stories set back and barely visible from the curbline. The design was understated, just a little austere, and an act of conspicuous consumption on the grandest scale. The problem of the acute-angled corner was dextrously resolved by chamfering, an act that some might consider a profligate waste of high-priced real estate, but which can be understood by the client.

The simplicity of the interiors was determined by the nature of Morgan's business, which did not deal with ordinary deposits and withdrawals. The first floor, housing the banking hall, was column free. Offices with fixtures of standard sizes and interchangeable parts ringed the hall and were set off by a neoclassical screen of pink Knoxville marble, with bronze grilles and columns of Skyros marble. The coffered ceiling had a round skylight in the center of it, through which light flowed because the second floor was shaped like a square doughnut and hugged the periphery of the building. The second floor housed the officers' private offices, with Morgan's planned for the corner and linked to the first floor by a private staircase. The offices were all oak-paneled, with Chippendale furniture and Oriental carpets. The third and fourth floors housed corporate dining rooms and other more mundane functions, including the janitor's quarters. A roof garden was on the fourth floor setback. In the basement were the vaults. And that was about all. There was no Downing's Oyster House in the basement, no towering office building with rentals to help pay the upkeep and maintenance, nothing but a large banking hall and a few offices for one of the most highly regarded pieces of property in the city's highest rent district. Morgan died in 1913, before he saw his dream become reality, but the building that was in his mind's eye assured him that its quality was high enough to be linked with his name.

The Woolworth Building

233 Broadway, between Barclay and Park Place
1913
BUILDER: Frank W. Woolworth
ARCHITECT: Cass Gilbert

When Frank W. Woolworth came to New York City in 1886, his first bank account was so small that the Irving National Bank hesitated before taking it. Twenty-five years later, the success of his five-and-ten-cent stores had earned him a place on the bank's board. Unlike Morgan, who built a diminutive building for his headquarters, Woolworth imagined something enormous for his. He had admired the Gothic Revival Houses of Parliament, and he determined that he would build something like them.

After a Hardware Club lunch with Louis Pierson, the Irving Bank's president, Woolworth pointed to a plot on the southwest corner of Broadway and Park Place and mentioned that he was considering it as the future site for the Woolworth Company headquarters. He could justify the cost on the basis of advertising and public relations value to a certain extent, but he was too sensible to let his dreams get in the way of profits. First he wanted to make suitable arrangements for financing. Woolworth asked Pierson if the Irving Bank was interested in a limited venture that would create the Broadway-Park Place Corporation to buy the land and put up the building. Woolworth would provide the initial financing, but the bank would buy stock in the company until it owned the realty company completely. What evolved early in 1910 was the Broadway-Park Place Company, with assets of $1.5 million, two-thirds put up by

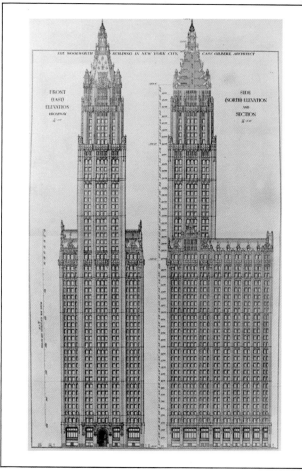

12

---

12. After several false starts, Frank W. Woolworth told architect Cass Gilbert to create a building that was taller than any other. Woolworth was not to be satisfied with just any design, and he returned one plan after another for refinement.

13. Although the Woolworth Building was finished three years before the 1916 zoning law mandated it, there was, nevertheless, a set-back tower with all four sides treated architecturally. Woolworth told Gilbert that he expected nothing less.

14

Woolworth, one-third by the bank. The bank would rent the entire second floor for a 25-year period and it would be able to nominate two of the five directors to the board, but the president would be Woolworth. Although the architectural details were not perfected, the general plans called for a 20-story building surmounted by a 10-story tower. In March, Woolworth paid almost $2 million for the five buildings on the southwest corner of Broadway and Park Place, and then he bought the two flanking buildings and announced that they would be retained as low structures to protect the light and air of the proposed building.

By November 1910, the Broadway–Park Place Company had changed its plans. Now the entire site would be cleared for a 45-story building that would be 625 feet high, thirteen feet higher than the Singer Building and second only to the reigning champion, the 700-foot Metropolitan Life Tower. The body of the proposed building was to rise 26 stories and be surmounted by a 19-story, 85-foot square tower rising from the building line. The style would be neo-Gothic, not the neo-Renaissance style of so many sky-

scrapers. The technology, of course, was indigenous to the new world in the twentieth century. The fixed locations of the steel frame established certain conditions that were not found in true Gothic buildings, but the lines were the vertical lines of Gothic architecture. "The economic conditions which call for the use of every bit of available space and at the same time provide ample light for rooms leave little opportunity for the arrangement of the masses," said

14. Even the most critical observer might accept the facade of the Woolworth Building as part of a well-preserved Gothic structure. The buttress terminal of an American Indian in full headdress, as seen in the bottom lefthand corner, shatters any illusions.

15. Perhaps it was the cruciform lobby, the neo-Romanesque ceiling mosaics, the neo-Gothic elevator doors and mail boxes, or any combination of the above that led the Episcopal bishop of New York to dub the Woolworth Building the "Cathedral of Commerce."

15

architect Cass Gilbert. "Story upon story of practically equal heights necessarily divide the structure, and each story, having the same functions, must be lighted with windows of practically the same area."

The startling news of a building of such magnitude coming hard on the heels of the Singer and Metropolitan Life buildings was eclipsed by Woolworth two months later. By January 1911, he had acquired the entire Broadway frontage with the purchase of the two lots on the northwest corner of Barclay Street and Park Place. Real-estate dealers knew that to assemble a large plot in this desirable section of the city was a feat. There were cases where anxious buyers, like Morgan, had waited for years, and even then some failed. To succeed in less than a year was remarkable.

Since the corporation's plans were changing, the relationship between Woolworth and the bank changed as well. Woolworth took an option to purchase at par all the realty company's stock that was held by the bank and thereby control more and more of the financing. The role of the bank was to diminish to little more than that of a tenant. To that end, Woolworth offered the whole second floor to the bank at an annual rent of $100,000. After obtaining some concessions, the bank said that Woolworth had a deal.

Woolworth admitted that he had been yearning to create a building taller than the Metropolitan Life, and he instructed Gilbert to enlarge his plans. Woolworth's idea was to have the main body of the building rise about 30 stories and be surmounted by an 85-foot square, 25-story tower, making 55 stories in all. In short, Woolworth had plans for the world's tallest building.

Cass Gilbert made dozens of sketches for the Woolworth Building, and each one was scrutinized by Woolworth, who returned many with his own suggestions. "I do not want a mere building," said Woolworth, "I want something that will be an ornament to the city." He insisted that all four faces be decorated, that the same architectural features and adornment on the front of the building be carried out on the side and rear walls, and he was willing to spend the additional money to get what he wanted. When Gilbert asked Woolworth how high the building should rise, he was told about 750 feet. When Gilbert wanted to know if that was the limit, he was told that it was the minimum.

To construct the foundations, Woolworth stuck with the city's most experienced firm and hired the Foundation Company, which sank 69 piers to bedrock through 84 feet of water. By February 1912, the Thompson-Starrett Company had erected the steel frame to the eighteenth floor on the firm foundation, and the builders had started setting

16

16, 17. Corbels in the Woolworth Building lobby humorously depict Woolworth counting out nickels and dimes and Gilbert cradling a model of the building.

the terra cotta facade at the sixth floor. When the building was finished, Gilbert informed Woolworth that he could not tell the height precisely, but he believed that it was 787 feet. Woolworth was not satisfied and had his own corps of engineers measure the height. Gilbert had been short in his estimate by about five feet.

There is little wonder that applications for office space began to be made as early as May 1911, although even the most optimistic plans did not anticipate completion until fall, 1912. The Tiffany Studios were manufacturing 24 street-level doors in polished steel with gold backgrounds. Greek marble was going to line the lobby walls and would be used for the stairs to the mezzanine. The finest glass mosaic would be used in the lobby for the three-story-high barrel-vaulted ceiling, and the same supplier, Heinigke & Brown, would provide the leaded glass for the back-lit ceiling in the west end. A corbel in the tradition of the Gothic stonecutters, representing Woolworth counting nickels and dimes, is at the southeast corner of the lobby's transept; a corbel at the southwest transept shows the architect cradling a model of the building. Corbels also depict others who were involved in the creation of the building, including banker Louis Pierson of the Irving Bank and Louis J. Horowitz, president of the Thompson-Starrett Company.

At the opening of the building in 1913, 900 dinner guests in the 27th-floor dining room honored the building and its architect. On cue from a Western Union telegraph operator, President Woodrow Wilson pushed a button in the White House that turned on all the lights in the new building. That night Cass Gilbert said that Woolworth's bankers had told him the building was unique in New York and probably so throughout the country, for it stood without a mortgage on it or a dollar of indebtedness. Woolworth had deferred as many payments as possible. "For the whole undertaking," said real-estate lawyer Robert McM. Gillespie, "we wanted $13 million, $5 million for the land, $1 million for the foundations, and $7 million for the building. Mr. Woolworth supplied $5 million." With Otto Markiewicz of Berlin, Gillespie set out to find the balance in Europe, where they raised about $8 million as a first mortgage on the building. By 1914, banker Pierson reported to Irving's board that Woolworth had already bought back all of Irving's 5,000 shares in the Broadway-Park Row Company. The Woolworth Building was his, and indeed every penny of the approximately $13.5 million that it cost had been paid. His building, said the *Times*, "stretches up, imperturbably august, a conquest of architecture. It storms the sky."

18. *A 1901 plan for a civic center by Henry F. Hornbostel and George B. Post called for a new Brooklyn Bridge terminal and a municipal building on the east side of Centre Street, City Hall Park stripped of all buildings except City Hall itself, and new buildings in the style of the Hall of Records on the north side of Chambers Street. Like so many municipal projects, the plan never came off.*

2

Political New York

The city's expanding bureaucracy in the 1880s forced the municipality to rent space in ever-widening rings around City Hall. By 1888, the city's annual rent bill was $93,750, or the interest at three percent on $3.2 million, a sum the city could spend for a fireproof municipal building that would house city agencies and put a stop to urban sprawl.

Many different roles and functions were suggested for the proposed municipal building. Some intended it to house only the agencies that were renting space, others only those offices that required fireproof quarters to protect precious documents, and still others wanted it to include all municipal functions, including the courts, the register's office, and the mayor's office. It was to be built on the site of a demolished City Hall or next door to a preserved City Hall or on some neighboring sites. Proposals by the score were put forward. Most were rejected, a few were approved, and some were modified beyond recognition.

All municipal buildings are inextricably entwined with politics and bureaucratic imbroglios, and after legislation was passed to finance a municipal building in 1887, it was politics more than real estate with which everyone had to contend. At first the building was to be erected on the site of the old jail in the northeast corner of City Hall Park, and

it was to harmonize architecturally with City Hall. Park defenders, including Andrew Haswell Green, opposed any new construction in City Hall Park on general principles. Two proposals called for a municipal building to be built atop the Manhattan entrance to the Brooklyn Bridge, and one of the grandiose plans would have commandeered Pulitzer's World Building and included a viaduct extending from the bridge across City Hall Park and along Park Row to Church Street, with offices overhead and stores below.

To determine at least an acceptable site for the Municipal Building, the city followed the usual bureaucratic procedure and created a commission. The commissioners envisioned a building on the east side of Centre Street that would straddle an arcaded Chambers Street. The objections were that the site's shape would result in a building with irregularly shaped rooms, and the existing elevated train structure would darken the lower stories and produce unacceptable noise levels. The site's biggest selling point was that at $2.3 million it was a relative bargain.

Mayor Thomas Gilroy ignored the commission's findings and in 1893 announced that the city would allocate all its money for construction costs and build on city-owned property. The mayor's decision was to tear down City Hall and build a five-story, $8 million municipal building of white marble on the site. The Architectural League sent a delegation to City Hall to request that the scale and renderings of the drawings be standardized, and to suggest that Columbia's Professor William R. Ware and architects Richard Morris Hunt and Napoleon LeBrun act as judges for the competition. The next day, an even larger delegation arrived, not to praise the project but to plead for preservation of the venerable City Hall.

Despite this plea, the competition was held, and more than 130 plans were submitted by September 1893. Four months later, the favored plan was reported to have one major drawback—the architect estimated that his proposed building would cost $13 million. Observers maintained that architects had a way of underestimating costs by about 50 percent, in which case the scheme would probably cost more than $20 million. Rumors then began to fly that the committee might either reject all the submissions or make a composite from features of the best plans. It was all an exercise in futility, since the legislation that had permitted the city to erect new buildings in City Hall Park was repealed. Cash prizes for the now-unrealizable building were awarded out of a sense of propriety, and first place went to John R. Thomas, who described his entry as a "building in the style of the Hotel de Ville in Paris, though by no means a copy." His design was later used, with modifications, for the Hall of Records.

Thomas's design also served as the linchpin for a grandiose plan for a civic center in 1901, when an improvement to the transportation complex at the Brooklyn Bridge was being discussed. Bridge Commissioner Gustave Lindenthal submitted a plan by Henry F. Hornbostel and George B. Post which would strip City Hall Park of all buildings except City Hall and create a new civic center on the north side of Chambers Street. Thomas's future Hall of Records provided the model for unified design and architectural regularity. On the east side of Park Row would be a bridge terminal with a 45-story office tower in the form of a campanile. Lindenthal wrote that the "whole forms a scheme of architectural magnificence rivaling the famous Place de la Concorde in Paris, Trafalgar Square in London, the Schloss Platz in Berlin, or the Rathhaus Platz in Vienna,

and has more than twice the area of any of them." The project entailed an expenditure of about $50 million, and it died unborn. The Municipal Building, however, would be built, and in accordance with the Commission's original suggestion.

Engine Company 31

87 Lafayette Street, northeast corner of White
1896
BUILDER: City of New York
ARCHITECT: Napoleon LeBrun

While debates raged over the need for a municipal building and the preservation of City Hall, the city remained in desperate need of firehouses. In 1894, a bond issue of up to $150,000 a year was authorized to acquire new sites for them. The land for Engine Company 31, as Mayor Gilroy could proudly point out, did not cost the taxpayers a penny, since the city already owned it. Construction costs, however, were another story. Whereas, the average engine company occupied a 25-by-200-foot lot, Engine Company 31 filled a 76-by-112-foot plot and housed a water tower and the headquarters for a battalion chief as well as the usual

19. Napoleon LeBrun used a scallop motif amidst neoclassical trim for the window heads at Engine Company 31. Scallop shells, or cockleshells, were worn as emblems by pilgrims returning from the shrine of Santiago de Compostela in Spain during the Middle Ages, and by the Renaissance the shells had taken on a sacred aura all their own.

20. LeBrun, who was the fire department's quasi-official architect by the 1890s, designed Engine Company 31 as if it were a Loire Valley chateau from the reign of Francis I. The city spent as much money proportionately for this firehouse as it spent for lesser ones.

firefighting unit. The estimated cost of $80,000 was about the same on a per-foot basis as the cost of the average 25-foot-wide firehouse, but it represented a substantial sum in the scheme of things, since the city was only appropriating $60,000 at a clip for firehouses.

An engine house had to stable the horses, garage the equipment, and house the firemen, whose lot in the 1890s was not a happy one. A fireman lived at the firehouse and, except for vacations, he was home only one night a week; by snacking at the firehouse, he could use his daily three-hour allotment for meal time to visit his family. A fireman's real home was his firehouse, and architect Napoleon Le-Brun made the facade of this one as domestic in nature as he could.

LeBrun, who had been a judge in the aborted municipal building competition and whose architectural firm had become the quasi-official architects of the New York City Fire Department, usually settled on something between Romanesque and classical for 25-foot-wide firehouses, but for Engine Company 31 he evoked a Loire Valley chateau from the reign of Francis I, a revival of the transitional style between Gothic and Renaissance that had been started in the 1880s by Richard Morris Hunt for the William K. Vanderbilt mansion. Appropriately, *Architectural Record* recognized that the engine company's upper stories seemed to belong "to a much more extensive and expensive type of residence," but nobody seemed to think that the style was inappropriate.

21. Architect John Thomas's adaptation of the Hotel de Ville in Paris won the competition for a Municipal Building that was never built. Since the city had paid for the plans, a fiscally sensitive reform administration decided to use them in modified form for the Hall of Records.

The Hall of Records

31 Chambers Street, between Centre and Elk
1906
BUILDER: The City of New York
ARCHITECT: John R. Thomas, replaced by Horgan & Slattery

In the 1880s, the Register's Office was housed in a building in City Hall Park that had started life in 1756 as a debtors prison. The city's irreplaceable records proving ownership on about $4 billion worth of property were thus less protected from fire than the average merchant's stock, a condition that lawyers regarded with anxiety. In 1889, the Association of the Bar of New York convinced Mayor Hugh Grant that a new hall of records was needed, but nothing came of the idea until 1896.

The city's proposal for a new Municipal Building had included a Hall of Records, but the state legislature authorized construction of a separate building to house the Register's Office on the west side of Centre Street between Chambers and Reade streets. The site was made extremely attractive when the Board of Estimate agreed to extend Elm Street south to Chambers, transforming the site into an entire block, with light and air on all sides (the street is now Elk Street). The site offered about 31,000 square feet of space and was worth about $1.4 million.

John R. Thomas, who had won the ill-fated Municipal Building competition, was appointed by Mayor William L. Strong to draw up the plans. Thomas's credentials included the Squadron A Armory and the extension and refurbishing of the New York Stock Exchange. In political circles, he was known for having saved the state about $1 million by writing ironclad contracts and by rejecting suppliers' work and materials that were not up to snuff during the construction of the Elmira penitentiary. These were qualifications that appealed to Mayor Strong, the reformer who came to office in 1895 after the Lexow investigations had revealed widespread municipal corruption. Fiscal integrity

22. The entrance to the Hall of Records, lighted by four bronze electroliers made by the Gorham Company, is flanked by sculpture groups by Peter Martiny. The art commission complained that the architects who were overseeing the construction were not submitting plans for their approval.

was the basis of Strong's reform, so he decided that since the city had paid $7,000 for the award-winning design for the Municipal Building, Thomas should adapt the design for the Hall of Records, which would house both the Register's Office and the Surrogate Court.

A politician's idea of reform, however, is not necessarily that of an architect. The American Institute of Architects had been arguing against direct appointment of architects, and regardless of the antecedents in this case, the AIA's New York Chapter held that the city should have instituted a competition to assure a diversity of choice. Qualified architects felt cheated. Every architect's ambition, said chapter president John M. Carrere, was to erect monumental structures. Nonetheless, Thomas's appointment was upheld, and his Parisian design was approved with minor modifications by Columbia's Professor Ware, architectural critic Montgomery Schuyler, and Henry G. Marquand, the president of the Metropolitan Museum of Art.

When the city received construction bids in 1897, three of the twelve were made by contractor John Pierce, including one for Hallowell granite, which is noted for its whiteness and the durability of its color. At $1,997,000, Pierce's bid on Hallowell granite was the highest, but so was his reputation, and he won the contract.

In 1898, Tammany Hall returned to power, which heralded the end of reform. Mayor Robert Van Wyck quickly tried to frustrate both Thomas and Pierce into resigning so that Tammany cronies could be appointed. One of Van Wyck's first official requests was for the addition of five stories atop the eight-story Hall of Records to accommodate more of the municipal bureaucracy. What he wanted was a whole new building, with new plans, new bids, and new contractors. Van Wyck only gave in when fire underwriters told him publicly that the eight stories were in scale to eleven stories in an ordinary building, which was difficult enough to protect from fire—anything higher was almost impossible. Frustrated, Van Wyck took another tack, self-righteously proclaiming that he would take a hard look at Pierce's contract, and if he found anything fraudulent, he would demand a new one. Failing once again, he went after Thomas's plans for the interiors. Armed with figures provided by architects Arthur J. Horgan and Vincent J. Slattery, Van Wyck claimed that the costs could easily be reduced from $2.5 million to 1.5 million. Horgan & Slattery were the Tammany architects. "If a scow of the street-cleaning department needed repairing, Horgan & Slattery would supervise the work and get the usual fees," said the *Times*. "Repairs to fireboats, the building of engine houses, and

23

24

Although the law did not require it, Van Wyck then said that he would only accept the lowest bidder for the work on the interiors. When the bids were opened in July 1900, they ranged from $1.95 million to $2.45 million, and the lowest just happened to be a bid by Tammany's nemesis, John Pierce. Several anonymous contractors now accused Thomas of showing the specifications to Pierce and refusing them to others until only a few days before the letting of the contract, too late to make proper estimates. The allegations were dropped as mysteriously as they had been made.

Tammany took one more shot in the dark. In December 1900, some of the judges in the New York County Courthouse, the very symbol of Tweed Ring venality, said that the plans for the Hall of Records could be easily expanded to include a new courthouse that would allow the judges to vacate their damp and drafty quarters. To add credence to their claim, they said that the foundations for the Hall of Records were big enough to support a much larger building. If their proposal required new plans, the judges said that the city should pay off the architect and contractor and get on with it. They were wrong about one thing. The building was to be erected on compressible soil, and each portion of the foundation had to be proportional to the load that it had to bear so that the settling of the structure would be equalized. Thomas said that it was the "same old story, the history of every public improvement in New York. As soon as a project was nearing completion, someone always comes forward with a new scheme." Thomas was already complaining of indigestion; in August, 1901, he suffered a heart attack and died.

Thomas's death gave Van Wyck the chance he had been waiting for. Within the week, Horgan & Slattery were appointed to oversee the construction. One of their first acts was to give all the sculptural work for the facade to Philip Martiny. There were no arguments against Martiny's competence, but the National Sculpture Society said that the work should have been apportioned among different sculptors. Horgan & Slattery also alienated the Municipal Art Commission, whose role was to approve public art, by consistently failing to submit samples of the sculptural

hundreds of odd jobs, large and small, were found for the favored architects." Thomas told Van Wyck that the proposed changes would ruin the structure. It had taken two years to bring the building to its present stage and would require almost as much time again to redesign it. "Well," retorted Van Wyck, "we don't want an opera house made out of what is intended to be an office building. If it's going to take you all that time to do this work, we'll get another architect." Thomas reduced the anticipated costs of the interiors to $1.9 million.

23. Architect John Thomas was not a Tammany man, and upon Tammany's return to power the venal politicians and their flunkies tried every trick to have Thomas removed. Thomas persevered as long as his health held out, and the city was blessed with its grandest Beaux-Arts staircase.

24. The complexity of the staircase at the Hall of Records would have been the envy of court architects to any number of French kings. Precedents from many chateaux—from Chambord to Blois to Versailles—contribute to the amalgam.

25

and decorative work or by submitting only bits and pieces. When the statuary for the pair of pedestals in front of the Hall of Records was shown, for instance, only one figure of one of the groups was displayed. No fault was found with the proposal, but the commissioners did not feel that they could approve the entire design until all the figures had been seen in context. Slattery facetiously described the art commission as "men of wealth who give their artistic training to the city free of charge."

Tammany's last crack at milking the Hall of Records came when department heads were given their choice of interiors after the fact, resulting in alterations to every floor. Tammany's changes, said the Muncipal Art Society, resulted in the "unmeaning ostentation of showy marble slabs" at a greater cost than would have been spent to carry out Thomas's original plans. And it turned out that much of the marble upstairs was not marble at all, but something called "plaster enrichment." The alterations delayed the opening another year and brought the cost to an estimated $8 million, to the joy of Horgan & Slattery, no doubt, who were getting their ten percent.

25. The Hall of Records contains the Surrogate Court, where countless destinies have been determined. This courtroom is designed to command respect for the authority of the law, and the symbol of the law itself—in traditional blindfold—is found carved into the marble fireplace.

26. Andrew Carnegie, J. Pierpont Morgan, and about 300 fellow members of the Chamber of Commerce petitioned the government to acquire the property at Bowling Green as the site for the Custom House. The site was clearly begging for a building of monumental proportions.

The United States Custom House

At Bowling Green, bounded by State, Bridge, and Whitehall Streets
1907
BUILDER: General Services Administration
ARCHITECT: Cass Gilbert

The Federal government's biggest moneymaker in the nineteenth century was the Customs Service, and its biggest port was New York, which contributed twice as much to the federal coffers as all other ports combined. In 1863, the Customs Service moved into the Merchants Exchange at 55 Wall Street, which had been the city's largest building devoted to business when it opened in 1842. By 1887, the crowded conditions led to the obvious conclusion that the Customs Service and the appraisers stores were again in need of expanded quarters.

A workable scheme was evolved by 1891. The appraisers stores were to be built uptown near the bulk of foreign shipping, and the Customs Service would be headquar-tered on Bowling Green, which was convenient by elevated railroads to the east and west sides of Manhattan and an ideal site from an aesthetic viewpoint. As one of the site's boosters said, it seemed "as if this particular location had been kept unimproved and preserved in order that New York might have a public building worthy of the city and the nation." The idea was to sell the Wall Street building for $4 million and apply the proceeds to constructing the new buildings. Until they were ready, the government would continue to occupy 55 Wall Street on a rent-back basis at an annual rate of four percent of the purchase price for the new owners.

It was not until 1898 that somebody nibbled at the bait of 55 Wall Street. Who made the offer was not immediately revealed, and the amount was not the anticipated $4 million, but $3.25 million. Within two days of the announcement, the Secretary of the Treasury said that the Bowling Green site would be used for the new Custom House, with construction costs set at $3 million. James Knox Taylor, the supervising architect for the Federal government, was pushing to start work.

The guidelines for the architectural competition called

27

for a six-story, U-shaped building, with the open-ended rectangular court in the rear. The specifications were prepared by Taylor, who was also to represent the government as a judge on a three-man commission with the two other commissioners chosen by the twenty competitors. The competition resulted in a tie between Carrere & Hastings, who submitted a rather fussy Beaux-Arts design with nautical trim to symbolize seafaring commerce, and Cass Gilbert, who submitted a neo-French Renaissance design with statuary representing the seafaring nations on the cornice and four single figures on blocks at the basement level. After modifications, the commission was awarded to Cass Gilbert, whose plan was described as a "roomy structure of plain design with sculptural embellishments. . . . There is no dome, spire, or steeple, the principal decorative feature being a group of statuary."

Senator Thomas Platt, always looking out for the good of his constituency and party, baldly opposed the selection of Gilbert on the grounds that he had only recently arrived from Minnesota and was not a member of the Republican organization of New York. A few architects who had entered the competition had a more ethical reason to raise a fuss and they complained to President McKinley that the selection committee had been rigged. Commissioner Thomas R. Kimball, who had been employed by Gilbert in Minnesota, had not been nominated by any of the competing firms, unless it was by Cass Gilbert, and he refused to comment. Complicating the issue, supervising architect Taylor had been in partnership with Gilbert. The petitioners claimed that neither qualified as disinterested judges and that Gilbert had been the front-runner from the outset. The brouhaha subsided at the request of the New York chapter of the AIA, who viewed it as unseemly.

After the commotion had blown over, Gilbert decided to modify his plans to include groups of figures representing four continents instead of the single figures on the basement level. Daniel Chester French and Augustus St. Gaudens were asked if they would like to split the work, which would pay $13,500 per group. St. Gaudens declined because he did not have the time, so French found himself on the way to his most successful sculptural commission. Gilbert's plan for the cornice statuary provided a large measure of freedom for the sculptors, who included St. Gau-

dens's brother Louis (who designed *Portugal*) and Karl Bitter (who designed the cartouche flanked by allegorical figures representing a peaceful and strong nation).

Bids for the construction of the building were not so easily arranged. The law forbade the request of a specific material from a particular quarry, which resulted in bids that included varying qualities of limestone, granite, and marble, and prices that ranged from $1.9 million to $3 million. John Pierce of Hall of Records fame was awarded the contract for his bid on Fox Island granite at almost $2.2 million, but the cost did not include mechanical equipment or interior finish, which would cost another $1.8 million and bring the total close to $4 million. Clearly the Custom

28

27. Cass Gilbert's winning design for the United States Custom House. Cries of foul play were heard, with other entrants claiming favoritism.

28. Imperious *Europe*, crowned and enthroned and leaning on the world's knowledge, makes the kind of social commentary that infuses all of Daniel Chester French's sculpture groups for the Custom House.

House could not be completed within the appropriated $3 million, and it was illegal to begin work on a government building under these conditions. Either Congress would be blackmailed into making later appropriations, or the building would be left uncompleted. Pierce was awarded the contract anyway and told to start work up to the first story. Congress relented and appropriated the balance.

The exterior was finished by January 1906, and it was a facade that Gilbert could be proud of. He had taken great care in its construction, going so far as to fit plaster casts of capitals into their niches to determine from the street whether their scale and placement were correct. By October, the interior decorations had not yet been installed, although about $7.2 million had been spent, and Washington was balking at appropriating funds for the mosaics and murals for the transverse hall, rotunda, and chief offices. And to the surprise of the Customs Service, the new building was not for its exclusive use. Such disparate Federal agencies as the Isthmian Canal Commission, the Secret Service, the Bureau of Animal Husbandry, and the Life Saving Service were sharing it as well.

The sale of the former Custom House at 55 Wall Street was by then an object of intrigue. The purchaser turned out to be Standard Oil's bank and an "influence" in government—the First National Bank. The price of $3.25 million had never been considered good, and the deal, which favored the buyer at the expense of the city government, was

not much better. The bank received about $128,000 a year in rent-back fees, which amounted to about $1.2 million, while paying the Federal goverment $3.2 million in installments that were spread out over the time it took to build the new Custom House. But the government had held the deed until the last installment was paid, and as nominal owner for nearly nine years did not have to pay real-estate taxes to the city. The bank took possession of 55 Wall Street in 1907 for about $1.2 million less than the 1898 sale price of $3.25 million, and it had paid no taxes in the interim.

And that is only half the story. In the early 1890s, Thomas R. Jackson, the architect in charge of Federal buildings in New York City, said that the construction of 55 Wall Street was strong enough to support the addition of three or four stories atop it, and he urged the government to expand and renovate the building. Not only did nobody in government pay him any heed, supervising architect Taylor wanted the new building so much that he went so far as to denigrate the Wall Street site because the streets were too narrow and the surrounding buildings too tall, which conspired to deprive the site of light and air. First National, however, had obviously heard Jackson and did to 55 Wall Street precisely what he said should have been done. The bank hired McKim, Mead & White to superimpose three stories atop the building and remodel the interior. Jackson was only wrong about the price. He had estimated $1.5 million in 1893 for refurbishing costs, and the bank spent $2.3 million in 1910.

30

First Precinct Police Station

Old Slip, between Water and South Streets
1910
BUILDER: The City of New York
ARCHITECTS: Hunt & Hunt

The plight of the city's police stations was so great in 1906 that $2 million was set aside to purchase new sites and replace the more decrepit station houses. As the police commissioner quickly discovered, real-estate prices were so high that he was forced to restrict the number of new

29. French's statue groups representing four continents—Asia, America, Europe, and Africa—contribute to the balance and harmony of the Custom House's facade. Less robust statuary had been called for in Gilbert's early plans.

30. Richard Howland Hunt and Joseph Howland Hunt entered their plans for the First Precinct House in the Architectural League Show of 1908. Two years later the building was ready.

sites and use as much city-owned property as possible. It boded well for the First Precinct. Since the city already owned the land under the old station house, the department only needed the $225,000 in construction funds.

Richard Howland Hunt and Joseph Howland Hunt, the sons of Richard Morris Hunt and heirs to his practice, were asked to prepare the plans, which Mayor George B. McClellan approved in 1908. The Hunt & Hunt building filled exactly the same amount of land—30 by 165 feet—as its predecessor, built only 24 years earlier but by then condemned for poor sanitary conditions. The obvious difference was that the Hunt & Hunt station house was much grander, with no brick anywhere in evidence.

The showcase for the firm's design was the Architectural League's annual show in 1907. The elevation showed an intentionally rugged building, a rusticated fortress more Florentine than a Florentine palazzo. With fear of riots and insurrections, this aura of impregnability might have been appropriate, but the building was basically designed to be a holding ward—a mini-prison—and the lower two floors in the west end of the station housed prisoners' cells. In 1910, the policemen of the First Precinct were able to move from their temporary quarters into this neo-Renaissance palace, where they found the third and fourth floors fitted up as dormitories, and a gymnasium in the center of the fourth floor.

31

31. More Florentine than Florence, Hunt & Hunt's rusticated First Precinct House exudes an aura of impregnability. The architects were the sons of Richard Morris Hunt.

32. Originally scheduled to be topped by statuary, which never materialized, the Bernini-like colonnade acts as a screen and grand entranceway for the Municipal Building.

The Municipal Building

Centre Street at Chambers Street
1916
BUILDER: The City of New York
ARCHITECTS: McKim, Mead & White

In 1903, Mayor Seth Low resurrected the idea of combining a municipal building with a public transportation complex. Like the commissioners ten years before, he wanted the building to straddle Chambers Street on the east side of Centre Street. The major difference was that the site that could have been bought for $2.3 million would cost $6.7 million instead. The Municipal Building was intended to house a multiplicity of city departments, as well as a terminal for the Brooklyn Bridge, Williamsburg and Manhattan bridge trolleys, an elevated station through the second

story, and a subway station in the basement for the new BMT loop. To the complications of several transit lines coming together were added those of an odd polygonal site, streets on every side, and one street passing through the middle.

The responsibility for construction fell to the commissioner of bridges, who invited twelve firms to enter the architectural competition in 1907. The jury gave first runner-up to Howells & Stokes, whose design, said architect and city chronicler I. N. Phelps Stokes, was "if not actually the prototype of the . . . upward tapering type of skyscraper with highly accentuated vertical lines, at least marked an important step in that direction and had a far-reaching effect upon the design of the modern skyscraper."

McKim, Mead & White took the first-place prize with a pseudo-classical design that lacked the grace of some other entries but was considered to be in the tradition of municipal buildings. One advantage of the design was its avoid-

33

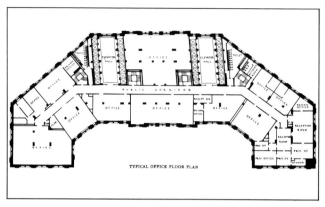

34

instead of bedrock, the city's superintendent of buildings refused to approve them. Digging another 75 feet to 135 feet might cost another $300,000, an investment that William J. Schiefflin's Citzen's Union, a watchdog of the city's physical plant as well as its fiscal doings, agreed would be well made. But the bridge commissioner said the corporation counsel had advised him that he was not legally bound to heed the will of the superintendent of buildings, so he awarded the contract for shallow foundations. The ensuing uproar convinced the commissioner to cancel the bid, and the Foundation Company, which had built the foundations for the Singer Building and would build them for the Woolworth Building, was awarded the $1.4 million contract to take the foundations to bedrock.

The Thompson-Starrett Company had won the overall construction job, and Thompson-Starrett's president, Louis

ance of courtyards. The flattened V plan allowed offices to face outwards. Linking the wings on the lower floors would be a Corinthian-style colonnade, which in its original design was topped by statuary like Bernini's colonnade at St. Peter's. And an outsized and multilayered Choragic monument supporting a statue of Civic Fame would crown the structure.

The 1907 plans called for a huge building, 23 stories high and 448 feet wide at street level, containing about 27,000 square feet of office space per floor. The city only required eleven floors immediately, but the additional floors, went the collective wisdom, would be filled as they were needed. Two stories were added in the revised plans of 1908, which made the building 559 feet high, and the third tallest in town. Included were accommodations for many of the city's principal courts, which it was believed would abrogate the need for a new courthouse (it did not). But all the talk of incorporating an el station and trolley terminals was forgotten—only the subway was included, and the price tag was up to $8 million.

Because the plans called for foundations resting on soil

33. McKim, Mead & White's design for the Municipal Building was not universally hailed in 1907, but its neoclassicism was regarded as appropriate for government buildings. Louis J. Horowitz of the Thompson-Starrett Company hoped that the ruinous delays traditionally associated with city architectural projects could be avoided. Seven years later the Municipal Building was ready.

34. The floor plans for the Municipal Building tipped the scales in favor of McKim, Mead & White. By virtue of the flattened V shape, there were no dimly lit courtyards.

35. The Chambers Street arcade of the Municipal Building has a barrel-vaulted ceiling decorated in the highest tradition of Roman design. Based on vaulting in the sixteenth-century Palazzo Farnese, it is just the kind of detail that the firm of McKim, Mead & White would borrow from the Italian Renaissance.

36. The Municipal Building's roofline is a virtuoso display of neoclassical elements, with finials and belvederes leading from one choragic monument to another and finally to Adolph Weinman's crowning statue of *Civic Fame.*

35

J. Horowitz, was eager to get on with the job to show that his firm could avoid the ruinous delays that had harassed municipal buildings. But by 1914, the Municipal Building was far from complete, and the arrangements of the floors were criticized for being poorly planned. The irony was that from the outset McKim, Mead & White's facade had hardly been praised—it was the internal arrangement that had won the commission for the firm.

The interiors were finally finished in 1916, and the total construction costs came to about $9 million, which made the Municipal Building one of the most expensive sky-scrapers in town. At least the city was trying to achieve some very special things, but there is always that municipal beast with which to contend.

36

Madison Square Garden,
New York

37. *Architect Stanford White took his inspiration for the tower of Madison Square Garden from the twelfth-century Moorish Giralda Tower in Seville, Spain. The colonnaded street derives from any number of Bolognese or Milanese precedents. While the building was a source of joy and pleasure for the architect, it was also the scene of his final tragedy.*

3

Stanford White's Squares

The odds are that if you ask the name of the greatest clubman, first nighter, or host of the Age of Elegance, you'll hear Stanford White. You will also hear that he was the most generous and least mean-spirited of men, and possibly its most profligate and licentious as well. Likewise, every New York building of architectural pretension was attributed to him, to the point that it would have taken him several lifetimes to design them. But with white stone and yellow terra cotta he did begin to transform the city from a monotonously dull brown place to one of lightness and fascination, and the metamorphosis began in earnest with his design for Madison Square Garden.

The Madison Square Garden of the 1880s was an abandoned trainshed used by Phineas T. Barnum for circuses, concerts, or religious meetings. Never a graceful place, its acoustics were all wrong, and its only positive attributes were its size and location overlooking Madison Square from Madison Avenue at 26th Street. Barnum tried to assemble a corporation to build a new Madison Square Garden, but not even he could pull off the deal.

Hiram Hitchcock, the proprietor of the Fifth Avenue Hotel, was more successful. The National Horse Show of America was desperate for a good arena in New York City

and signed on as a major investor. Others included J. Pierpont Morgan, his friend and fellow banker Charles Lanier, coal man Edward J. Berwind, California millionaire Darius Ogden Mills, insurance man James T. Hyde, and Stanford White. Over two-thirds of the original $1.5 million capitalization went to the Vanderbilts for the cost of the land, and every penny of the balance and then some would be needed for construction.

Although White was a principal stockholder, an architectural competition was held to avoid ruffling the feathers of other architects. Columbia's professor William R. Ware awarded the prize to McKim, Mead & White anyway for a joyous and lighthearted design recalling the late Gothic of Spain and Northern Italy. White's original plan included shops, street stalls, and bachelor apartments, but the final building was completely public, except for five studio apartments in the tower.

The 300-foot tower, modeled on the Giralda in Seville, was Madison Square Garden's crowning architectural feature and White's monument to the city. When construction on the Garden began to go over budget, fellow investors began to consider the tower expendable, which so appalled White he began to tell reporters that they could say anything they liked about the building, but "for any sake, say it needs a tower." He then pestered contractor David H. King so much that King finally volunteered to put up half of the $450,000 to build the tower, just to keep White quiet. The full amount was finally raised.

To crown the tower, White's friend Augustus St. Gaudens created a monumental figure of the goddess Diana. In its first incarnation the statue was eighteen feet tall—too tall, so White paid for a new thirteen-foot version. ("Too Tall" Diana was later used by McKim to top the Agricultural Building at the Chicago World's Fair of 1893.) The *Diana* was described as a "female person as she might appear after she had locked her bathroom and is prepared to make her ablutions safe from prying eyes." To Anthony Comstock and his Society for the Suppression of Vice she was *too* naked, and although nannies might have shielded their charges' eyes from the statue, the Johnnies and clubmen would gather to gaze on the loveliness of her.

The three-story Garden was built of yellow brick, terra cotta, iron, and glass. Its design was like that of a railroad terminal. On the Madison Avenue side was the equivalent of a headhouse, which contained the grand staircase, a cafe and restaurant, a concert hall modeled after the Wagner Theater in Beyreuth, a combination theater and assembly hall, and, for the summer months, an open-air roof garden. Extending to Park Avenue was the equivalent of the trainshed for the 300-foot-long amphitheater, which had seating for as many as 5,000, including about 175 boxes. When the arena's floor was covered, as it would be for conventions, the capacity was easily 9,000.

The Garden's opening night was June 17, 1890, when most of the New York society would already have left the city for the summer, but there was a large turnout anyway. They heard a concert conducted by Edward Straus, watched a ballet, and in general had a "bully" time. Inspector Thomas Byrnes, Chief of the New York Detective Bureau, was alerted to the possible attendance of professional pickpockets. While scores of his detectives were scattered throughout the building, he stood behind a large curtain at the main entrance to watch arriving ticketholders.

From the outset, Madison Square Garden was a money loser. Its construction costs had come close to $1.65 million, which represented a fifty percent overrun, and its anticipated receipts of $210,000 a year were never realized. Down it came in 1925, to be replaced by the New York Insurance Company.

White, the Garden's unofficial impresario, would have been dismayed. He especially loved his tower studio, his "snuggery," where he worked and played and hosted parties. Mrs. Reginald deKoven, who lived with her composer husband on nearby Irving Place, said that one night a "crescent table was covered with old golden damask and spread with orchids. Lights twinkled in surrounding bay trees, a mandolin band shed music like a sparkling fountain, and about the table were women as lovely and varied in type as ever assembled." One of the women who was in attendance in White's studio for several years was the ethereally beautiful Evelyn Nesbit, a Floradora Girl who was perhaps sixteen when White started seeing her. By the time she was twenty, she was married to Pittsburgh millionaire Harry K. Thaw. He knew of the times that "Stanny" and Evelyn had shared together, and on a warm June night in 1907, Thaw walked up to White in the roof garden atop Madison Square Garden. From under his overcoat he pulled a pistol and shot White three times, and for Stanford White the lights went out.

The Farragut Statue

In Madison Square, south of 26th Street
1881
BUILDER: The Admiral Farragut Monument Association
SCULPTOR: Augustus St. Gaudens
ARCHITECT: Stanford White

In 1879, when the firm of McKim, Mead & White was being formed, the division of profits gave Charles Follen McKim 42 percent, William Rutherford Mead 33 percent, and White only 25 percent. How the spoils were divided that first year was almost academic, since they did not add up to $5,000. "If I can get a little work outside the office," said White, "I shall manage all right." Part of the little work was the pedestal for the Farragut statue.

Sculptor Augustus St. Gaudens had been awarded the Farragut commission in 1875, narrowly edging out the established John Quincy Adams Ward. To make the statue, St. Gaudens went to Paris, but he ran into delays caused by molds accidentally broken in casting or intentionally smashed when he deemed them bad, and by holidays in the south of France with McKim and White. By 1880, the Admiral Farragut Monument Association was complaining that St. Gaudens had spent too much time for too little in return. To St. Gaudens's despair, a plaster cast that was shown at the Paris Salon of 1880 only received an honorable mention. Adding to the gloom was the very real possibility that the City of New York might reject the association's gift if the presidents of the Metropolitan Museum of Art, the National Academy of Design, and the American Institute of Architects did not pass favorable judgment on the statue. To St. Gaudens's relief, the committee said that the work was beyond criticism.

38. Augustus Saint-Gaudens won the commission for the
Farragut statue by the skin of his teeth, edging out the established John Quincy Adams Ward by a vote of six to five. The
monumental scale and Catskill bluestone of Stanford
White's base caused a few problems.

The park commissioners' only objection resulted from a bureaucratic entanglement rather than aesthetic criticism. White's semicircular pedestal was a big chunk of Catskill bluestone. Everyone agreed that it was a brilliant and unprecedented design, but the commission required pedestals in city parks to be of a prescribed material and of approved proportions. Catskill bluestone was not on the list, and the scale transcended that of a mere pedestal. However, the regulation had previously been suspended and it was suspended again.

White then set out to get the site that he wanted, which was the north side of Madison square. The site was recommended by its "very quietness," and it was where the "aristocratic" part of the avenue began, with Delmonico's right opposite. Landscape architect Frederick Law Olmsted said that Madison Square was "sort of shiftless" and wanted the *Farragut* either in front of the Worth Monument on Fifth Avenue or in Union Square. The site selection committee decided in favor of White and placed the statue just south of 26th Street, where it originally faced west.

The statue's unveiling in 1881 was preceded by an hourlong parade down Fifth Avenue. Farragut was, after all, the U.S. Navy's first admiral, and many of New York City's leading citizens came to pay him honor. St. Gaudens was there, but he was not featured, and White's presence, if made, was not noted. Their collaborative effort, nevertheless, was appreciated, and the *Farragut* was instantly regarded as one of the city's finest pieces of public statuary. Hailed as a great breakthrough, the *Times* said that it was the "result of intelligent co-operation of the two professions which ought never to be disassociated—sculpture and architecture."

39. Actor Edwin Booth felt that he owed a debt to his profession, and the gift of the Players Clubhouse was his way of paying it off. Stanford White volunteered his services gratis and saw to the remodeling of the interiors and the addition of the neoclassical brownstone portico, including the Renaissance-style torchères.

The Players

16 Gramercy Park South, between Park Avenue South and Irving Place
1888
DONOR: Edwin Booth
ARCHITECT: Stanford White

A son of tragedian Junius Brutus Booth and brother of John Wilkes Booth, Edwin Booth was already on stage at the age of sixteen. By his fifties, he felt that he owed a debt to his fellow actors and to the profession in general, so he formed The Players, an association modeled on London's Garrick Club. Actors John Drew, Lawrence Barrett, and Harry Edwards joined, as did theater managers Augustin Daly and A. M. Palmer and writer Brander Matthews. Some founders and charter members, like Mark Twain, were only tangentially related to the theater. Others, like General William Tecumseh Sherman, simply enjoyed the association of actors.

One of the objects of The Players was to collect records of every description—paintings, curios, playbills—associated with the history of the stage in general and the American stage in particular. To form the library's nucleus, Booth contributed his own collection of theatrical pictures and books.

But Booth also planned to make a gift of a clubhouse, and club treasurer William Bispham found the 1845 building on Grammercy Park that was ideal for conversion to a clubhouse. Booth's only stipulation was that he retain an apartment in the house. Stanford White offered his architectural services gratis, "an offer," said Charles C. Baldwin, "that was, of course, accepted." To provide more room within, White removed the stoop and added a two-story, neoclassical portico in its place. He remodeled the interiors, combining his unusual flair for decoration with his ideas on comfort. Many of the rooms had odd nooks and crannies, window seats with fur throw rugs, and hooded and tiled fireplaces. The dining room had mahogany wainscoting and tables to match, with silver tankards and pewter pots for decoration, and, naturally, a quotation from Shakespeare: "Dear Actors, eat no onion or garlic, for we are to utter sweet breath." From its opening day, The Players had enough watercolor and oil paintings, line engravings, mezzotints, old woodcuts, and photographs to cover every inch of wall space. It was, said the *Times*, "born, like Minerva, grown up, clothed, and well educated."

Edwin Booth's room remained as he left it. "Nothing has been altered," wrote Daniel Frohman in 1935. "A book upon the table is still open at the place where he finished reading. And as one steps over the threshold, it is like stepping back into the nineteenth century. It makes one think how fleet a thing is time measured in eternity."

The Chancel of the Church of the Ascension

Fifth Avenue and Tenth Street, Northwest Corner
1888
DONORS: Julia and Serena Rhinelander
ARCHITECT: Stanford White
ARTISTS: John LaFarge, Louis St. Gaudens,
D. Maitland Armstrong

Fifth Avenue's first church and the city's first brownstone church was the Ascension, which was erected in 1841. Ascension was an austere, almost puritanical church that avoided display as inconsistent with the sacred purpose of the structure. Its rector was Dr. Manton Eastburn, a "low churcher" who bought the land behind the church to foil the introduction of a deep papist chancel, ensuring that architect Richard Upjohn could not come up with any of his "high church" ideas. By the 1880s, however, display was as fashionable for sacred as it was for mundane purposes.

In 1884, Julia and Serena Rhinelander set out to glorify the church and commemorate their parents by donating $37,000 for a reredos and a painting for Ascension's chancel.

40

Their father had inherited a sugar importing and refining business, and their mother, Mary Rogers, had inherited the property along Sixth Avenue between Carmine Street and Waverly Place. The family estate was valued at $50 to $75 million and was divided among seven heirs, including Lispenard Stewart and William Rhinelander Stewart.

It was Julia and Serena Rhinelander's nephew, William Rhinelander Stewart, who advised the family on the administration of the Rhinelander Real Estate company as its lawyer. He also represented the sisters in the selection of a supervising architect for the work to be done on the chancel of Ascension. He chose Stanford White, making Ascension the earliest New York church to fall under the spell of White and the group of artists he assembled. White and his Young Turks would add neo-Renaissance decoration to this neo-Gothic church with the same conviction Renaissance artists had shown when they tried to obliterate what they considered the barbarisms of the Gothic.

By 1886, White's Siena marble reredos covered the lower half of the chancel wall, and mosaics by D. Maitland Armstrong, famous for his stained glass, were set in. Hovering above the altar were two angels in high relief sculpted by Augustus St. Gaudens's brother Louis, whose career had begun in carving cameos. Ascension's greatest masterpiece is the altar painting of *The Ascension* by John LaFarge. The scaffold and huge white curtain covering *The Ascension* remained in place about three years while LaFarge worked on the painting, prompting White to tell the church's rector that the delay was "perfectly hellish." Dr. E. Winchester Donald replied, "Thank you; I'm a clergyman, White, but you express my sentiments admirably." When the painting was finally finished in 1888, neighboring Grace Church, where William Rhinelander Stewart was a member, congratulated Ascension on the completion of its "work and labor and love in making God's house beautiful."

Stewart believed that *The Ascension* was considered the finest altar painting in America, and many art historians agree. The chancel's assemblage is firmly rooted in the Renaissance: LaFarge's *Ascension* in Raphael, White's reredos in Bramante, St. Gaudens's angels in Donatello, and Armstrong's kneeling angels in Giotto. Even the painting's gilt frame echoes the Renaissance, with its oblique angle creating perspective and leading the eye into the scene. The congregation owed "much to the Misses Rhinelander," said the *Times*, "whose princely gift [LaFarge's] painting is, but they owe more to the good luck of having an artist of character." The same might be said for White, St. Gaudens, and Armstrong.

---

40. The redecoration of the chancel of the Church of the Ascension was under Stanford White's direction. John LaFarge painted *The Ascension*, Louis Saint-Gaudens carved the chalice-bearing angels, and D. Maitland Armstrong set the kneeling angels in mosaic. The artists happily stamped their neoclassicism on Richard Upjohn's Gothic Revival church.

Washington Arch

**In Washington Square, Fifth Avenue at
Waverly Place**
1892
BUILDER: Washington Arch Committee
ARCHITECT: Stanford White

The City of New York spent about $175,000 in 1889 celebrating the centennial anniversary of George Washington's oath-taking. The festivities included a recreation of Washington's triumphant return to New York, observances on the site of the swearing-in ceremony, parades on Fifth Avenue that passed through no fewer than two memorial arches at Madison Square, and a ball overseen by society's very own Ward McAllister. With all the official hooplah, the hit of the celebration was a wood-and-plaster arch that straddled Fifth Avenue just north of Washington Square on a line with Washington Mews. The arch was the brainchild of William Rhinelander Stewart, whose counsel had resulted in Stanford White's redecorating the Ascension. With the sales pitch that the arch would make Washington Square a focus of the centennial, Stewart had gone to his neighbors on Lower Fifth Avenue to raise the funds. He then went to Stanford White and asked him to design it.

White obliged with a simple but finely delineated neoclassical arch whose slender piers stood on the sidewalks. A statue of Washington in the uniform of the Continental Army stood atop the lintel. The statue ostensibly bore the patina of age, and claims were made that it had originally been erected at the Battery in 1792 and was the first statue to honor a citizen of the United States. Either White was selling a bill of goods or had been sold one, because the story was hogwash. Despite the bogus statue, New Yorkers liked the arch, and Jeanette and Richard Watson Gilder used the pages of *The Critic* to urge that a marble version of the same design be created as a permanent fixture of the city.

The idea of shifting it into Washington Square came from many quarters, including White, himself. No doubt Stewart wanted to see it in the square, since then he could view it from the front parlor of his home at 17 Washington Square North. Real-estate man Orlando B. Potter, one of the few critics of the site, said that Fifth Avenue would become useless as an artery through the park. He also objected that the arch would be an impediment to the elevated railroad he wanted to see built through the square. His voice was lost in a chorus of praise for the project.

The Critic was convinced that the "money would be freely subscribed for a work of art that would be so conspicuous an ornament to the city." New York had spent very little on monumental projects, and in fact, arch-rival Brooklyn was in the course of creating a memorial arch at Grand Army Plaza for $250,000. A goal of $150,000 was set for White's

41

permanent arch, and Stewart, who turned out to be a masterful fund raiser, set out to find it. He intuitively knew publicist's tricks and used them all. Newspapers and magazines needed fillers, so he planted any story that had a ring to it, however artificial. When the $50,000 mark was passed, with a $100 contribution from none other than Mrs. William Rhinelander Stewart, the story ran. When contributions came in from the famous, such as $100 apiece from actor Edwin Booth and Mayor Hugh J. Grant, the stories ran. When three boys were willing to contribute the proceeds from the first issue of their newspaper, *The Chimney Seat*, which was scheduled to be published as soon as they could get it out, the story ran. When contributions were sluggish, Stewart made "limited time" offers. For every contribution of five dollars or more in February 1890, the donor received a photograph of the Centennial medal

---

41. Washington Arch was the brainchild of William Rhinelander Stewart, who had asked Stanford White to direct the refurbishing of the chancel of the Church of the Ascension. He turned to White again for the arch, and at its unveiling White's design for it was recognized as a harbinger of neoclassical things to come.

sculpted by Augustus St. Gaudens or a print of an original lithograph by Edwin Blashfield, with lettering by Stanford White. Stewart's biggest coup came when Paderewski gave a benefit performance with the Boston Symphony Orchestra at the Metropolitan Opera House. Piano manufacturer William Steinway underwrote all the expenses, and the fund was raised by $4,300.

Some architects questioned the feasibility of recreating the original design in stone without providing more structural support. Architect Maurice Fernochan, who was in practice with Richard Morris Hunt, was convinced that without modifications the arch would "come down to the ground in a heap," so it came as little surprise to some when Henry B. Marquand, president of the Metropolitan Museum of Art and chairman of the committee for the erection of the arch, announced at the groundbreaking ceremonies in 1890 that the marble version would not be a facsimile of the wooden arch after all.

White instead designed a single span, 30 feet wide and 47 feet high, which he proudly pointed out was grander than any single-span memorial arch of antiquity. It also differed from its "classical predecessors in being generally lighter, in the prominence of its frieze, in the reduced height of the attic, and lastly and most important, in the absence of Orders." The cornerstone was laid with appropriate ceremony on Decoration Day, 1890, and two years later only three blocks of marble remained to be set in position to complete the first phase of the work, which called for yet another ceremony. Carved into the pieces of Tuckahoe marble were the initials RWG, SW, and WRS, and, with the aid of block and tackle, Richard Watson Gilder set his in place, then Stanford White, and finally, the indomitable William Rhinelander Stewart.

By 1895, the $133,500 that the arch had cost to that point had been collected from the populace in general and from the likes of William H. Vanderbilt and John Jacob Astor IV in particular. However, the biggest contributors of all were never listed in the regular postings of donors; builder David H. King had agreed to waive his fee, and Stanford White had agreed to waive his commission.

When Henry Marquand announced that the design would be completely new, he said that the arch represented the "beginning of a new and pure taste in the art of architecture," which proved true. The arch was one of the earliest manifestations of the City Beautiful Movement, which held that cities could be places of beauty if they were embellished by grand vistas, neoclassical design, and public sculpture. Chicago's Columbian Exposition launched the movement on a national scale and created the American Renaissance. Ironically, it was the exposition that kept the relief figures of Victory from being placed within the spandrels of the arch until 1893, when sculptor Frederick MacMonnies finished his work on the Great White City.

Judson Memorial Church

55 Washington Square South, at Thompson Street
1893
BUILDER: Berean Baptist Church
ARCHITECTS: McKim, Mead & White

By the 1890s, the neighborhood north of Washington Square was as patrician as it had been when it was developed 50 years before, but the neighborhoods east and south of it were filling up with immigrants and tenements, and the nativists were becoming restless. When Henry Marquand spoke at the laying of Washington Arch's cornerstone, he chided those who feared that the square would soon be surrounded by immigrant-inhabited tenements. Marquand wanted to know if the tenement dwellers would dishonor the memory of Washington by their mere proximity, and whether by virtue of their poverty they should be precluded the right to beautiful architecture. Dr. Edward Judson, the minister of the Berean Baptist Church on Bedford and Downing streets, was asking the same question, and he set out to bring some beauty into the lives of his immigrant congregants by way of an ecclesiastical complex that would serve them better and would act as a memorial to his father, a missionary to Burma.

Just as the real-estate community studied maps of different sections of the city to forecast possibilities for investment, so Dr. Judson carefully studied Manhattan. He concluded that the south side of Washington Square would be strategic because it was on the border of a densely built-up tenement district, yet it was only a stone's throw away from a respectable and aristocratic neighborhood. Although he hardly had enough money to warrant his actions, Dr. Judson bought the 130-by-100-foot plot on Washington Square South for $132,500 in 1888. And because he believed that the church was to minister to people who had so little beauty in their lives, he asked Stanford White to design the complex.

Behind buff brick and terra cotta, White artfully masked the complexity of the buildings, which included the 102-foot-long church, a home for children in the 165-foot-high campanile-like tower, and a young men's lodging house equipped with a library and a gymnasium. The estimated construction costs were $188,000, but prices would escalate and Judson's congregation was hardly wealthy. The combined cost of the land and buildings rose to a reported $450,000 by the time the complex was finished. The only sizable single contribution was $40,000 from John D. Rockefeller, but by 1893 Dr. Judson had miraculously netted all but $35,000 of the final bill.

Stanford White only designed four churches and one church porch in his entire career, and Judson Memorial—whose design was strongly influenced by Rome's Romanesque basilicas and whose detailing was in the manner of

42. Dr. Adonirum Judson, the rector of Judson Memorial Church, wanted Stanford White to create an ecclesiastical complex for his congregation because so few of his parishioners had beauty in their lives. The result is a vision of the early Renaissance from the hills of Tuscany.

the early Renaissance of Northern Italy—ranks as one of his gems. As in many of his projects, White's friends joined in the work. John LaFarge designed stained-glass windows, and Augustus St. Gaudens reportedly planned the marble reliefs on the chancel wall. At the same time, White oversaw some beguiling touches. At the corner of the building is a marble fountain that was given in memory of Duncan Dunbar, the minister of the MacDougal Baptist Church. The story was that Dunbar's supply of fresh water had given out on a sea voyage, which taught him the value of a drink of water and made the idea of a fountain in his memory especially appropriate.

The week-long dedicatory ceremonies included a series of talks on problems facing society and immigrants in particular, including sickness, ignorance, child neglect, and the influence of saloons. One of the addresses was by the vice- and Tammany-fighting Reverend Dr. Charles Parkhurst, for whom White later designed the Madison Avenue Presbyterian Church overlooking Madison Square.

Appellate Division, New York Supreme Court

27 Madison Avenue, northeast corner of 25th Street
1900
BUILDER: City of New York
ARCHITECT: James Brown Lord

The Appellate Division was created in 1894 as the state's highest court. There was no question that the court's role demanded a building with dignity and authority; the question was where to put it. For the justices to come in close daily contact with the lower-court judges whose decisions they review was not deemed judicious, which ruled out the downtown Civic Center. South of the Civic Center was the financial district with prices to match. An alluring piece of property was the former site of the Sixth Avenue Car Barns east of Sixth Avenue between 43rd and 44th streets, especially since the Association of the Bar of the City of New York had just purchased a portion of the site for its new quarters. This would have given the justices a congenial place for respites and the use of the 50,000-volume library for research. The justices, however, found a site overlooking Madison Square, whose residential quality appealed to them. And for at least three of the seven justices, the site meant a comfortable twenty-minute walk from home; for a fourth, a thirty-minute walk. A congressman owned most of the property, and when it was condemned at a valuation

44. Marble walls and benches, gilded capitals, and stained glass were all part of James B. Lord's goal of revivifying the glories of the past. The Van Buren in this stained glass is no doubt Martin, but the Fish could be any one of the New York Fish family in the New York Bar—Nicholas I and II, and Hamilton I and II.

43. Architect Daniel Lord re-created the spirit of Palladian London in his design for the Appellate Division Courthouse. The statues atop the cornice were not in place on opening day, but their absence did little to still visitors' enthusiasm for the courthouse.

43

44

plans. If the plans were satisfactory, Lord would become the supervising architect with a commission based on the schedule of payments of the American Institute of Architects.

Lord's plans called for a courthouse that was residential in scale—three stories high by 49 feet on Madison Avenue and 150 feet on 25th Street—a white marble palace of justice that would have made Inigo Jones proud. Allegorical statuary would abound on the outside, while the interiors would be filled with Siena marble, onyx paneling, murals, and stained glass. The justices liked Lord's plans on all levels, including the prosaic ones, such as the assurance of privacy that Lord guaranteed in a private entrance and stairs and corridors leading to their quarters. He even equipped the elevator with two doors, one for public areas, the other for the justices' quarters.

Lord's estimate was $659,000. When the low bid came in at $638,969, there was joy. When the construction costs

of $370,000, the city's controller raised his eyebrows over the specter of croneyism, but the deal was made anyway.

The state had given the justices the right to select an architect without a competition, and they chose James Brown Lord, who, in their opinion, was simply the most competent. This time the charge of the old-boy network could be justifiably leveled—architect Lord's grandfather had established the law firm Lord, Day & Lord, and his father was one of the practicing attorneys. The choice stood, and for $3,500 Lord was asked to draw up preliminary

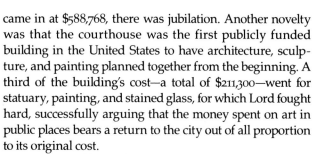

came in at $588,768, there was jubilation. Another novelty was that the courthouse was the first publicly funded building in the United States to have architecture, sculpture, and painting planned together from the beginning. A third of the building's cost—a total of $211,300—went for statuary, painting, and stained glass, for which Lord fought hard, successfully arguing that the money spent on art in public places bears a return to the city out of all proportion to its original cost.

Lord, himself, was filled with contradictions. His aesthetic self was willing to give the sculptors absolute freedom within the framework of neoclassicism, and he placed their work on a par with his. His aristocratic self, however, made him rather fearful of the artistic temperament, according to muralist Henry Siddons Mowbray. As a result, he disassociated himself from the artistic output to the point where he had John LaFarge arbitrate any differences on his behalf. Lord also believed that competitions were demeaning, so he asked Augustus St. Gaudens and Daniel Chester French to select the artists for him. With no public competition, there were rumblings. A group of sculptors protested that a committee of "several men who together assume the functions of a national art tribunal and all too often arrogantly pose as arbiter in both local and national affairs," were making unilateral decisions. Lord turned a deaf ear to the noise and sailed on.

When the courthouse was unveiled at a private viewing in December 1899, about a year and a half after its scheduled completion, only the Madison Avenue caryatids were installed. The missing statuary did little to dampen anyone's enthusiasm, but the building's glory filled one of the

46

45. Edwin Howland Blashfield, whose murals decorated Collis P. Huntington's house, William K. Vanderbilt's mansion, and the Waldorf-Astoria Hotel, said that when the time came to decorate the Appellate Division, "we tried so hard to give full measure that I fear we overdid it."

46. The Appellate Division's lawyers' cloakroom, which shares a common wall with the courtroom, has hooks for top hats and slots for canes. Some of the richly diffused light that enters the courtroom comes through the stained-glass window.

justices with mock misgiving. On the first day in the new courthouse, Justice Barrett quipped that he was fearful that he and his colleagues "may be expected to live up to it. . . . All these brilliant men, the sculptors, painters, glassmakers, seem to have conspired with the architect to woo our spirits back from these sombre robes and waft us back to youthful dreams of fairyland."

The Flatiron Building

(Originally, the Fuller Building)
175 Fifth Avenue, Broadway at 23rd Street
1902
BUILDER: George F. Fuller Company
ARCHITECT: Daniel H. Burnham

In 1855, Amos Eno bought the Fifth Avenue block at 23rd Street that, by virtue of its triangular shape, was called the "Flatiron." Eno was convinced that his $32,000 investment would be worth $1 million one day, and he was not far off the mark. Although the site was hardly developed to its

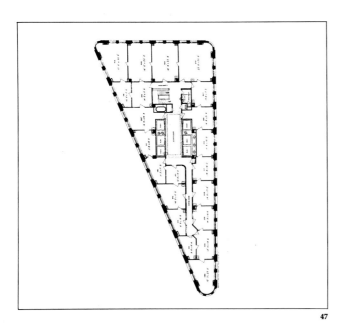

47

47. The Flatiron Building's floor plan shows that the famous site is not shaped like a real flatiron, which is roughly an isosceles triangle, but is shaped more like a right triangle. Ill-named or not, the configuration contributed to the kind of economical layout that builder Harry Black appreciated.

48. Although never the world's tallest building, Daniel Burnham's Flatiron Building captured the essence of the dramatic new age of skyscrapers and stole the hearts of millions. On a more prosaic level, the Fuller Company had paid a price for the site that set a real-estate record in the neighborhood, and the builders wanted to take full advantage of their investment.

48

maximum in the 1890s, the Eno Estate was collecting $42,000 a year on it, which meant a healthy four percent on a million dollars. During the '90s the Eno heirs started selling off some of the estate's vast holdings, and Samuel and Mott Newhouse, who held extensive copper mining interests in the West, wound up with the northern half of the Flatiron for $750,000. The price for the 3,700 square feet came to over $200 a square foot, an amount never before paid for lots in the vicinity of 23rd Street. The Newhouse brothers announced that a very tall building was regarded as an architectural and engineering impossibility because of the Flatiron's peculiar shape and size, so their intent was

49

terra cotta walls to look like an Italian Renaissance palazzo, the building gave an appearance of strength, allaying the fears of many, but the wind still continued to bring notoriety to the corner. One day in 1907, painter John Sloane noticed that the "pranks of the gusts about the Flatiron Building . . . were interesting to watch. Women's skirts flapped over their heads and ankles were to be seen." The corner's attractions became so famous that post cards portrayed men standing on the corner watching all the skirts go by, and sometimes the crowds grew so large that a policeman would be stationed at the corner to keep men from loitering. Stories have it that the policeman would shoo away the oglers by saying, "Hey, you on Twenty-three, skidoo."

to build a twelve story building that would have stores on the first floor and offices and bachelor apartments above. The scale of the neighborhood was changing, and bigger things were brewing.

In 1901, Harry S. Black's Fuller Company purchased the entire Flatiron block for almost $2 million. As evidenced by his Trinity and U.S. Realty Buildings, Black liked narrow sites for their efficiency, and he announced a colossus, a 300-foot high, steel-framed skyscraper that would take full advantage of the site—with 120,000 square feet of rentable floorspace. When the building was going up, *Architectural Record* said that it was "quite the most notorious thing in New York," if only because it was being constructed on such a "stingy piece of pie." But Charles Follen McKim, whose offices at 160 Fifth Avenue commanded a fine view of the building's progress, marveled at the rate of construction, which McKim said was about one story a day, in itself a good enough advertisement for Fuller. Although it was never New York's tallest, the Flatiron Building captured the imagination of citizens and visitors alike, and served as the symbol of the dramatic new age of skyscrapers.

Architect Daniel H. Burnham designed a frame with an elaborate set of bracing and cross-bracing. Despite its technological breakthroughs, some people were convinced that the building would topple with the great gusts of wind for which the 23rd Street corner was famous. Decorated with

The Colony Club

120 Madison Avenue, between 30th and 31st Streets
1907
BUILDER: The Colony Club
ARCHITECTS: McKim Mead & White

The idea for the Colony Club came to Mrs. J. Borden Harriman in the summer of 1902. She had to leave Newport to run a few errands in the city, but the Harriman townhouse was full of painters and plasterers and checking into a hotel was out of the question. A gentleman could stay at a hotel or his club, but New York matrons were discouraged from checking into hotels alone and they had no club at which to stay. So Mrs. Harriman and a few like-minded women decided to build a clubhouse in the belief that they had as much right to the creature comforts as men. As if that were not enough, these women brazenly dubbed their club a club, separating them from the usual women's groups that ordinarily called themselves associations or leagues. "Club" had a bad image, connoting high living rather than moral and social uplift.

The initiation fees were set at $150, with annual dues of $100, which made the Colony as pricey as the most expensive men's clubs. Its admission standards were also as exclusive, and the club's system of governing was copied from the Union Club. To finance the clubhouse, members were asked for contributions. All three of J. Pierpont Morgan's daughters were members, and Morgan agreed to subscribe $10,000 if nine others would do the same. August Belmost II was willing, and William C. Whitney offered to put up $25,000 if the women built a clubhouse as large as the Metropolitan Club. They did not, but they commissioned its architect, Stanford White.

White actually became more than the club's architect. According to Mrs. Harriman, he was an instructor in ar-

49. The Flatiron Building was dependent on a steel frame for support. Nevertheless, Daniel Burnham gave the building a rugged face that ostensibly contributed to the support of the building, but the fabric of the curtain wall is terra cotta, which is of little value in compression.

50

sophistication to interior decoration, "like a witch sweeping the cobwebs out of the sky," said Mrs. Harriman. The interiors had all the comforts of a first-class clubhouse. On the top floor was a glass-enclosed winter garden heated by a pair of porcelain stoves that were custom made in Paris. On the upper floors were a full gymnasium, a running track, and squash courts, and in the basement was a swimming pool that measured 20 by 55 feet. The pool, finished in white marble, was the second largest in any club in the country, and was exceeded abroad only by the Empress in London.

The Colony represented a community of interests and attracted a diversity of members, including society leaders like Mrs. John Jacob Astor IV, literary women like Jeanette Gilder, coeditor of *The Critic*, actresses Maude Adams and Ethel Barrymore, and professional women like Elsie de Wolfe. The members made only one mistake. The law said that a church could have the state refuse a liquor license to any institution within 200 feet of the church's front door. Across the avenue was the Madison Avenue Baptist Church, whose board of deacons was exercising its right. The Gotham Hotel was experiencing a similar problem, and although the Colony Club was never as flagrant in flaunting the law as the hotel, the club adopted basically the same policy. Elizabeth Marbury, chairman of the board of governors, said that there was nothing to stop members from keeping anything they wanted in their lockers. "Anyhow," said Miss Marbury, "even if we didn't have lockers, there's a place around the corner. Any member who wanted to send out and get a drink could do so." Certainly somebody was, because accounts of meals included mention of $75 wine bills, as well as champagne dinners.

Without liquor sales by the club, profits were bound to be effected, and with or without a liquor license, some skeptics were sure that the club would fail anyway. The Princeton Club was convinced that the Colony would never open, so the Princetonians put their plans for a new clubhouse in abeyance, believing that they could pick up the building for a song. The club did not fail. In fact, it made an $8,000 profit its first year. The Colony Club was a natural, of course, and long overdue. One club member who was both the wife and mother of clubmen, called home one evening soon after the club had opened. "Don't wait dinner," she said, "I'm dining at my club." She then turned to Mrs. Harriman and said triumphantly, "My dear, I've been getting that message for years—now I'm giving it."

chitecture and gave the building committee a rare opportunity, for he made the members study the "examples of Colonial architecture from which he was drawing his inspiration. He went to Annapolis to look at a balcony. The facade he chose from a beautiful mansion in Charleston. . . . With all his sense of appreciation of the richer architectural moods of the Renaissance in Italy and the grand French days, he was quick to kindle at the beautiful simplicity of the early American, so designed for democratic living in the new world." The clubhouse's fine details shine through, from the patterned brickwork to the club's monogram worked into the railing above the cornice. The brickwork, said Charles C. Baldwin, is "small—almost dainty—and . . . built entirely of headers, expressing so nearly as architecture can the 'tone' and atmosphere of an exclusive women's club." Unfortunately, the building's balcony, which was supported by cast-iron Corinthian pillars, was truncated by city edict. To keep the feeling of what was, the balcony was metamorphosed into a railing, and the pillars became pilasters.

At the instigation of White, Elsie de Wolfe interrupted her stage career to design the interiors. She brought a new

50. The Colony Club was America's first women's club to construct its own clubhouse. Stanford White gave it a dainty facade from the American Georgian period; charter member Elsie deWolfe, who was later Lady Mendl, designed the interiors.

51

52

The Prince George Hotel

14 East 28th Street, between Fifth and Madison Avenues
1906
BUILDER: Charles F. Rogers
ARCHITECT: Howard Greenley

The hotels Seville, Martha Washington, Madison Square, Arlington, and Prince George were built within a few years of each other in the neighborhood around Madison Square. These hotels did not have the bustling atmosphere of a Waldorf-Astoria or a Knickerbocker or an Astor, nor were they resplendent with marble and gilt. They were designed for guests who were seeking quietly genteel and comfortable elegance.

The original plans for the block-through Prince George were drawn up by A. N. Allen, but owner Charles F. Rogers changed his mind and chose Howard Greenley to design the $800,000 hotel in 1903 in the restrained French Renaissance style that was becoming *de rigeur*. Greenley, a 1901 graduate of the Ecole des Beaux-Arts who was associated with Arnold Brunner for the first two years of his career, began his own firm the year of the Prince George commission. (He went on to design the interiors for Lord Duveen's

New York mansion and to serve as the president of the Architectural League for 25 years.)

Greenley used painted surfaces and woods to carry the interior decoration, and with baronial accessories such as Caen stone fireplaces he managed to create an atmosphere of richness without vast expenditures. The throne-lined corridor ran from street to street with public rooms off it. On one side was the cafe, on the other the tearoom and the dining room. Dominant colors in one room were picked up in a minor role in the adjoining room. The dining room was decorated in subdued tones of green with buff trim, with a fresco in reds and blues as a foil; the tearoom's frescos in a lattice-and-vine design picked up the dining room's greens and reds. Since the tearoom occupied the center of the hotel and had no natural light, the trick was to bring a sense of the outdoors into the room. Electric lights were neatly tucked into the vines that hung from the trellis, and lights were concealed behind the opalescent glass cartouches above the pilasters. George Innes, Jr., son of the great Hudson River School artist, painted a series of panels representing the seasons, and Howard Greenley designed the faience fountain with its ornamental pond lilies, irises, and other aquatic plants. The fountain statuary was especially appropriate for a hotel owned by Charles Rogers, the son of sculptor John Rogers.

The Prince George was open only a little more than two years when Evelyn Nesbit Thaw shook up its quiet demeanor. The 22-year-old Mrs. Thaw had been set up in a residence at 446 Park Avenue while she was a star witness at Harry K. Thaw's second trial for the murder of Stanford White. Her menage consisted of two maids, a footman, a chef, and a chauffeur for her electric brougham, but her lease expired at the end of March 1907, and was not renewed. Her lawyer told Col. A. E. Dick, the manager of the Prince George, that Mrs. Thaw was looking for a quiet hotel. A drawing room, bedroom, and bath, as well as a maid's room, were engaged, with the manager's blessing. Only a few days after Mrs. Thaw moved in, she was involved in a minor *scandale* in the dining rooms of the Knickerbocker Hotel. Mrs. Thaw, it seems, was attracting too much attention with her gentleman escort, the same phenomenon that occurred every time Mrs. Thaw walked alone through the lobby of the Prince George. Her appearances, however, seemed seldom enough. The room clerk maintained that she only used her rooms about every other night, but the commotion that she created and the complaints that Col. Dick received were enough reason for him to ask her to give up her suite. For Evelyn Nesbit Thaw, whom St. Gaudens described as a "woman with the face of an angel and the heart of a snake," it was one more humiliating step down from the glory that was Stanford White.

51. Howard Greenley's facade for the Prince George Hotel is filled with the kind of neo-French Renaissance detailing that was becoming popular for hotel- and apartment-house design in the early 1900s. One of the difficulties in applying anachronistic motifs is that an ideal in one scale can become overblown in another.

52. Everything about this mantelpiece derives from the period of Francis I, except the British icons. The royal standard and three feathers of the Prince of Wales are no doubt there to symbolize Prince George, who had become the Prince of Wales in 1901 and who would become George V in 1910. Naming the hotel the Prince George was a ploy to attract English visitors and give the place a tony cachet.

53. Builder Charles F. Rogers was the son of sculptor John Rogers, who produced his sculpture groups not far from the Prince George. This faience fountain in the Tea Room is not a Rogers, however—it was designed by the Beaux-Arts trained architect Howard Greenley.

54. *The Waldorf-Astoria was built in two stages by bickering members of the Astor family. Only a stone's throw away from the grand hotel was Murray Hill, a neighborhood whose exclusionary covenant did not allow such crass commercialism in its midst.*

4

The Murrays' Hill

In the early 1800s, the farm that was on the high ground between today's Lexington and Madison avenues from approximately 34th to 38th streets was owned by Mary and John Murray. In 1847, their heirs drew up a covenant that restricted the use of the land to brick or stone private dwellings of at least two stories. The only exceptions were churches and private stables, which meant that the kind of industry ordinarily associated with the edge of a nineteenth-century city was banned, and the Murrays' Hill was on the edge of the city in 1847, with Madison Avenue not even cut through north of 42nd Street.

The Murray clan clung tenaciously to its property, but John Thompson, who owned a parallelogram of land that roughly stretched from Madison to Sixth avenues between 32nd and 36th streets, sold his farm to William Backhouse Astor in 1826 for $25,000, and the Astors sat on it. Caroline Schermerhorn Astor was the one who saw the property's possibilities, and by 1856 she had cajoled her husband William into building a mansion in the vanguard of the so-cially-acceptable limits of Fifth Avenue, on the southwest corner of 34th Street. A brownstone mansion was erected in which an art gallery was installed that could be turned into a ballroom. (According to Ward McAllister, Mrs. Astor's social advisor, the ballroom could only accommodate 400 guests comfortably, and Four Hundred became the magical number for New York society with a capital "S.")

Mrs. Astor's brother-in-law, John Jacob Astor III, followed the leader and erected a mansion next door, on the northwest corner of 33rd Street. In 1890, he bequeathed the house to his son, William Waldorf Astor, who decided not to live in it. Fifth Avenue to the south was losing its grip as a first-class residential district, and dreaded business was beginning to creep in. W. W. Astor had considered living as far uptown as Riverside Drive between 112th and 113th streets, but he chose the northeast corner of Fifth Avenue and 56th Street instead.

Stories have it that during the Newport season of 1890, Caroline Schermerhorn Astor began to be known as *the* Mrs. Astor, which enraged William Waldorf Astor. So far as he was concerned, he was the male head of the family, and if anybody was to be addressed as *the* Mrs. Astor, it would be his wife, not his aunt. To spite her, the story goes, he decided to build a hotel on his 33rd Street property that would literally overshadow her.

The Astor family was not new to the hotel business. In

1836, John Jacob Astor had built the six-story, 300-room Astor House on lower Broadway. It was the city's most influential hotel of its time, with innovations that included interior plumbing, public rooms, and seventeen bathrooms. It was described as an ornament to the city and a monument to its proprietor, and William Waldorf Astor was determined to continue the tradition at his Waldorf, even naming the hotel for himself in the fashion of the Astors. As manager, Astor hired George C. Boldt, the pet of the rich and fastidious patrons of Philadelphia's Bellevue, and Boldt oversaw every detail in the preparation of the twelve-story hotel, which had a 100-foot frontage on Fifth Avenue and a 275-foot depth on 33rd Street when it opened in 1893. Architect Henry J. Hardenbergh gave the 500-room hotel a robust, dignified, and comfortable appearance in a style that was described as German Renaissance, which allowed odd balconies, turrets, and elaborate decoration.

William Waldorf Astor might have built the Waldorf to spite his aunt, but when the plans were promulgated in 1890 there was a rumor that the residence of Caroline Schermerhorn Astor might be torn down and the site used for a sister hotel. Boldt certainly had a clue, because he told Hardenbergh to plan for the eventuality of extending the hotel to 34th Street, and he had Hardenbergh design the Waldorf's lobby floor to be high enough above the level of 33rd Street to compensate for the hill on the avenue. If there was to be a combined hotel, the ground floor would be on a single level.

By 1891, William Waldorf Astor had tired of America's coarse ways and retired to genteel England, where his money bought him a baronetcy and a little respect while his estate managers carried on. With his abdication, John Jacob Astor IV, Caroline's son, became the titular head of the family, and with their move to 65th Street imminent, the second half of the hotel could begin to be planned officially. The hotel was originally to be called the Schermerhorn, in honor of young Astor's illustrious mother, but cooler heads prevailed and the hotel was named in honor of Astoria, the fur-trapping colony in Oregon that represented the beginnings of the great Astor wealth. At sixteen stories, the Astoria dwarfed its sister, and with a 100-foot frontage on the avenue, a 350-foot frontage on 34th Street, and a 75-foot wing on 33rd, the L-shaped Astoria wrapped around the Waldorf.

The Astoria had 550 rooms, making the combined Waldorf-Astoria the biggest hotel in the city, with 1,050 rooms when it opened in 1897. The main dining rooms extended along the entire Fifth Avenue side of the lobby floor, and it was decorated with a frieze by Charles Yardley Turner. The entire second floor was given over to public rooms that could be used for private "entertainments." The ballroom held more dancers than Mrs. Astor's ballroom ever would, and it could be turned into a theater, with a capacity of more than 1,100 guests seated on gilt chairs and still more in the double-tier boxes that ran around three sides of the

room. The ceiling was decorated by a 44-by-65-foot mural by Edwin Howland Blashfield, who was fresh from his triumph at the Library of Congress, where he had painted the ceiling under the dome. But the Waldorf-Astoria's most impressive feature was Peacock Alley, the marble-clad corridor where the rich and hopeful came to show off their finery. Out-of-towners and New Yorkers alike were seldom as happy as when they were in Peacock Alley, either putting on a vain show or taking one in.

The De Lamar Mansion

233 Madison Avenue, on the northeast corner of 37th Street
1906
BUILDER: Joseph Raphael De Lamar
ARCHITECT: Charles Pierrepont Henry Gilbert

Murray Hill's most expensive house was undoubtedly the mansion of Joseph "Captain" Raphael De Lamar. The 50-by-100-foot plot alone cost $250,000 in 1902, and the projected construction costs were $325,000. The actual combined cost probably came closer to $700,000, some say $1 million.

De Lamar could well afford it. After becoming the master of his own ship at the age of 23, the Dutch emigrant entered the salvage business in New England. When gold fever bit in 1878, he went west to Leadville, Colorado, where he made his stake, but where he also realized that he knew nothing about mining. He enrolled in chemistry and metallurgy classes, came to understand what he owned, and sold out for about $20 million two years later. De Lamar was elected to the Idaho Senate in 1884, became bored with the West and came to New York City, where he married. Daughter Alice was born in 1896, after which the family lived in Paris, where De Lamar bought elaborate bronze-mounted furniture, and where he bought art, "the sort of paintings," said his daughter Alice, "collectors bought in 1900 in heavy gold frames." While in Paris, De Lamar and his wife were divorced, and he returned to New York with Alice.

55. Murray Hill's most expensive house of the period was this Beaux-Arts extravaganza that C. P. H. Gilbert designed for Joseph De Lamar. Some estimates place the cost of the land and the house together at $1 million.

55

Architect Charles Pierrepont Henry Gilbert had also gone West, where he had learned the trick riding he continued to practice in New York at the Squadron A Armory. Gilbert bore two of Brooklyn's most famous names as his middle names, and represented solid New York gentry, with membership in the Sons of the Revolution, Society of Colonial Wars, Society of the War of 1812, and New York's most prestigious clubs. De Lamar gave Gilbert a free hand in the design of the house.

Alice De Lamar, then about eight years old, was shown the 130-room mansion of Senator William A. Clark of Montana that was rising on Fifth Avenue and 77th Street, and she was told that her new home would look just like it. Understandably, both houses seemed forbidding and gloomy to a child, and they soured Alice's appreciation for things Beaux-Arts evermore. De Lamar's house is, nonetheless, uncontestably one of the grandest expressions of the Beaux-Arts in the city, a great French-style *palais* from its concrete base to the copper cresting atop its mansard roof. Contractor Charles T. Willis saw to it that Gilbert's specifications were carefully followed, and Gilbert called for the highest quality. Steel was used for columns and beams, and the house was completely fireproof. Interior partitions were built of terra cotta to prevent the spread of

fire laterally, and the Roebling System of flooring—concrete poured atop metal arches—was used to prevent the spread of fire vertically. The street and avenue facades were given a facing of granite, the terra cotta bay windows were given a copper facing, and the mansard roof is tile and copper. The house boasted two Otis elevators, one for passengers, which only rose to the fifth floor, the other for servants, which was about three-by-five feet and rose from the basement to the attic. Gilbert estimated that an elevator added a minimum of $2,000 to the overall cost of a house, a small price to pay, and he believed that any house that cost over $25,000 deserved at least one.

The layout and vast number of rooms were what you would expect in a mansion. The ground floor had the dining room in the east end and the library and billiard room overlooking the avenue. "A fountain with plants and marble figures [stood] at the foot of the stairs," said Alice De Lamar. "The floor above [had] the ball room, . . . and the music room with a gilt grand piano and vitrines for all sorts of bibelots. . . . The art gallery room [had] walls painted Pompeian red . . . and [was] filled with paintings. . . . In the art gallery was [Hiram] Power's *Greek Slave.*" (This was one of the nineteenth century's most popular statues. There were six replicas, and De Lamar probably had one of them.) "Among the paintings, the most prominent item was Bougereau's *Aurore*, which was supposed to be his masterpiece. We had that picture in Paris in 1898, long before the Madison Avenue House." The most valuable object in the house was the large Persian rug, which Miss De Lamar believes is in the Getty Museum. There were also large windows of Tiffany glass that were lit electrically from the back, and Alice's father took her to the Tiffany factory to see them being made. On the third floor were De Lamar's large bedroom and bath, the breakfast room, and two guest rooms and baths. "Above was a floor with my bedroom and bath, the sewing room or library for myself, and a guest room and bath," said Miss De Lamar. "On the floor above that was a number of servants' rooms and the housekeeper's room, and above that the laundry room and the flat roof behind the mansard, where a great deal of coal soot used to collect, and where the dogs were permitted to run. The mansard tower opposite the laundry was equipped as a gymnasium, but it was useless because of the coal soot." For all the house's luxury, the heat never seemed to reach the radiators on Alice's floor, and the temperature was seldom above 60 degrees.

The house was filled with sadness. In 1904, De Lamar practically decided to sell the unfinished mansion. "His desire to be the owner of one of the finest dwellings in the city and the costliest one on Murray Hill," said the *Times*, "is not nearly so strong as it was . . . when he bought the site." De Lamar was described as the "Mystery Man of Wall Street" by his associates, and as "taciturn and aloof" by the *Dictionary of American Biography.* "The ball room never got used for that purpose. . . . My father was in his late 60s

57

59

58

57. Off the grand foyer on the second floor were the ballroom (stage right) and the Pompeian Room (stage left), while suspended above was the musicians' gallery.

58. De Lamar's Pompeian Room depicted classical themes in its frieze (one of the panels shows Ulysses defying Circe), as well as muselike interpretations of sculpture, drawing, architecture, and the other arts. This room held Hiram Powers's *Greek Slave.*

59. Tucked into the corner of De Lamar's Pompeian Room is one of a pair of Tiffany windows. De Lamar took his young daughter Alice to see some of the glass being manufactured at the Tiffany Studios.

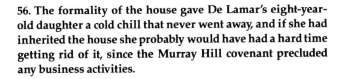

56. The formality of the house gave De Lamar's eight-year-old daughter a cold chill that never went away, and if she had inherited the house she probably would have had a hard time getting rid of it, since the Murray Hill covenant precluded any business activities.

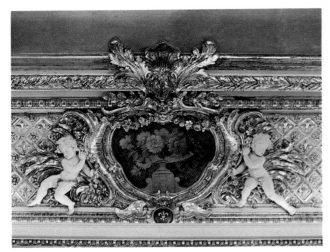

61

when he moved in there, and had taken to his 'carpet slippers' pretty much and did not care to entertain guests. . . . Once a year I had a birthday party of a few kids from my school."

When pneumonia killed the seventy-five-year-old De Lamar in 1918, his estate was valued at over $32 million. Alice was bequeathed $10 million, two yachts, and Pembroke, De Lamar's mansion on Long Island's North Shore. The balance, including 233 Madison Avenue, was divided equally among the medical schools of Harvard, Johns Hopkins, and Columbia. The medical schools set out to sell the mansion as soon as the will was probated and in 1922 they believed that they had made a sale to the American Bible Society. The society's role, however, was not only to sell the Bible figuratively but to do so literally, and the Murray Hill covenant clearly specified that buildings erected as dwelling houses were restricted to that purpose. The Appellate Division agreed that the sale would violate the covenant, so the million-dollar house was finally sold to the National Democratic club for less than $300,000. For Alice De Lamar, the house had remained a gloomy place and she was glad when the war provided the excuse for her to get out of it. She never set foot in it after its contents were auctioned off.

---

60. The ballroom was never used as such during De Lamar's stay in the house. As his daughter said, he had "already taken to his bedroom slippers."

61. The De Lamar house is now the Consulate of the Polish People's Republic. Polish craftsmen were brought to this country especially to restore the house, which had been sorely neglected during its middle years as the Democratic Club.

The Pierpont Morgan Library
33 West 36th Street, between Madison and Park Avenues
1906
BUILDER: J. Pierpont Morgan
ARCHITECTS: McKim, Mead & White

One of Murray Hill's most famous residents and ardent defenders was J. Pierpont Morgan. In the 1870s, he and his family lived at 6 East 40th Street, just off Fifth Avenue, but throughout the decade Morgan kept eyeing the three brownstone mansions that the Stokes-Dodge family had built on Madison Avenue between 36th and 37th streets. In 1880, Morgan got his chance to buy the house on the northeast corner of 36th Street. It was large, comfortable, unpretentious, and understated, nothing like the houses the Vanderbilts were building on Fifth Avenue. It suited his needs perfectly, and after minor modifications, in 1882 the family moved in.

Morgan, the banker's banker, was doing innovative things with money on a huge scale at the end of the nineteenth century, and he was acquiring works of art on an equally huge and innovative scale. His collecting was not in the same league with that of the average millionaire in the market for a languorous Barbizon scene for his walls or a marble bust for the hall. Morgan sought finer things, rare books and manuscripts and medieval triptychs and Chinese porcelains. By 1900, his comfortably large house was getting uncomfortably cramped, and Morgan decided to build a private library next door in which he could properly store his treasures.

Morgan's property extended 157 feet east of Madison Avenue and was separated from his neighbor's property by an eighteen-foot alley. In 1900, William Salomon, chairman of the board of the Baltimore & Ohio, sold Morgan the neighboring 75-by-100-foot plot, giving him a 250-foot frontage on 36th Street. By the spring of 1902, Morgan had purchased two more lots and owned all the property between his house and the corner lot on Park Avenue. He cut off 28 feet from the eastern end of his property for a house for his daughter and son-in-law, the Herbert L. Satterlees, and the site between their new house and his was "to be laid out architecturally and turned into a garden (135 by 100 feet)," said Charles Follen McKim to his partner William Rutherford Mead. On the site, Morgan proposed to "build a little museum building to house his books and collections." Morgan authorized the firm to go ahead with both commissions.

Morgan had already rejected a rather top-heavy Baroque design by Whitney Warren for the library, and it is surpris-

62. The library of J. Pierpont Morgan is modestly described as a Palladian garden house, but the pure neoclassical facade masks the fact that this was a very expensive toy for a very rich man. Architect Charles Follen McKim saw his chance to play as well, and convinced Morgan that the library should be constructed according to the pure building technique of the Erectheion in Athens, where perfectly cut stones were assembled without an ounce of mortar.

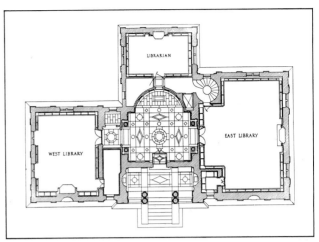

62

ing that Morgan's plan in general was not rejected by his neighbors. The Murray Hill Covenant clearly outlawed museums, though the museums the Murray clan had in mind were doubtless more like Barnum's side shows than the private library Morgan conceived. If there were any questions of propriety, Morgan did the right thing politically and sought the approval of some neighbors. By bringing them into his confidence and creating an advisory board, he was able to calm any qualms his neighbors had about the ticklish subject of harmony with the prevailing brownstone fronts. The library was not to dwarf the houses nearby and it would be tastefully designed in white marble. One neighbor suggested that white marble might give the impression that Morgan had decided to have his mausoleum next door to his house. Consultation with McKim led to the choice of Knoxville marble, with a hue of pinkish gray to diminish the lugubrious effect.

McKim, Mead & White presented a pair of designs to Morgan in 1902. One was a rather dry neo-Greek temple with a portico topped by outsized anthemia, a design that doubtless would have led everyone to believe that Morgan was indeed building his mausoleum. The other design was reminiscent of an Italian garden structure, a discreet and graceful building with a Palladian-style loggia set into it. It appealed to Morgan.

McKim understood that the library was tantamount to a big toy for Morgan, and since money was a minor obstacle for his client, here was an opportunity for McKim to play as well. McKim told Morgan that he had dreamed of building after the manner of the Greeks. He had tried to insert the blade of his knife between the stones of the Erectheum in Athens and had been unable to do it. He wanted to follow

63. Morgan's corner house was torn down after his death and a new wing was built to designs by James Wistar Morris. The front door to *the* library is now used only occasionally, and the usual visitors enter McKim's wing from the area northeast of the West Library, which was Morgan's den.

the Greeks' example, but it would cost a small fortune and no one would see where the additional money went. Morgan was planning to spend about $350,000, and he asked how much extra. "Fifty thousand dollars," answered McKim. "Go ahead," came the reply. As a result, McKim had the marble cut so that the tongues and grooves perfectly fitted together, with no mortar used.

The brick foundations were set in 1903. Three years later, the building was completed at a cost of over $1,150,000, over three times the original estimate. The price did not displease Morgan, but, according to muralist H. Siddons Mowbray, Morgan complained that, "it wasn't his library that was being built, but McKim's." It was McKim who conceived the masterpiece and oversaw its construction; it was McKim who got to scour Rome for imperial porphyry and varicolored marbles; it was McKim who saw that craftsmen and artists of the highest order were hired for the work. It was McKim, in short, who was the creator.

What Morgan got for his million-plus dollars was as close to perfection as anybody got in the Age of Elegance or any other time. It was the *London Times* that anglophile Morgan allowed to review the library, and the *New York Times* arranged with its sister paper to reprint the article and the editorial that accompanied it. This period in American design is often called the American Renaissance. Money created this rebirth of classical antiquity, just as money had created the Renaissance in Italy, France, and England. The

66

65

London Times compared Morgan with Lorenzo the Magnificent in the catholicity of his taste, and said that the making of a library like Morgan's was the "outcome of the age of millionaires. These gentlemen of vast means abound in America. . . . One out of ten has taste; one out of a hundred has genius. Frick and Widener come under the former category, but the man of genius is Morgan. . . . [He] is probably the greatest collector of things splendid and beautiful and rare who has ever lived."

The library has burglarproofing that includes some extraordinary measures, such as steel shutters that noiselessly roll up at night to cover the windows. And there is a sanctum sanctorum that the *London Times* reported is "actually a safe. One enters by a thick steel door fitted with a combination lock. The walls of the room are of steel. . . . It has all been so cleverly done that nothing but the door indicated that one is in the veritable vault."

---

64. McKim's chaste version of the Italian Renaissance greeted visitors as they arrived in the library's entrance hall. To the right is the East Library, to the left is the West Library, or Morgan's study, and straight ahead, through one of the city's loveliest doors, was the librarian's office.

65. Morgan's West Library, or study, is where he held court and played the role of the Medici prince. Steel shutters silently roll up to cover the windows at night.

66. The East Wing of the Morgan Library is a bibliophile's paradise regained. A touch of irony is the theme of the Flemish tapestry above the fireplace—it is called *The Triumph of Avarice*.

The west end of the library houses Morgan's den, paneled and gilded in the best robber baronial tradition. Here Morgan could hold court. The East Room is ringed by balconies that provided access to the bookshelves. (Some of the most valuable books are in asbestos-lined cases on glass shelves, protected by a light ornamental grille.) Here H. Siddons Mowbray painted the frescoes for the 30-foot high ceiling. The tinted glass was not looted from some European treasury, as the fifteenth-century fireplace and Flemish tapestry had been, but was imported from France and only cost $522.

While the library was being constructed, Morgan began to stake his claim on a family compound in Murray Hill. The four-story home on the east end of his property for his daughter and son-in-law was finished in 1903. The following year, son J. P. Morgan, Jr., returned from London amidst rumors of his father's imminent retirement. He rented a Stanford White-designed house around the corner at 22 Park Avenue. In the meantime, Morgan paid $500,000 for the William E. Dodge house, which sat on a 65-by-157-foot plot next door to Morgan on Madison Avenue. The month his son arrived, Morgan bought the last of the three-house complex, the Anson Phelps Stokes house on the southeast corner of 37th Street. The asking price for the house and its 65-by-100-foot plot was $1 million. After alterations, J. P., Jr., moved into it, and the middle house was torn down to provide more space for gardening.

The real-estate community was convinced that the activity by the likes of De Lamar and Morgan would only strengthen values in Murray Hill. Ironically, the changes that were wrought and the high quality they produced sowed the seeds of trouble. Because Murray Hill was so genteel and privileged and becoming ever more so, it also became desirable as a place to do business. Small shops had already filtered into some of the basements and parlor floors of brownstones on the periphery of Murray Hill. And 34th Street, with its crosstown horse cars, had all the hustle and bustle of a main street.

B. Altman & Co.

355 Fifth Avenue, between 34th and 35th Streets
1906
BUILDER: Benjamin Altman
ARCHITECTS: Trowbridge & Livingston

Broadway and Sixth Avenue between 14th and 23rd were dubbed "Ladies' Mile" because of their concentration of department and speciality stores. The city's biggest stores were there, many on full-block frontages, including Siegel-Cooper, "The Big Store—A City in Itself," Simpson Crawford, Hugh O'Neill, Macy's, Stern's, and B. Altman & Co.

Altman's founder, Benjamin Altman, was born on the Lower East Side in 1840. Despite his lack of formal education, by the time he was 25 he was operating his own dry goods store on Third Avenue and 10th Street. By the mid-1870s, Altman had a store on Sixth Avenue at 19th Street that occupied a 150-by-184-foot lot. In 1896, his expanded store occupied the entire avenue frontage. Altman, however, did not own the land upon which his store was built. The 18th Street corner was held on a 21-year lease, and the 19th Street corner was an Astor leasehold. Nevertheless, Altman's future partner, Michael Friedsam, announced in 1900 that Altman had acquired more of the site and that further expansion was imminent. "When the work will begin I am not in a position to say," said Friedsam. "It may be one year, two years, or ten. Our business has increased so rapidly that we must have more space."

It was all a virtuoso display of the art of dissembling, all an elaborate ruse. As early as 1895, Altman had bought the house on the southeast corner of Fifth Avenue and 35th Street, just beyond the bounds of the Murray Hill Covenant. In 1901, he bought the house at 363 Fifth Avenue, which was in the middle of the block. Aiming to acquire the entire block, he did not want his acquisitions known, because he knew that rumors raised prices. Each deal was negotiated separately and discretely. Sensing commercial opportunities, some owners simply refused to budge, others were only willing to rent. By 1904, however, Altman felt he had secured enough land to announce that he was moving to the fashionable East Side. He paid dearly for his hasty announcement. In March 1905, he bought 5 East 34th Street for $250,000 and 3 East 34th Street for $265,000. These were Fifth Avenue prices, not crosstown street prices. However, with the exceptions of the corner lot on Fifth Avenue at 34th Street and the entire Madison Avenue front, with those two purchases he nearly owned the block. Despite the holdouts, Altman was ready to build. He hired the firm of Trowbridge & Livingston, who designed a neo-Italian Renaissance palazzo that would cost an estimated $2.5 million. The sandstone, imported from France, is the same that brings the lovely warmth and softness to so many buildings in Paris.

The eight-story Altman store is distinguished by its classical proportions and its attention to detail. Marc Eidlitz & Son were charged with overseeing construction, and they made sure that the best materials and workmanship went into it. The Hecla Iron Works ran advertisements extolling their contributions, "examples of iron stair work, railings, elevator screens, lamps, etc., which for richness and intricacy of design have never been surpassed in this country. In addition to this, the duplex electro-plated finish gives an appearance of solid bronze, and for all practical purposes it is equal in every respect, while the cost is considerably less than the latter."

The arrangement of the merchandise was duplicated from the Sixth Avenue store so that old customers could quickly adapt to the new store. Only the ambience was grander. Galleries were arranged around a central court lighted by a great dome of glass. On overcast days and late afternoons, electric lights hidden in globes above the dome substituted for sunlight. A great merchandising idea was introduced in the millinery and gown department on the third floor, where a large room was outfitted with mirrors on all four walls. One of the mirrored walls was a panel that could be slid back to let the sun shine in, so fabric could be examined under both natural and artificial light.

Altman was a patient man and continued to negotiate with the property owners who were blocking his progress. The Madison Avenue holdouts were Mrs. Margaret A. Howard, who owned the 75-by-100-foot plot on the northwest corner of 34th Street, and William Waldorf Astor, who owned the balance. In 1910, Altman struck a deal with Mrs. Howard. She had bought the three lots twenty years before

---

67. Benjamin Altman's Fifth Avenue store, designed by Trowbridge & Livingston, was tasteful and unobtrusive to the point that Altman never put up a sign to advertise the store's presence.

for $190,000. Altman paid her $750,000. Then he dealt with William Waldorf Astor. The policy of the Astor Estate was to hang on to property, leasing it for periods of 21 years and then either renewing the lease on their terms or taking title to the land and everything on it, including improvements, if the lessee did not agree to terms. The Astor Estate had been Altman's landlord before, and Altman might have learned that sometimes the estate made mistakes and rented property on long-term leases with renewals based on the property's valuation at the time the original lease was signed. Altman accepted a long-term lease from the Astor Estate with renewals that were described as liberal.

Altman's only stumbling block now was the northeast corner of Fifth Avenue and 34th Street, which was occupied by the Knoedler Art Gallery. In 1905, Roland Knoedler had refused to budge. So far as he was concerned, his quarters were good enough, and his lease would not expire until 1911. However, in 1910, the art dealer announced that he was moving to the northwest corner of 46th Street and Fifth Avenue, where he planned a building to rival Joseph Duveen's, his only real competition.

Knoedler's original reluctance to oblige Altman was no doubt based on a certain vindictiveness. When Altman started collecting art, he went to Henry Duveen, Joseph

Duveen's uncle, rather than Knoedler. Altman was a collector of the first rank, amassing a collection that was one of the few that could hold a candle to Morgan's. Like Morgan, Altman would build a private art gallery. In 1909, he bought the house at 1 West 50th Street, which was next door to his mansion at 626 Fifth, and had it torn down and replaced by a brownstone building designed and constructed by the same firms that did his Fifth Avenue store. Altman's gallery was a two-story-high room measuring 38 by 52 feet and it was filled with paintings. Just as a portion of Morgan's collection was given to the Metropolitan Museum of Art to create the Pierpont Morgan Wing, so *all* of Altman's collection, valued at $15 million and described as "without question the most splendid gift that a citizen has ever made to the City of New York," went to the Metropolitan and created the Altman Collection. Altman's respect for Morgan was tremendous, and one of his most treasured possessions was a catalog of the Morgan collection inscribed "To my friend, Benjamin Altman," which Altman would show with evident pride to the few visitors he allowed in his gallery.

Altman was not, however, another Morgan. In this age of clubs, Altman belonged to none, and he cared less for society. His physician said that although Altman's name was widely known in the worlds of business and art, he doubted if 100 people in the city knew Altman by sight. Altman was even reluctant to publicize his art purchases for fear that the publicity might be misinterpreted as advertising for his store. In the last years before his death in 1913, he led a secluded life, attending to business at home or corresponding with art dealers and fellow collectors.

This man of taste and fortune was only partially responsible for solidifying Fifth Avenue as a commercial street. The Gorham Company moved into a McKim, Mead & White–designed store on the southwest corner of 36th Street, Tiffany & Company into another on the southeast corner of Fifth Avenue and 37th Street, and by 1907, Fifth Avenue between 26th and 50th streets was a "bustling thoroughfare, jammed with carriages and motors, crowded with shoppers and passersby, and redolent with the fumes of wealth and business," according to the *Architectural Record.*

Altman had built a store that was big, but it was also

tasteful and minimally intrusive. He respected his neighbors to the extent that he never erected a sign. But in 1909, builder/developer Margaret S. E. Cameron announced that a 17-story office building was about to be erected at 185 Madison Avenue, on the northeast corner of 34th Street. Some of the proposed building would stand within the restricted area of the covenant, so Morgan and other Murray Hill neighbors slapped an injunction on Cameron and took her to court, where the plaintiffs lost. They took the case higher, to the Appellate Division, where they lost again. There were already the hotels Vanderbilt and Waldorf-Astoria on 34th Street, as well as Altman's, and the court said that the character of the street had changed to the extent where it was already a business artery.

Adding to the discomfort of Murray Hillers, one of their own broke the covenant. Mrs. Collis P. Huntington, the widow of the West Coast railroad speculator, leased her private stables at 126 East 38th Street to the White Cross Milk Company, and the noise of the milk cannery kept the neighbors awake all night. They complained, and won their case in court. But a milk cannery is clearly a nuisance in any residential district, covenant or no covenant, and the decision might have been different if the business had been something less nocturnal and bothersome in its nature, such as a dressmaker.

Conservative Murray Hill residents maintained that apartment houses broke the covenant, but in 1913, the South Church sold its property on the southeast corner of Madison Avenue and 38th Street to developers who claimed that an apartment house fell within the interpretation of a building that was limited to residential, non-commercial use. They made their point, and in 1915, the Havemeyer mansion on the southwest corner of Madison Avenue and 38th Street was coming down, with a sixteen-story apartment house planned for the site. Then, in 1920, the White-designed home of Charles T. Barney on the northeast corner of Park Avenue and 38th Street was replaced by a 15-story apartment house. The final blow came in 1923 when the Court of Appeals, after a thirteen-year fight, granted permission to the Astor Estate to build an office building on the west side of Madison Avenue between 35th and 36th streets. And so it went, with bits of Murray Hill being chipped away.

---

68. **Altman's 34th Street marquise was manufactured by the Hecla Iron Works, which was so proud of its work at Altman's that it ran advertisements celebrating its achievements.**

69. *The Baroque image of Bradford Gilbert's Grand Central Station was grafted onto the original depot in 1898. With the coming of Grand Central Terminal in 1913, the site would become the center of one of the city's greatest real-estate developments and a source of great revenue for the already wealthy Vanderbilts.*

5

Vanderbilt's Grand Central Terminal

The neighborhood now dominated by Grand Central Terminal was on the outer edge of development in mid-nineteenth-century New York and dubbed "the end of the world." Nonetheless, Commodore Cornelius Vanderbilt moved his passenger depot to Park Avenue at 42nd Street in 1869. In 1857, the City Council had banned steam engines south of 42nd Street, making it necessary to uncouple passenger cars at the edge of the city and haul them by horse to the depot at 26th Street. Vanderbilt therefore went about assembling a real-estate package to encompass almost all the land between Lexington and Madison avenues from 42nd to 48th streets. The only major holdout was some Goelet property on the west side of Lexington Avenue.

Grand Central Depot was ready by 1871. Designed by John B. Snook, the station was red brick with stone quoins. Its Second Empire roofline was dominated by three pavilions with mansard roofs that were reminiscent of the Tuileries, which surely appealed to the parvenu in Vanderbilt. The depot's most remarkable feature was not its facade, however, but the 530-foot-long train shed, which was 200 feet wide and about 60 feet high at its apex, a huge space framed by arched trusses of wrought iron and glass. The depot was "by far the largest, stateliest, most costly and most commodious edifice devoted to like purposes on the continent," said the *Tribune*, "an ornament to our city and a credit to our architecture." By the 1890s, the depot was too small, so atop it and around it arose a more baroque image designed by Bradford L. Gilbert. Three floors were added, the facade was covered by rusticated stucco resembling stone, and the pile was topped by copper-clad cupolas.

When the Gilbert-designed depot was ready in 1898, it was indeed more central to the life of the city. There were already several major institutions in the neighborhod. In the vanguard had been Temple Emanu-El, on the northeast corner of Fifth Avenue and 43rd Street since 1868. St. Bartholomew's Church had occupied the southwest corner of Madison Avenue and 44th Street since 1876. Sherry's, designed by Stanford White, had stood on the southeast corner of 44th Street and Fifth Avenue since 1896. Diagonally across the avenue stood the uptown Delmonico's, designed by James Brown Lord and opened in 1897. And the neighborhood was rapidly becoming the realm of exclusive men's clubs.

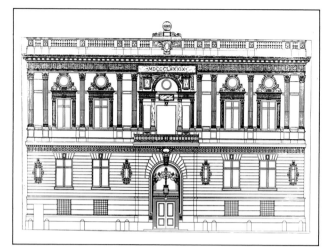

70

The Century Association

**7 West 43rd Street, between Fifth Avenue and
Avenue of the Americas
1891
BUILDER: The Century Association
ARCHITECTS: McKim, Mead & White**

The Century was an association of painters and writers and those who were interested in promoting a taste for the fine arts. It had started at a meeting of the Sketch Club in 1847 and was dubbed the Century because its membership was originally limited to 100, a number that swelled about eightfold by the 1880s. The association's clubhouse at 109 East 15th Street was becoming uncomfortably cramped, with hardly enough wall space to display its art. Younger and more affluent members were willing to spend as much as $200,000 for a suitable site in the newly emerging clubland on or off Fifth Avenue in the 40s and 50s. The idea of moving was anathema to some Centurians, however. They feared that a new and grander clubhouse might result in an intrinsically different Century, one with a more formal and restrained manner.

Despite the qualms of a few of the older members, four 25-by-100-foot lots were purchased on 43rd Street in 1889 for $150,000, less than had been anticipated, and McKim, Mead & White were hired for the $160,000 job. Stanford White was given the principal responsibility for the design, and he created a clubhouse in the Italian Renaissance style that was indeed grander, though not pompous. The basement of light stone and superstructure of cream-colored brick resembled the London clubs of Pall Mall and St. James Square, and it contrasted with average New York clubhouses whose facades were drab and dreary.

71

For those who were concerned that the "unrestrained intercourse of congenial and cultivated minds" would be lost, there was little to worry about. White created public rooms that were large, certainly, but above all they were comfortable. He even included a loggia opening onto the street for quiet chats on warm evenings. "White was most happy in maintaining a strong suggestion of New York interiors," said Herbert Croly, founder and editor of the *New Republic.* "No atmosphere could have been more appropriate for the apartments of a club with the traditions of the Century." And the Century's traditions were strong,

70. A new "clubland" had developed on and off Fifth Avenue north of 42nd Street by the 1890s. The Century Club, a five-minute walk from Grand Central, was designed in 1889 by McKim, Mead & White, with Stanford White in charge.

71. The only major change to Stanford White's neo-Renaissance design for the Century Club is barely perceptible—the Palladian loggia that was once open is now glassed in and has been incorporated into the dining room.

with a membership list that reflected achievement, not necessarily wealth. Membership was considered by some the equivalent of the French Academy.

Although the move drove dues from $35 to $50 a year, it did not drive away scholars, authors, or "other gentlemen of

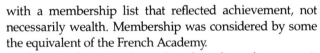

moderate means"—Augustus St. Gaudens, for instance, joined in 1890. The decade also saw the likes of Vanderbilt lawyer Chauncey Depew, banker and U.S. vice-president Levi P. Morton, and political reformer Carl Schurz mingling with sculptor John Quincy Adams Ward, artists Louis Comfort Tiffany and John LaFarge, book collector Samuel P. Avery, and architects James Renwick, Richard Morris Hunt, Charles F. McKim, William R. Mead, and Stanford White. It was just this mingling of the arts and business that led one observer to remark that artists could not afford to stay away from the association, where they were offered the chance "to sell pictures to the rich men who are now pressing to get in." Only one thing kept out such talented people as Elsie de Wolfe, Mary Cassatt, and Edith Wharton, and that was the association's restrictions against women.

---

72. Large, comfortable rooms, such as the Century's lounge, were a Stanford White hallmark. This came as a relief to the Centurians, who were reluctant to consider moving to a new and grander clubhouse for fear that a stuffy atmosphere would inhibit lively conversation.

73. As if he were designing a great hall in an English Renaissance mansion, Stanford White had the walls of the Century's dining room covered by wood paneling and its ceiling decorated in an elaborate pattern in plaster.

New York Yacht Club

37 West 44th Street, between Fifth Avenue and Avenue of the Americas
1900
BUILDER: New York Yacht Club
ARCHITECTS: Warren & Wetmore

Another all-male enclave was the New York Yacht Club, where the members broke a strict house rule and held a special ladies' reception at the opening of its splendid new clubhouse in 1900. Clearly the members believed that their new quarters deserved to be shown off.

The former clubhouse at 67 Madison Avenue was a warm, woody place where the men, surrounded by their ship models, felt at ease. It was not considered the kind of place where one ordinarily spent a lot of time during the season, since the club's most important activities took place on the water, not within four walls. The club maintained seven East Coast "stations," floats manned by club servants and equipped with telephones, mail boxes, maps, and other necessities for a man on his yacht. The station at Newport was so elaborate that if it had been equipped with a restaurant and bar, it might have been described as a clubhouse.

Membership came from the ranks of gentlemen sportsmen, men who had enough money to maintain a yacht without having to ask how much one cost to operate. Cordial relations were maintained with other yacht clubs and sportsmen, including Sir Thomas Lipton, who, in the spirit of hands-across-the-sea camaraderie, was elected an honorary member in 1899. Membership had swollen from 324 in 1880 to more than 1,400 in 1897, and the club's fleet included over 150 ocean-going sailboats and over 150 steam yachts. The club's largest steam yacht was William K. Vanderbilt's *Valiant*, which at 312 feet was more than three times as long as the Fifth Avenue frontage of his house. J. Pierpont Morgan had tired of his 204-foot *Corsair II* by 1898 and had bought the 304-foot clipper-bowed *Corsair III*, considered by many yachtsmen the most beautiful steam yacht ever built. Not to be outdone, quantitatively at least, was Ogden Goelet, who owned two steam yachts over 300 feet long. In all, the club boasted 47 steam yachts over 150 feet long, 13 over 200 feet, and four over 300 feet.

When the movement was begun to build a new clubhouse, the majority of the members were content to leave well enough alone. They believed that new stations or even a new clubhouse on Long Island would be more appropriate. Even after a site had been found on 44th Street in 1898, there was reluctance, and when confronted with the question of whether to buy a 50-foot lot for $100,00 and put up an acceptable clubhouse or a 75-foot lot and erect a really proper clubhouse, most members chose neither. Out of the blue, J. Pierpont Morgan offered to buy the land and give it to the club, with only two strings attached—he would only

75

buy the 75-foot lot, and the annual dues would have to be raised from $25 to $50 to help pay for the construction costs. It was an offer the members could not refuse.

The New York Yacht Club had held the America's Cup since 1851, and it was in defense of the cup that the club lived and breathed, with syndicates regularly building sailing yachts to stave off worthy challengers. It seemed only meet and right and their bounden duty to build a shrine for the cup.

Seven firms were invited to submit designs. The winning design by clubmembers Warren & Wetmore had panache and a sense of glory. Paris-trained Whitney Warren recognized the club's special purpose in furthering naval architecture. He believed that the club's link with the sea should not be subordinated nor should anyone have to be reminded that the club represented more than a mere social club. Into the marble and limestone facade are incorporated nautical elements such as hawsers wrapped around anchors, and keystones with grotesques of Posei-

---

74. J. Pierpont Morgan gave land to the New York Yacht Club with the understanding that a proper clubhouse would be built on the property. Anything less would have profaned this (former) reliquary for the America's Cup.

75. The windows that look out from the Model Room were made to resemble the sterns of Dutch *jachts*. Architects Warren & Wetmore were concerned with making the Yacht Club's facade unmistakably linked with the sea, an idea that appealed to the likes of Colonel John Jacob Astor, who served on the architectural committee.

76

den himself. Most distinctive are the bay windows that resemble the sterns of small Dutch vessels, or "jachts."

Warren brought a great degree of freedom for arranging inner space in the 100-foot-deep building by designing an off-center entrance. Although every public room is on a different level, there is a wonderful logic to the design that allows each of these rooms to be reached off the main hall. The model room sits on the equivalent of the parlor floor behind the three bay windows overlooking 44th Street. A balcony, complete with a musicians' gallery, rings the room, and a back-lit stained-glass ceiling imbues it with roseate hues. The mantel, which was carved from a single piece of 45-ton Caen stone, achieves Baroque grandeur in both scale and detail. Lining the oak walls are half-models of members' ships. Cases hold full models of some of the world's most important yachts. This room is the heart of the clubhouse. Its soul rested with the America's Cup, which had its own place of glory in another room until 1984.

Except for the club's trophies, books, and models, everything about the 44th Street clubhouse was new when it opened. Since the land was free and the members wealthy, care and expense could be lavished on the place, and the cost of building and furnishing the clubhouse rose to $392,000. Morgan no doubt thought that it was money well spent.

76. Almost all the public rooms in the Yacht Club are on different levels, and until the visitor gets his bearings, the layout can be as confusing as the Promenade Deck of an ocean liner. This is the grand staircase; the door to the Model Room is up the stairs and to the left.

77. The Model Room, which is lined by the half models of members' yachts, seems to have the sway of a grand saloon. The volutes above the Caen stone fireplace are mysteries of the deep.

The Porch of St. Bartholomew's Church

Originally, Madison Avenue at 44th Street; now, Park Avenue at 50th Street
1903
DONOR: Mrs. Cornelius Vanderbilt II
ARCHITECTS: McKim, Mead & White

Despite Morgan's gift to the Yacht Club, the biggest name for giving in the neighborhood was still Vanderbilt. In 1877, Cornelius Vanderbilt II put up $75,000 for the Railroad Branch of the YMCA on the northeast corner of 45th Street and Madison Avenue so that his employees had somewhere wholesome to go between runs into and out of the station. The branch included a 7,000 volume library, a gymnasium, bowling alleys, a lunch room, just about all the accoutrements of a proper clubhouse. Cornelius and his mother also gave to the parish of St. Bartholomew's Church a mission house at 205 East 42nd Street that was described as the finest in the city, standing six stories high on a 75-by-100-foot plot and costing $250,000.

Cornelius Vanderbilt II, the commodore's grandson and namesake, could afford to be magnanimous, since he had a fortune that was estimated at $70 million. His charitable tasks included the chairmanship of St. Luke's Hospital and the Metropolitan Museum of Art, and stints as a trustee of Columbia College, General Theological Seminary, the Cathedral Church of St. John the Divine, and the American Museum of Natural History. He took from the New York Central and Hudson Railroad, where he was president, and gave to others.

Vanderbilt's death came in September 1899, and his funeral was held at St. Bartholomew's Church, which was on the southwest corner of Madison Avenue and 44th Street. Thanks to the sixty choir members who sang and Bishop Henry Codman Potter who officiated, the service generated so much publicity that the church itself came into the limelight. It was already recognized as the wealthiest congregation in the city, with forty-three known millionaires as congregants, but Vanderbilt was a Vanderbilt, which carried

with it a certain innate notoriety, and he had been the church's biggest and most consistent giver. In his will, Vanderbilt continued to give, leaving the church about $400,000.

Another Vanderbilt family gift to St. Bartholomew's was in the offing in 1902, this one in memory of Cornelius II. The gift from his widow and children was originally to have been a pair of bronze doors, but friends and family members encouraged a more substantial memorial to be placed in front of the church. What emerged was a whole new porch, conceived by Stanford White and sculpted by some of the finest artists of the day, including Daniel Ches-

78

ter French, Phillip Martiny, and Herbert Adams. White's inspiration was the triple porch of the Romanesque church at St. Gilles, which he had seen when he toured the south of France in 1878 with McKim and St. Gaudens, and his choice of materials was sumptuous—arches of limestone, columns of Cippolino marble, panels of Egyptian porphyry, and doors of cast bronze. These materials show White's sagacity at specifying the best, while the skillful carving manifests his wisdom at hiring the best. Of course, White's patrons could well afford the best, indeed were accustomed to nothing less than the best, and were willing to spend about $200,000 for the best.

78. The Vanderbilt Porch at St. Bartholomew's Church was a gift from members of the Vanderbilt family in memory of Cornelius Vanderbilt II. Designed by Stanford White and a host of sculptors and artisans, it was added onto the former St. Bartholomew's and incorporated as the centerpiece for the new edifice. To have done anything less, said architect Bertram Goodhue, would have been at once impertinent and unwise.

The Home Club

15 East 45th Street, between Fifth and Madison Avenues
1906
BUILDER: The Home Club
ARCHITECTS: Gordon, Tracy & Swartwout

Plans for a mysterious nine-story residential building were filed for a site just off Fifth Avenue in 1905. No advertisements heralded its coming or invited potential tenants to inspect the premises, nor was there discussion of the building on the real-estate beat. The building was called the Home Club and if it had been a club it would have been the city's most exclusive since its membership was limited to six families.

The Home Club was never intended to be a club in the true sense, although it had clubby amenities like a communal billiard room. It was really a limited venture cooperative apartment hotel where all apartments were custom designed to the specifications of the owners. The prime mover behind the Home Club was banker Pliny Fisk, who developed the habit of encouraging others to share expenses in cooperative ventures as an undergraduate at Princeton University, where he was largely responsible for the success of the Ivy Club, Princeton's first eating club. At the Home Club, Fisk and his family occupied the upper two floors, and he ordered a solarium and a children's playroom on the roof (this was well before rooftops were considered livable places by the upper crust). The other five families occupied fourteen- and sixteen-room simplex apartments, each with six or seven baths.

There were no kitchens in the apartments, since all food was prepared in the professionally equipped kitchen on the first floor and delivered by a special elevator to each apartment's pantry. The tenants simply left their orders with the kitchen staff in the morning for designated times during the day.

The Home Club also provided private rooms—and catering—that could be booked for large entertainments, such as balls or musicales. The entire second floor was devoted to an 18-by-59-foot ballroom with 25-foot-high ceilings and a banquet hall that measured 20 by 40 feet.

The palazzo-like facade, with details kept purposely small to give scale to the building, expressed the two-part character of the Home Club. The facade "might have been finer if built entirely of marble or stone," said architect Egerton Swartwout, "but the cost was prohibitive, and from the first sketches it was frankly designed for a brick and terra-cotta treatment." For the rear and side elevations, Swartwout wanted a simple version of the facade, but he wound up with "windows punched in the rear and side walls with a grim disregard of symmetry and design." According to Swartwout, the future tenants kept taking

79

European trips and were seldom available for consultation. When they were tracked down, they demanded changes that disrupted planning. As a result, no floor had the slightest resemblance in layout to any other.

The Home Club cost about $300,000 to build and required a huge staff to maintain. In addition to the usual janitorial and floor staff, it had a full kitchen staff and servants. Rentals were as high as $12,000 a year. Nowhere in the city was apartment living more expensive, nor was any multi-family dwelling more exclusive or chic.

---

79. Architect Charles Lamb's wife complained in 1908 that it was all very well for her husband's profession to "plan memorial arches, new boulevards, and that sort of thing," but why couldn't they think of something for housekeepers? Her solution was cooperative kitchens, which was just the idea that banker Pliny Fisk had instituted in the Home Club, where six families lived in splendor. As Egerton Swartwout's drawing shows, the Home Club was set off from the street by a balustrade, but even that could not protect the tenants from the vagaries of urban life.

New York Public Library, Astor, Lenox and Tilden Foundations

Fifth Avenue, between 40th and 42nd Streets
1911
BUILDER: The City of New York
ARCHITECTS: Carrère & Hastings

In 1885, Alderman President Adolph L. Sanger advocated the creation of a reference library that would be endowed by New York State, built on land owned by New York City, supported by contributions from the citizenry, and kept open at all reasonable hours for the accommodation of students and working people.

The Lenox Library already stood on Fifth Avenue and 70th Street, which had been established in 1870 by James Lenox's gift of more than $1.25 million, and the Astor Library was on Lafayette Street, which opened in 1854 and was endowed by the ordinarily parsimonious John Jacob Astor. These libraries, however, were private and were described as working libraries for serious persons, to distinguish them from the smattering of lending libraries. Their great failing was the limitation of their hours. The Astor, for instance, was only open from 10 A.M. to 4 P.M., Mondays through Fridays, effectively shutting out the average working person. Clearly the libraries that were funded by private munificence were not meeting universal needs. The editorialists pointed out that every great center of civilization had a great library that was open to the public, with London's British Museum held up as an example. It was open from 9 A.M. to 8 P.M., and books were delivered within fifteen minutes from the time the call slip was submitted. As a result, London attracted scholars from all over the world. New York had the books. What it needed was a public library whose collection and convenience could match any other.

The seeds of a great reference library began to germinate in 1886, when Samuel J. Tilden bequeathed $4 million to establish a library in his name. By 1892, however, there was neither a public nor a Tilden library. Tilden's heirs had whittled down the bequest to $2 million, which did not leave enough for the trustees to meet the goal of a comprehensive library. They began to consider merging the Tilden Trust with other libraries to create a great public library supported by private contributions, just as Alderman Sanger had suggested. Tilden trustee John Bigelow said that if the city provided a building, the Tilden Trust and other institutions could provide the books and funds. Without waiting around for official responses, Andrew Haswell Green, another Tilden trustee, paved the way legally by getting a bill through the state legislature that allowed the private libraries to consolidate.

The trustees of the Lenox Library warmed to the idea, and by 1894 William Waldorf Astor and other Astor family members were likewise interested, since consolidation would reduce their responsibility to the Astor Library. If the two libraries and the Tilden Trust merged, the result would be 400,000 bound books and a $3.5 million endowment. After delicate negotiations, New York's great reference library, officially known as The New York Public Library, Astor, Lenox and Tilden Foundations, came into being in 1895, with a goal of being open from the earliest a student could be expected to need books until the latest that a daytime working man might need for research or literary recreation.

All they needed was a site. The trustees considered Columbia University's Madison Avenue campus between 49th and 50th streets, where existing buildings could be used for storage and a new building could be erected on the vacant land. However, the trustees soon realized that their job was not to go into the real-estate business but to extend the usefulness of libraries. They decided that the new building should be built on property that required a minimum outlay, which meant property either already owned by one of the members or contributed by the city or state.

The Tilden mansion on Gramercy Park was neither fireproof nor big enough, and the litigious nature of the heirs made the venture risky. The Astor Library was too far downtown and too small. The Lenox Library on 70th Street was well constructed and strong enough to suport three additonal floors, and the site could include the entire block if certain restrictions were removed. The only major drawback was its location, which was considered too far uptown and too difficult to reach. The one site that appealed to everyone, as much for its centrality as anything else, was the Croton Receiving Reservoir on Fifth Avenue between 40th and 42nd streets. To everyone's relief, Governor Levi P. Morton signed the bill in 1896 that empowered the Parks Department to turn over the land to the trustees of the library, and the Board of Estimate authorized construction and maintenance of a suitable, fireproof building whose construction costs were not to exceed $2.5 million.

The library's first librarian was Dr. John S. Billings, M.D., best known in library circles as a bibliographer and for his "Index Catalogue of the Library of the Surgeon-General's Office." After consulting with Columbia's Professor William R. Ware and various librarians, including his counterpart at the Library of Congress, Billings conceived a massive building measuring about 350 by 225 feet, with two interior courtyards creating a squared figure eight for the general floor plan. The west end of the building was to be seven tiers of stacks with the main reading room perched above, a configuration that would allow fast and easy delivery of books. Billings said that a domed circular reading room was undesirable, because it was a waste of space and difficult to heat. He wanted the ceilings as low as pleasing proportions demanded. The reading room could fill the

81

80. Dr. John S. Billings, the first director of the New York Public Library, did not want a glossy facade, but architects Carrère & Hastings convinced the normally frugal municipal government that the building deserved nothing less than marble.

81. Designed by the Italian-trained sculptor Raffaele J. Menconi and cast by the Tiffany Studios, the bronze flagpole bases in front of the library are filled with symbolism: the turtles, which support the entire weight, represent time; the figure shown here represents conquest (the three others represent discovery, adventure, and civilization); and the bas-relief medallions represent the races of man.

82. Dr. Billings saw that the main reading room was constructed over the stacks to facilitate the delivery of books and to make the room light and airy. To save on heating bills, he suggested that a glass screen divide the room so that half could be closed off when not in use.

83. The marble vault in the great hall, now called Astor Hall, is a genuine self-supporting vault. The city had agreed to pay $2.5 million on construction but ended up paying almost four times as much, partly as a result of decisions such as the one to use pure masonry construction in places.

80

83

82

west end of the building without being encumbered by supporting columns, and the room would be quiet, bright, and easily ventilated. He also wanted a glass screen to divide the room, so that one half could be closed off to save heating bills. Further economies would be realized by constructing the fireproof building with brick and terra cotta. The pamphlet for the architectural competition, which contained Billings's general guidelines for the design, was published in 1897 and prompted the *Times* to say that the library was to be a "librarian's library," not an "architect's library.... The fulfillment and reconciliation of the practical requirements are to be the basis of the design rather than an ideal form for the exterior." It meant, in essence, that form was to follow function.

The architectural competition was in two parts. The first was open to any architectural firm in metropolitan New York and only required sketches. Finalists would be awarded $400 apiece. The second competition would invite the six best designers of the first competition and six established firms to provide finished drawings, each of whom was guaranteed $800. Billings said that this system was followed because "the larger firms of established reputations ... [had] agreed among themselves to enter no competition where the names of the architects were not known and where there was not renumeration for each competitor." Almost ninety entrants were attracted to the first competition, and some very good architects finished in the money, including Joseph H. Friedlander, Henry Hornbostel, and Whitney Warren.

The invited competitors, who included Cyrus L. W. Eidlitz, George B. Post, and McKim, Mead & White, were asked to provide floor plans for each story, elevations for the facades on Fifth Avenue, 42nd Street and Bryant Park, and two sections for principal rooms. The "decidedly superior" design of Carrère & Hastings was approved unanimously by the library board and the Board of Estimate.

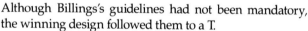

84

85

Although Billings's guidelines had not been mandatory, the winning design followed them to a T.

Since the city was to pay the construction costs, the library's trustees launched a not-too-subtle campaign to woo voters and swing opinion. In 1900, they spent $3,500 on a plaster of paris model of the winning design and displayed it in the Astor and Lenox Libraries, the Governor's Room in City Hall, the Architectural League Show, and Buffalo's Pan American Exposition, anywhere that people might see it and the critics might praise it. The scheme worked so well that Billings's plan for a money-saving facade of brick and terra cotta was scrapped. The specifications had urged an inexpensive facade, but limestone was mentioned as an acceptable alternative. Carrère & Hastings made a strong pitch for white marble, which was durable yet easy to carve, and which takes on a soft quality over the years without losing its sparkle. To erect a marble building the size of the library required 530,000 cubic feet of marble, which would make the library second in size to the Capitol. Marble was more expensive than limestone, and far more expensive than brick and terra cotta, and it meant that the estimated cost would rise from $2.5 to $3 million. To compound the problem, prices rose by 25 percent between 1897 and 1899, and the estimated cost of the building suddenly escalated to $5 million.

The city would spend more than it bargained for. Carrère

& Hastings specified only the purest marble from the quarry in Dorset, Vermont, and about 65 percent was waste (the marble was not "wasted," but used for other buildings, including Harvard University's medical school). The waste slowed down delivery and threw construction schedules out of kilter, but it was far from the only hindrance.

The library was a hybrid that forced the architects to be faithful to two masters, since it had to placate both the board of trustees and the city. Because the city was paying construction costs, it was a public work, which by its very nature suggests a certain inertia. Accounts of the amount of official red tape varied, but every contract, no matter how trivial, had to pass through a series of hands. The architects consulted with the library's trustees before preparing their detailed drawings, specifications, and applications for contracts, and consulted with them again once the plans were prepared. If approved, the papers were sent to the Park Board, where, after approval, they were submitted to the corporation counsel. The counsel sent them to the controller, from whom they went to a public hearing, back to the Park Board, and finally out for bids. The Park Board chose the bid that it considered best, which was not always the lowest, an imperiousness that sometimes led to court fights. After acceptance or adjudication, the contractor had to deliver. If he was anything like the marble contractor, things were snarled.

84. Unlike the vault in Astor Hall, the vault above this landing is plaster; it was a concession to economic reality. The subject of the John W. Alexander portrait is Mrs. Henry W. Draper, who gave thousands of books to the library in the early 1900s and bequeathed about $450,000.

85. The library's oak study tables, which are a comfortable four feet wide, were designed by Carrère & Hastings, who incorporated the city seal as a decorative element. (The chairs are not original.)

86. The main building of the New York Public Library is a humanist's idea of a sacred place, and the grand staircase demands that the library be approached with reverence. The statue in the niche portrays John M. Carrère, who was killed in an automobile accident. He lay in state in the great hall in 1911, just weeks before the library opened.

87. The designs for the Trustees Room furniture were accepted with the understanding that the gilding for the teak table and chairs would be eliminated. Woods that were used in the library include Circassian and French walnut and American oak.

86

Work progressed painstakingly. To be nearer the site, Carrère & Hastings set up an office in a house they bought and remodeled at 28 East 41st Street. Since the contract gave them five percent on the total cost of the building, including any fixtures and furniture that they designed, they could afford the move. They also set up a shop on the grounds to build ¾″ and ⅞″ scale models of balusters and portals and Corinthian columns for study, which the *Architectural Record* described as an innovation in architecture. The reporter also spied "behind a fence on the site . . . in a plausible enough simulacrum of the white marble, a whole bay of the building to be." The model of the single bay was built of staff, fiber-reinforced plaster on a wood frame, and it showed the proportions and details. If one bay was good, then a multiple of the design, or the whole wall, would be good.

And the facade was good. John M. Carrère said that a building that is monumental in character should not be merely an expression of the individual preference of the architect, it should take into account the "highest development of architecture as exemplified in its last great historical period," which, to the Paris-trained Carrère, compelled him "to go to the eighteenth century, to . . . the best of the Louis XVI epoch—to such buildings as the Louvre or the Place de la Concorde. . . . It is the logic of history, as one may call it, that has been mainly considered. Hence the building will not be an exponent of any one style to the exclusion of others, but may be characterized as belonging to the modern Renaissance, . . . with such modifications as the conditions and needs of our own age have suggested."

The contract for the interior was let in 1907 and came to $3.8 million, or $1.3 million more than the original estimate for the entire building. But by then the idea was accepted that a building of the character of the public library called for the best materials, upon which even fiscally conservative mayors concurred. There were concessions, of course. The main reading room, which was to have been lined in marble, instead has plain brick walls finished in plaster and wood, and plaster was often used for domes instead of marble. The vault in the main entrance hall, however, is a genuine, self-supporting system, and the purists in Carrère & Hastings won their point again, using only masonry construction in the grand staircase, with no steel supports. Decisions like that brought the official cost of the construction to $9,002,523.09, or about 87 cents a cubic foot. Between the time that Mayor Seth Low laid the cornerstone bearing the date MDCCCCII and the time the library opened in 1911, the value of the site had risen to an estimated $20 million, which confirmed the sagacity of the trustees who inveigled the city into not only paying for the construction of the library but providing its site as well.

Charles Scribner's Sons

597 Fifth Avenue, between 48th and 49th Streets
1913
BUILDERS: Charles Scribner's Sons
ARCHITECT: Ernest Flagg

In 1912, Charles Scribner's Sons bought a 53-by-100-foot plot at 597 Fifth Avenue for over $500,000. The seller was Emma F. Taylor, the daughter of former Governor Roswell P. Flower, whose brownstone home had stood on the site. The move by the prestigious publisher was one more striking illustration of the northward migration of retail trade. Since

88. France's Belle Epoque is seen in the facade of the bookstore of Charles Scribner's Sons. Architect Ernest Flagg, who had studied at the Ecole des Beaux-Arts in Paris and who was fluent in French architectural practices, was the Scribner court architect, a role that he owed partly to his sister, who was Mrs. Charles Scribner.

1894, the firm had occupied 155 Fifth Avenue, between 21st and 22nd streets, where its store, said the *Times*, paid Fifth Avenue the "homage of an enchanting literary atmosphere."

Ernest Flagg, the architect of Scribner's first Fifth Avenue store, was asked to incorporate the same features in the new building—a large store with a double-height ceiling ringed by a mezzanine, with offices on the upper floors. By 1913, when the new building was completed, Flagg had also designed the firm's printing plant at 311 West 43rd Street, Arthur Scribner's residence at 39 East 67th Street, and Charles Scribner's residence at 9 East 66th Street. Flagg's sister Louise just happened to be married to Charles.

The Scribner Building was considered one of the few aesthetically pleasing business structures in the choice new retail district, ranking with the Knoedler Art Gallery on 46th Street and the Duveen Gallery at 56th. The building's facade of Indiana limestone, iron, and glass, is filled with beguiling details, including a pair of joyful cupids stretching a stone ribbon emblazoned with the firm's name across the doorway. The most distinguishing feature is the store's metal-framed, double story window, which is imbued with the spirit of Paris, where Flagg had studied. "The neoclassical style he learned is evident in many of his buildings," said current chairman of Scribner's and Flagg's greatnephew, Charles Scribner, Jr. "He believed that architectural beauty lay in the harmony of simple proportions based on the ratios of integers." His design for the lower floors of the Scribner Building is reminiscent of the design of Charles Guirard de Montarnal for the upper floors of 118, rue Reaumur, one of the award-winning designs in a competition sponsored by the Municipal Council of Paris in 1897, when the municipality sought to encourage a high level of design for the city's new buildings. Adding to the Parisian ambience within the store are walls and ceilings painted white with gold trim, and a graceful staircase that would be right at home at the Petit Trianon in Versailles.

This is a true steel-framed skyscraper, and Flagg took extraordinary precautions against fire. The only wood in the entire building is in its furnishings and fittings, and he used a system for the floors that combined steel, for tensile strength, and poured concrete with sizable pebbles thrown in, for compressive strength. When electricians recently tried to install new lights in the building, said Chairman Scribner, it took several hours just to drill a few holes.

89. The sinuous curves of the balusters in the Scribner staircase come closer to Art Nouveau than any other fixture in the city. The staircase leads to the balcony that rings the bookstore.

Grand Central Terminal

89 East 42nd Street, at Park Avenue
1913
BUILDER: New York Central Railroad
ARCHITECTS: Associated Architects—Reed & Stem, Warren & Wetmore

450 Lexington Avenue

450 Lexington Avenue
At the southwest corner of 45th Street
1910
BUILDER: New York Central Railroad
ARCHITECTS: Associated Architects—Reed & Stem, Warren & Wetmore

The new Grand Central Terminal was created by a technological development and precipitated by a fatal accident. In 1902, an engineer ran a red light in the smoke-filled open cut on Park Avenue, and the resulting loss of fifteen lives had the state legislature ban steam engines in Manhattan by 1908. This meant that New York Central's operations had to be electrified at a time when the electrification of railroads was in its infancy.

William J. Wilgus, the New York Central's chief engineer, was ready. As early as 1899, Wilgus had conceived of electrified trains operating in tunnels and entering a double-decked terminal. The Park Avenue tunnels would go from a single level to two levels south of 50th Street, and the tracks would fan out and occupy an area from west of Lexington to east of Madison Avenue from 50th Street as far south as 42nd Street. Wilgus imagined a real-estate development of monumental proportions that encompassed about seventeen blocks above the underground tracks that would incorporate the revolutionary idea of air rights, which had been "unenjoyable with steam locomotives requiring open air, or great vaulting spaces for the dissipation of their products of combustion. . . . Thus from the air would be taken wealth." It was alchemy, pure and simple, making the New York Central Railroad heir to real estate that could suddenly be exploited. Thanks to skyscraper construction, office buildings, hotels, and apartment houses could be supported by steel piers that were placed between the set of tracks.

No less than McKim, Mead & White and Daniel H. Burnham entered plans that attempted to carry out Wilgus's ideas, but the competition winners were Reed & Stem of St. Paul, architects whose reputation was barely known beyond the few cognescenti whose arcanum included railroad station design. Reed & Stem's drawings called for a block-busting twenty-story tower on 42nd Street, with a "Court of Honor" on Park Avenue north of the terminal. One of the guidelines had stipulated that Park

90. Architects Warren & Wetmore said that the triple portal they had designed for Grand Central Terminal would serve as a splendid gateway to the city. The terminal was planned as the linchpin for a monumental Beaux-Arts complex of office buildings, hotels, and apartment houses built above the tracks of the New York Central Railroad.

90

Avenue traffic was to flow freely through the property, and the average entry showed street-level tunnels punched through the terminal. Reed & Stem devised an "elevated circumferential plaza" that took traffic by ramp around the periphery of the building. Charles Reed also conceived a system of ramps within the terminal, allowing passengers to go "upstairs" or "downstairs" without setting a foot on stairs. And he believed that there should be a major arrival room with a high, skylit roof, because even in the halcyon days of train travel, with velvet and plush everywhere, long-distance travelers still experienced a degree of claustrophobia. He wanted them to know that they had indeed arrived when they got to Grand Central, that they were somewhere. He had gotten there by being Wilgus's brother-in-law.

With little public explanation, Reed & Stem were soon persuaded to accept a parternship with the architectural firm of Warren & Wetmore, who had proposed its own scheme after the fact. Once again nepotism entered the scene; Whitney Warren just happened to be a cousin of William K. Vanderbilt. Reed & Stem's role was relegated to engineering, while Warren & Wetmore were given the glorious responsibility of design, and a grand plan evolved that was the realization of Wilgus's air-rights scheme. Absolute harmony was sought, with the cornice lines on Park Avenue restricted to the height of the terminal, with tall buildings rising from the setbacks, with none of the clash of styles that is the hallmark of the average city. Here was to be a Beaux-Arts extravaganza, using the principles of contrasting scales for overall effect, and neoclassical elements and statuary for detail.

Whitney Warren's early plans were run of the mill, but a calligraphic sketch of 1910 captured the essence of the final design and set down the basic elements of the 42nd Street facade, with its three Roman arches, colossal columns, and even the escutcheons. Warren's philosophy on the "reasoned art," as he called architecture, was that there was precedent and tradition for all purposes, that "every motive and element should have its reason for being, and in all compositions, no matter how simple, the elements must explain themselves and justify their presence." Warren's triple-arched facade was like a triumphal arch in an ancient city or the decorated portal of a walled city, crowned by a sculptural group that would "stand as a monument to the glory of commerce as typified by Mercury, supported by moral and mental energy—Hercules and Minerva." Following his French predilection, Warren hired Jules-Alexis Coutan to sculpt the group, and, discarding Reed & Stem's idea of a skylit roof over the concourse, he asked French society artist Paul Helleu to create a painting for the barrel-vaulted ceiling.

The building contractor was the veteran John Pierce, who provided Stony Creek granite from Connecticut for the lower facade and Bedford limestone from Indiana for the upper facade. The stone for the interior walls is not

91

91. The grand staircase at Grand Central is like a minuet in stone. Just as Rome's Spanish Steps diverge and come together again, so the terminal's steps diverge between the Vanderbilt and the Concourse levels, then come together to diverge again between the Concourse and the Lower levels.

92. The "carvings" above the lunette windows are not carved at all. The decoration—in this case, a winged wheel—is made of terra cotta and is stamped out of a mold.

93. This marble water fountain is neoclassical in its detailing, from the link border to the garland. Details like this, in a human scale, add to the glory of Grand Central.

94. Rich enough in details and large enough in scale for a royal portal, this entrance leads from Grand Central's waiting room to the men's room, downstairs.

95. Grand Central has public areas that are richly decorated but off the beaten track, such as this marble-walled lobby at 15 Vanderbilt Avenue. The Hecla Iron Works provided the bronze for the staircase, and the inspiration for the S-curve might have been provided by Michelangelo.

94

ton avenues, part of the site later occupied by the Waldorf-Astoria Hotel. The tracks in the basement were a boon for the post office, since sacks of out-of-town mail could be dropped by chute directly to the waiting trains below.

But the post office only got about half the area it had anticipated, and 450 Lexington Avenue represents even less of the original plan. The building was to have filled the entire site between 43rd and 45th streets, with the lower six stories constructed of a steel frame that would support a twelve-story tower when either the railroad needed more space for itself or when the rental market was ready for more space. The site between 43rd and 44th streets, however, was occupied by the temporary train depot during construction, so only half the plinth was built, and the twelve-story tower never was added. Though truncated, 450 Lexington is an exemplar of the Terminal City itself.

The business of the New York Central Railroad was business, not monument building, and the railroad had

stone at all, but a terra cotta-like substance stamped out of a mold to simulate Caen stone. The wainscoting and ornamental trim are genuine Bottocino marble, and the floors are Tennessee marble. The Hecla Iron & Bronze Works furnished about $2 million worth of bronze screens, bronze and iron window frames and railings, and iron elevator fronts, marquises, and train gates.

The first substantial hint of Terminal City's uniform cornice lines and overall style was the office building at 450 Lexington Avenue, which was designed to house the general executive offices of the New York Central Railroad. In 1902, the Goelet Estate had offered the half block site west of Lexington Avenue from 43rd to 45th streets to the Federal government for $1.3 million, but the government was not buying. Two years later, the New York Central purchased the property for an undisclosed sum, and the post office agreed to be the main floor tenant. Like the terminal, the base of the building is Stony Creek granite, with Bedford limestone above. Like other Terminal City buildings, it was constructed over the tracks of the train yards. All electricity, steam, and hot water were provided by a power plant on the north side of 50th Street between Park and Lexing-

95

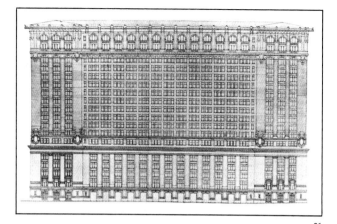

96

97

Warren & Wetmore design a contingency plan for the air rights above the terminal, where a twenty-story office tower was planned but likewise never built. In some cases, the railroad skimped, but good returns on moderate investments could make the railroad change its mind. In 1911, for instance, it claimed that natural light was needed to illuminate the train yards, so the company was not going to cover the medians along Park Avenue south of 50th Street. Local property owners pointed out that the yards below the projected buildings would be in darkness and concluded that natural light was expendable where the profit motive existed. When the railroad realized that the property valuation on the periphery of its development was rising at an annual rate of 25 percent, it concluded that its own property would be enhanced even more if the money was spent to cover the medians and create an unbroken promenade, so it changed its mind. Within about fifteen years of the terminal's construction, a swath of prestigious buildings was erected on the railroad-owned property, including the hotels Commodore, Barclay, Biltmore, Chatham, and Park Lane, eleven office buildings, ten apartment houses, and one club. None of them matched the glorious plan that Warren & Wetmore had visualized, but Park Avenue took on its trappings of luxury nevertheless and Wilgus's economic theory became economic fact. The New York Central's outlay for the undertaking was put at $180 million. By 1923, its improved property was valued at about $328 million.

In the meantime, Fifth Avenue's residential bastions had been falling. The Windsor Hotel, between 46th and 47th streets, burned down in 1899 and was replaced by the Windsor Arcade, which should have telegraphed the cheapening of the avenue, since it was designed to give a Fifth Avenue address to small shops that could not have ordinarily afforded Fifth Avenue prices. In 1909, Helen Gould was the only one who was still holding the residential fort at 47th and Fifth. In 1911, W. & J. Sloane announced its plans for an eight-story store on 47th Street and Black, Starr & Frost had bought a corner lot on 48th Street where

99

96. The plan for 450 Lexington Avenue was indicative of Warren & Wetmore's scheme for Terminal City. Setback towers were to rise from low-lying buildings whose cornices were on a line with the terminal's.

97. The balance and harmony of a classical approach to design is thrown out of whack in the never-finished 450 Lexington Avenue. It is the rump end of a plan for a building whose base was to be twice as long and whose setback tower was to rise from the cornice.

98. Warren & Wetmore brought a wonderfully rhythmic feeling to the openings in 450 Lexington Avenue. They created a similar effect in the coffered ceiling of the terminal's lower level.

99. The lower walls of 450 Lexington are faced in Stony Creek granite with Bedford limestone above, the same facings that were used for the terminal. This entrance leads to the Grand Central Branch of the U.S. Post Office, for which the first floor was designed.

the jewelers were planning a $250,000 building designed by Carrère & Hastings. Then Columbia University, which had restricted its Elgin Garden site between Fifth and Sixth avenues from 47th to 51st streets to residential purposes, lifted its ban against commerce.

More than the buildings were changing on the avenue—the whole tone, the tenor of the avenue was changing. The *Times* said that during the fashionable hours in the 1890s, the avenue "seemed *en fete,* gay, full of animation and color, a reflection of the luxurious life of the great city, [with] thousands of handsome carriages filled with beautifully gowned women, whose toilets, much in evidence in victorias and broughams, added a vivid effectiveness to the parade." By 1909, however, the appearance of the avenue was becoming monotonous, "for in place of prancing, high-stepping horses, glistening harness, and servants in rich liveries, one finds a ceaseless procession of the machines which are beginning to outnumber the carriages." The automobile had arrived.

The commerce and the automobile proved too much for the aristocratic members of the Home Club. In 1906, the "club" had been considered the last word in luxurious apartment living. Only seven years later, the neighborhood had become so commercial that the building's original purposes were abandoned. Its ballroom had only been used a few times in the last few years, the last of its tenants were gone, and the building stood abandoned and empty. The lower floors were altered for trade, and the upper floors, which had housed such luxurious apartments, were divided up as bachelors' apartments.

The congregation of St. Bartholomew's Church regarded the changes in the neighborhood as dimly as the residents of the Home Club. The Tiffany Studios had occupied the defunct Manhattan A.C. clubhouse at 347 Madison Avenue since 1905, and by 1914 Brooks Brothers was planned for the site at 346 Madison, the Biltmore Hotel was already across the avenue, and traffic noises were interfering with the Sunday services. The congregation decided to move to the exclusive new district on Park Avenue, between 50th and 51st streets, which was closer to where the majority of the congregation lived. The rector believed that the New York Central would abide by its announcement to impose height restrictions on its property south of the church, where setback towers would rise from a uniform cornice line of seven stories. The low scale of the church would fit right in, as would the church's costly memorials, so the Vanderbilt porch, which had been added to the Madison Avenue church, was brought along and included as the centerpiece of the Park Avenue church. To have done anything less, said architect Bertram Grosvenor Goodhue, would have been at once impertinent and unwise. The railroad's grand plan, however, did not come off, since the railroad did not impose its own restrictions. Unlike St. Bartholomew's, which sometimes had to answer to a higher authority, the railroad only had to answer to its stockholders.

100. *Newspaperman Adolph Ochs arranged for the Times Building to be built with the IRT subway tracks in the first basement, and it was the IRT's August Belmont II who arranged for the city to change the name of Longacre Square to honor the arrival of the newspaper. Hotels such as the Astor, seen on the right, were being constructed at the same time, as were theaters, which would become synonymous with the newly named Times Square.*

6

The Times'
Square

Adolph S. Ochs, the president and publisher of the august *New York Times*, failed in his attempt in the early 1900s to buy the property on Broadway at Park Place that ultimately became the site of the Woolworth Building. In the long run, he was probably just as happy that negotiations fell apart, because the influence of Park Row as the newspaper district was waning and the trend was northward. In 1893, for instance, the *Herald* had moved into a McKim, Mead & White-designed building at what became Herald Square, where Broadway and Sixth Avenue cross at 34th Street, and the *Times* was not to be outdone.

Longacre Square, at the confluence of Broadway and Seventh Avenue at 43rd Street, was ripe for development and the triangular plot between 42nd and 43rd streets was alluring. It was controlled by Charles Thorley, the florist who popularized violets and long-stem flowers, the first to add the decorative touch of a ribbon to a bouquet, the first to deliver flowers in glass boxes, and the first to cultivate the idea of cut flowers as interior decoration. By the 1890s, he was the florist to the Four Hundred, with commercial clients that included George W. Boldt of the Waldorf-Astoria. He was no stranger to real estate and had taken control of the Broadway site when a friend of his in real

estate was grousing about business. Thorley saw the "To Let" sign on the plot at Longacre Square and said "Get me that." The site was leased to him for $4,000 a year for 21 years with four renewal options, and Thorley's friend got the commission.

Thorley hired Henry F. Kilburn to design a $60,000, eight-story, steel-framed building for the 42nd Street side of the plot, and in 1899 he negotiated a twenty-year, $25,000-a-year lease with the Pabst Brewing Company, who turned the building into the Pabst Hotel. Under the management of James B. Regan, the hotel was doing fine, but, unfortunately, the Pabst Rathskellar stood in the path of the projected Interborough Rapid Transit subway as it turned from 42nd Street to go north on Broadway. If a building blocked the path of the subway, the rapid transit board could condemn the property, but in this case they didn't have to bother. Thorley broke his lease with Pabst in 1902, and then ostensibly struck a deal with Ochs. With the understanding that the IRT would have tracks and a station in the basement of the projected Times Building, the entire site was Ochs's for a published figure of $27,500 a year, with renewal privileges.

Before construction could begin, the Pabst Hotel had to be demolished. Wreckers were familiar with tearing down structures with load-bearing walls, but here they were presented with the first demolition of a steel-frame building. At first blush, the George A. Fuller Company believed that the building could be taken apart and re-erected elsewhere, but both the idea and the building were scrapped. Fuller was also given the problematical job of construction. Ochs's presses and August Belmont's subway were both competing for the same space, and where to put what was neatly resolved by running the subway through the basement and installing the presses in the sub-basement, where the newspaper could take advantage of vault privileges and extend its space to the curb line. The structures had to be kept totally independent of each other so that the vibrations of one did not effect the other, and delicate construction details had to be resolved between architect Cyrus L.W. Eidlitz and the subway's chief engineer, William Barclay Parsons. The skyscraper was supported by steel piers spaced so that they did not interfere with the tracks; likewise, the roadbed was supported on steel piers that passed through the sub-basement without interfering with the presses. When the excavation for one was going on, so was the excavation for the other, which drew scores of sidewalk superintendents, including Ochs, who went to the extreme of renting a room at the Cadillac Hotel so that he could watch progress from the northeast corner of Broadway and 43rd Street.

Architect Eidlitz had decided that a neoclassical design was inappropriate because the trapezoidal lot precluded a harmony of balance, so he took Giotto's Gothic campanile in Florence as his model. The skyscraper's "monumental proportions and architectural beauty," said the *Times*, "will make it a landmark." The original estimate for the building was $1.5 million, but Ochs wound up borrowing at least another million to finish the job. He told his mother that it was money well spent, since the building was "a beauty, and even though the $2.5 million that went into it cost some anxieties, it is there and it will be a monument to one man's daring."

Ochs wanted the building to be a tourist attraction as well as a billboard for his newspaper, but he never planned on occupying the entire building, only the sixteenth floor as the preparation room and the six tower floors as the editorial offices, with the presses in the sub-basement. The rest would be rental space. Over a year before the building was ready for occupancy, a three-column advertisement began to run in the *Times* proclaiming that "space may now be reserved in the Times Building," which was in a "conspicuous situation, . . . with streets 100 feet wide surround[ing] it on all sides, so that every office in the building will have an abundance of light and air. There will be no dark corners on any floor—no place where lights will burn continuously." Legitimate news stories on the building's progress often ran adjacent to "paid" advertisements, and the stories often repeated the building's salient selling points. When the cornerstone was laid, for instance, the story included the fact that electricity would be used for all sources of power except heating, which was steam.

The Times Building was boosted as being the world's tallest on one count and the almost-tallest on another. If the building was measured from where the steel structure began 57 feet below the surface of the street to the top of the building, 363 feet above the curb, it added up to 420 feet, which eclipsed the Park Row Building. The other claim, equally specious, was that if its elevation above sea level were taken into account, the Times Building was 412 feet high, only three feet lower than its downtown competition.

The assumption has generally been that Ochs, who wielded tremendous power, was instrumental in changing the name of Longacre Square to Times Square, but it was accomplished at the suggestion of August Belmont II, the IRT's financier. In the spring of 1904, Belmont told his board that he was considering designating some subway stations after important local institutions, and he wanted the station at Broadway and 42nd Street to be the Times Station. He also said that because of the conspicuous position held by the newspaper, the square on which the Times Building stood should be called Times Square, and the city agreed. Belmont also believed that no station was liable to be more important than Times Square, and he was right—within the first year that the subway was open, 1905, about 5,000,000 passengers paid their fares at Times Square. Entertainment, like population, follows transportation, and theaters were taking a firm hold around Times Square.

The Lyceum Theater

149 West 45th Street, between
Avenue of the Americas and Broadway
1903
BUILDER: Daniel Frohman
ARCHITECTS: Herts & Tallant

Producer Daniel Frohman decided to leave his Lyceum Theater on Fourth Avenue and 23rd Street in 1902 and build a new theater in the vanguard of the northward migration.

101. Although Times Square was just emerging as the new theater district, producer Daniel Frohman selected a side-street site for his new Lyceum Theater because he considered Broadway too noisy and crowded. Herts & Tallant designed an extravagant neoclassical building with a Mansard roof and bull's-eye windows that might have been part of a hunting chateau in France.

He wanted a side-street site that was near the new subway at Times Square for convenience yet far enough from Broadway for tranquility, and the 88-foot frontage he found on 45th Street had the added virtue of a 16-by-100-foot lot in the rear that went through to 46th Street. It meant that the workings of the theater could extend through the block, with a stage door in the rear. Frohman put down about $110,000 and planned to build a $230,000 theater.

A strange ceremony marked the laying of the cornerstone in 1902. Thirteen bricks were removed from the old Lyceum and installed in the cornerstone of the new one, because, so far as Frohman was concerned, thirteen was a lucky number. When actor Edward "Ned" Sothern was about to sign his first contract with Frohman on a Friday the thirteenth, Sothern reneged, asking if the signing might not be put off until the next day. Frohman told him

---

102. Muralist James Wall Finn's most ambitious theatrical work adorned the Century Theater. At the Lyceum, he only painted the three small but lively panels in the foyer.

103. This voluptuous newel post in the Lyceum lobby is not indicative of public sculpture during the Age of Elegance, when an ostensibility of prudishness reigned and even modest nudes such as Augustus Saint-Gaudens's *Diana* could cause an uproar.

that there were thirteen letters in the name Edward Sothern, thirteen letters in his own name, thirteen in the name of the theater, and thirteen members in the play. Sothern signed, and with David Belasco as stage manager, starred first for Frohman in *Highest Bidder*, a title that had thirteen letters, as did the names of Sothern's fellow leading actors, Herbert Kelcey and Georgia Cayven. Only someone who was deathly superstitious would have gone to the trouble to figure it all out, but someone also figured out that Frohman's run on thirteen would continue—thirteen months after the laying of the corner stone, the new Lyceum opened.

During construction, Frohman determined that he wanted a studio, which he would come to regard as his home, office, banquet hall, and director's room. In one corner is a little door that opened to a view of the stage, and from which Frohman and the author of the play in rehearsal would watch, discussing what should be changed, what could be strengthened.

The auditorium only occupies about one third of the total space, reported the *Times*. Above it was a large rehearsal room whose stage was a facsimile of the main stage, including identical curtains and footlights, which meant that two rehearsals could be held simultaneously. Below the stage are storerooms for sets. Since the main stage could be lowered fifteen feet, one set could be removed and another installed and sent up without any disturbance. The rest of the building is used for the components that make up a successful backstage, including carpenters' and set painters' shops, rooms for costume designers and wardrobe mistresses, as well as dressing rooms.

The Lyceum was described as a model of comfort. A ventilating system forced fresh air through silk gauze screens and sprays of water. The air was then either warmed or cooled, depending on the weather, and injected into the theater via four-and-a-half-inch ducts. The balcony is cantilevered, so the view from the rear of the orchestra is as unobstructed as from the front. The orchestra seats were a generous 22 inches wide, with 38 inches from the back of one chair to the back of the one in front, and they were covered in leather. Frohman had heard about a church deacon who asked one of his parishioners what he thought of the new minister, to which the parishioner responded, "Well, he's either got to make his sermon shorter or his seats softer." Not knowing what kind of theatrical sermons he would be preaching, Frohman said that he wanted to make

---

104. Daniel Frohman's study in the Lyceum Theater, where he worked and entertained, is now the office of the Shubert Archives. One could walk through the French doors onto the roof, which prompted Frohman to wonder if his studio thus did not qualify as the first penthouse in town.

sure that his seats were as comfortable as possible.

The interior colors were muted, ranging from deep yellows to warm reds and browns, with draperies of golden yellow. The wainscoting was relieved by gold leaf dulled to an almost imperceptible tone. In the vestibule are murals by James Wall Finn, who had painted the ceilings of Sherry's ballroom. One of Finn's subjects in the Lyceum is Mrs. Sarah Siddons, the great English tragedian of the early nineteenth century.

The glory is the facade, an imposing neo-Renaissance design that theatrically masks this early Times Square arrival. Statues originally stood within the bays, but they have fallen victim to time. The grand buttercup-fluted Corinthian columns, complete with lyre fleurons in the capitals, still stand triumphant.

The Lyceum opened with *The Proud Prince*, which provided Frohman with one more perfect cue. When he was called to the stage for an opening-house speech, he said "maybe you think that you have been seeing *The Proud Prince* this evening, but you are mistaken. I am the proud prince."

The Lyric Theater

213 West 42nd Street, between Broadway and Eighth Avenue
1903
BUILDER: Eugene Clifford Potter
ARCHITECT: Victor Hugo Koehler

An entrepreneur who was fast to see the possibilities of 42nd Street as a theater district was real-estate operator Eugene Clifford Potter. For the Lyric, Potter hired architect Victor Hugo Koehler, who never achieved great fame, but who designed a gem of a building in brick and terra cotta, with its roots firmly planted in seventeenth-century Italy. The Lyric had two entrances, one under an elaborate glass-and-iron marquee which sprang from a deep portico on 42nd Street, the other on 43rd Street. Twenty-foot-wide corridors led to each side of the auditorium on 43rd Street, which provided the double advantage of grand entrances and fast exits in the event of fire.

Though the house was shallow, columns supported the balcony and gallery, which impaired sight lines. The interior motif was the lyre intertwined with theatrical masks, all set into a color scheme of apple green and old rose, with plaster reliefs picked out in gold. In the boxes, wicker armchairs were mixed equally with straight-back chairs, the armchairs, no doubt, for the gents, the straight-back chairs for the ladies.

The Lyric was built for the production of light opera, and Reginald deKoven, who made a modest fortune from his operetta *Robin Hood*, became its proprietor. DeKoven's idea was to use the theater for his own productions of comic

105

operas and to rent it for others. His timing, however, could not have been worse. DeKoven was serving as the president of the American School of Opera, which filed for bankruptcy in the spring of 1903. With no school, there was no stock company, so deKoven unloaded the theater on two young producers, Sam and Lee Shubert—*the* Shubert Brothers—who promptly moved their offices into the new building.

Builder Potter's prescience paid off. Six years after the Lyric opened in 1903, there were seven theaters on 42nd Street between Seventh and Eighth avenues, more, it was said, than on any other block in the world. One of the few remaining available sites was being held at about $6,000 a front foot, roughly three times what Potter had paid.

---

105. Speculator Eugene Potter early saw the possibilities of Times Square and built the Lyric Theater to house the light opera of Reginald deKoven. He likewise saw the possibilities of Park Avenue as a residential thoroughfare and built the Montana Apartments between 52nd and 53rd streets.

106. The front entrance to the Lyric Theater was through a narrow lot on 42nd Street. For the 43rd Street facade, behind which sat the auditorium, architect Victor Hugo Koehler designed a neo-Italian Renaissance facade and West Side builder Clarence True supervised the construction. Together they built a sidestreet gem.

The Belasco Theater
(Formerly the Stuyvesant)

111 West 44th Street, between Avenue of the Americas and Broadway
1907
BUILDER: The Stuyvesant Theater Company
ARCHITECT: George Keister

107

One of Potter's 42nd Street neighbors was Oscar Hammerstein's Republic Theater, which was rented to David Belasco. Belasco had a penchant for naming theaters after himself, so the Republic became the Belasco. Changing the name, however, did little to improve his plight of carrying a lease that might not be renewed. Belasco wanted his own theater, where he could implement his ideas on design, lighting, and seating.

Spectacular effects were Belasco's forte, and the ends to which he went and the money he was willing to spend to achieve them were well known. (A 1920s *New Yorker* cartoon showed an ocean liner being tossed about in a stormy sea, with bolts of lightning crashing through the sky. "My God," says a passenger, "Belasco must be aboard.") His fame was also based on his craft. He both wrote and produced plays, and although he did not always originate effects, Belasco "never employed a familiar idea without improving upon its previous application," said one reviewer. "No matter how familiar the situation or the device, it takes on a quality of freshness as a result of his theatrical dexterity."

Belasco's dream of his own theater began to materialize when Meyer R. Bimberg, acting on behalf of some of Belasco's friends and patrons, created the Stuyvesant Theater Company in 1906. The $275,000 capitalization was intended to give Belasco what he wanted, but the cost of the 125-by-100-foot plot came to $302,000, and the cost of the theater was put at $300,000 more. Again, they dug into their pockets.

The subdued neo-Colonial facade of Harvard brick and white stone belies the sumptuous interior that included a ceiling of 22 stained-glass panels showing heraldic shields of 21 great playwrights, including Shakespeare, Goethe, and Molière. The 22nd shield commemorated the theater's namesake, Peter Stuyvesant, who never saw a theater during his stay in New York because there were none. The Stuyvesant's heavy wood chairs were upholstered in rich, dark-brown leather, with Belasco's emblematic bee embossed on the rear of each chair. The prevailing colors were deep browns, blues, and greens, offset by ambers and oranges. Around the proscenium arch are mural paintings symbolizing music and poetry, grief and tranquility. The lighting, more like daylight than the normal glare in theaters, was worked out between Belasco and lighting experts

Nimis & Nimis. The stage is 80 feet wide and 27 feet deep, and its floor can be opened at any section. Designed for plays, the Stuyvesant had fewer than 1,100 seats. And since the design was broad and shallow, there was no need for opera glasses.

The Stuyvesant was New York City's first theater built under a revised fire code. To avoid another catastrophe like the Brooklyn Theater fire, where 296 theatergoers were caught on interior stairs and unable to escape, exits were required to give out onto genuine fire escapes, so the Stuyvesant was built with a circumfluent ten-foot passageway. On the orchestra level alone there were nineteen exits, one exit for every twenty orchestra ticketholders. The entire theater could be vacated in three minutes.

By 1909, Belasco had followed Frohman's lead and was ensconced in a studio-apartment built to his specifications in the theater. An eclectic collector, he filled his warren with religious artifacts and military mementos that ran the gamut from suits of armor to a lock of Napoleon's hair. Belasco's bedroom was furnished *a la japonais*, with a miniature Japanese garden installed outside the window.

In 1910, he changed the name of the theater. The 42nd Street Belasco was rechristened the Republic and the Stuyvesant became the Belasco.

---

107. Architect George Keister's rather subdued Palladian-style facade belies a sumptuous interior for David Belasco's showcase theater. Belasco, known for his expensive theatrical effects, inveigled his backers into spending $600,000 for the site and the building.

The Algonquin Hotel
(Originally the Puritan)

59 West 44th Street, between Avenue of the Americas and Fifth Avenue
1902
BUILDER: Puritan Realty Company
ARCHITECT: Goldwin Starrett

With its site straddling the exclusive Fifth Avenue district and Times Square, the Algonquin was built as the theater district began to emerge. The fireproof, red-brick and stone building opened as an apartment-hotel called the Puritan, with full restaurant services available to residents and non-residents alike. It represented the "last step in excellence in this class of structure," said the *Tribune*, which was not usually given to hyperbole. As a lure to an apartment-

108

109

hotel's sybaritic life, the *Tribune* said that the Puritan had set out to solve the "vexatious servant problem" by providing servants who were thoroughly trained, quiet, respectful, and efficient. If things did not go properly, it was not the tenant who had to concern himself, it was the management. The Puritan advertised that it combined all the advantages of housekeeping and hotel life, that its staff provided every requisite for the comfort of cultured people. Nevertheless, if a guest insisted on his own maid or valet, rooms could be rented for them at one dollar per day.

Opening day found three-quarters of the Puritan's apartments rented, with rates that ranged from $420 a year

---

108. The Algonquin was one of the neighborhood's earliest hotels to cater to the theater crowd. Its comfortable lobby became a meetingplace for actors and theatergoers, residents and transients, while the dining room became famous for its roundtable, where writers and wits gathered in the 1920s and '30s.

109. This correctly detailed portico leads from the Algonquin lobby to the gentlemen's room downstairs. It was this attention to detail that partly accounted for the Algonquin's popularity.

for a single bedroom with bath to $2,520 a year for a suite that included a parlor, a combination library and dining room, three bedrooms, and three baths. The layout of the ordinary New York apartment was "along a long and narrow corridor which suggests the cabin passageways middecks of an ocean liner," said the *Tribune*. The Puritan's layouts were arranged in "square groups with the private hallway providing alluring angles." The apartments were fitted with floors of oak and with mantels and bookcases of mahogany, but furniture was supplied by the tenants. Meals could be taken in the apartments or the dining rooms, and there was the choice of dining *a la carte* or boarding at $12 a week.

The Puritan was never ostentatious. Its opulence lay in its reserve, its quiet ways, in management's attention to detail. The hotel was modern and up-to-date, with a telephone in every room. The tenant could summon his carriage, reserve theater tickets, or ask the house barber to come up and trim his hair and give him a shave in the privacy of his own room. If the tenant chose to go downstairs to the Puritan barbershop, he might find it decorated as a wisteria bower for the occasion. He might also find thespians there, since according to photographer and city chronicler Joseph Byron, it was where "many an actor had his face shaved and his hair cut to his liking."

It was renting agent Frank Case who wanted to change the hotel's name from the Puritan, a cold and forbidding name whose meaning "contradicts the meaning of innkeeping," said Case. When Manager Albert T. Foster told him to come up with a better name, Case determined that it would be an American name, not a Marseilles, Piccadilly, Heather, or Lido. He went to the public library "to find," as he described it, "the first and strongest people in this neighborhood, stumbled on the Algonquins, liked the word, liked the way it fitted the mouth, and prevailed upon the boss to accept it." Case admitted that the Algonquins were not especially hospitable to strangers, but in time the name came to have a new meaning quite separate from tomahawks and scalping. And soon the idea of naming hotels after local tribes had spread down the block to include the Iroquois.

The Knickerbocker Hotel

142 West 42nd Street, southeast corner of Broadway
1906
BUILDER: Colonel John Jacob Astor
ARCHITECTS: Marvin & Davis and Trowbridge & Livingston

The Astor Place subway station had terra cotta plaques on its walls that depicted beavers to celebrate the beginnings of the Astor family's great fortune; it also had a direct entrance from the platform into the new Wanamaker store. The Times Square station had a direct entrance into the Times Building and an entrance from the east end of Track One (now the Shuttle) that was marked "Knickerbocker." The doorway led directly into the Knickerbocker Hotel, whose seal, like the Astor Place plaques, incorporated a beaver. In this case, it was within an escutcheon topped by a crown and flanked by a pair of stout Dutch burghers. The message was that the Astor Hotel on Times Square was not the only Astor hotel in the neighborhood. The Knickerbocker was one too.

The Astors owned virtually all of Times Square, thanks primarily to John Jacob Astor's proclivity for buying property on the edge of the built-up sections of the city and holding the property until the northward flow of population had caught up with it. In 1803, very early in the game, Astor and William Cutting bought the Medcef Eden farm for $25,000. On today's street pattern, the Eden farm's 70 acres include most of the blocks on a northwesterly angle between 41st and 48th Streets from east of Broadway to west of Eleventh Avenue. Astor took the half on the high ground nearest Broadway and Cutting got the western half.

In 1890, the Long Acre property was divided among third and fourth generation Astors, with John Jacob Astor IV owning about half, and his father William and uncle William Waldorf splitting the balance. A lot of the property had been developed by small-time lessors, and the rowhouse rents could not compare in magnitude or ease of collection with those produced by lessors of major buildings, such as hotels. The Knickerbocker was built by John Jacob Astor IV who, at twenty-eight years old in 1892, had inherited about $50 million from his father's estate. Some of his investments were more colorful than one would expect. When the Spanish-American War broke out, for

110. The Knickerbocker Hotel was built by Colonel John Jacob Astor on land that his family had owned for over a hundred years. The Astor Hotel, also on Times Square, was built by the colonel's uncle, William Waldorf Astor.

111. Maxfield Parrish's *Old King Cole and His Fiddlers Three* was commissioned for the Knickerbocker's oak-paneled barroom, and it is indicative of the quality of the hotel's decoration. Today the three-paneled painting hangs in the St. Regis Hotel, another hotel built by Colonel Astor.

instance, he provided a fully equipped artillery battery, for which he was made a lieutenant colonel. He proceeded to deck himself out in a uniform that was definitely not government issue and to keep the title.

The Colonel threw his talents and some of his fortune into the Knickerbocker, just as he was throwing them into the St. Regis Hotel at the same time. There was one difference—the Knickerbocker offered Fifth Avenue luxuries at Broadway prices, ranging from two dollars a day for a single without bath to a three-room suite with two baths for twenty dollars a day.

Between the time the plans were drawn up by architects Marvin & Davis and the interior fittings were being installed, the neighborhood changed to such an extent that to continue with the original plans was tantamount to building a dowdy dinosaur. Colonel Astor realized the problem and ordered the interiors torn out and redone to the plans of Trowbridge & Livingston. Astor was listening to his lessee, James B. Regan, the same young man who had managed the ill-fated Pabst Hotel diagonally across the street. The *Times* pointed out that "it isn't every hotel man who plans his hotel to suit his own ideas, but that is what James B. Regan has done. In every particular his wishes have been deferred to by the architect and the owner." It meant that Astor spent an additional $1.2 million on the interiors, bringing the cost up to about $3.5 million.

The Knickerbocker had little plaster and less gilt. In the lobby there were pillars of Pavannazza marble, and a heroic figure of Father Knickerbocker, the hotel's namesake and the symbol of New York aristocracy. In the cafe there was an Indian battle scene by Frederic Remington that was set amidst hangings of gold and mirrored walls. In the oak-paneled barroom, which opened off the cafe, was Maxfield Parrish's *Old King Cole and His Fiddlers Three*. The dining room had a ceiling modeled after one at Fontainebleau, and there was a pair of fountains sculpted by Frederick Mac-Monnies with cupids coyly playing amidst Parian marble bowls. To make the dining-room floors easier to clean and to keep odors from clinging to carpets, there were plain marble floors. Regan spent seven months in Europe seeking the fittings he wanted. He returned with solid gold service for forty-eight and Sevres china. Antique heraldic banners lined the Grille Room, which was designed in the style of the Elizabethan period, and banners fluttered in the corridor leading to the IRT. Among the European pillage was chef Alexandre Gastand, whom Regan stole from London's Hotel Carlton. Regan's trip abroad convinced him of the superiority of French service, and he attempted to duplicate it. Each floor had its own clerks and service personnel, with pantries for serving food. Typical of both America and Astor was a dependency on gadgets. Each pantry was connected with the kitchen by electrically

heated dumbwaiters to keep the food warm on its trip from the kitchens, and there was pneumatic cleaning; there were also two icemaking machines with a capacity of eight tons a day.

The Knickerbocker was an instant success, "a veritable triumph of Science and Art in every feature of construction and equipment," if its advertisements are to be believed. In 1908, the hotel gave little diaries as keepsakes to its patrons. The diaries included a full-page color photograph of the hotel, points of interest, places of amusement and the IRT's subway stations, with the Times Square station singled out as the Knickerbocker stop. In 1907, manager Regan began to provide baggageless patrons with pajamas, combs, and brushes at no charge. For anyone detained in town unexpectedly, it was a great convenience. Then some of Regan's friends were unable to attend a dinner because they were not equipped with proper attire, so he outfitted them. The next plateau was the maintenance of a wardrobe, from which complete evening outfits would be provided. The valet would measure the guest in his room and return to spread out a full-dress or tuxedo suit, starched shirt, cravat, and pumps—free of charge.

In 1909, Regan hosted a dinner for fellow hotel managers, for whom he transformed the ballroom into an Italian garden. Gravel paths wound their way through real sod, with vases and bronze figures contributing to the landscape.

The hotel men drank vintage 1838 champagne from gold-rimmed goblets, ate off the gold service, and sat on gilt chairs. For favors, desk clocks of Russian leather embossed with gold monograms were given, and Enrico Caruso sang.

The Knickerbocker was one of Caruso's favorite places. The Metropolitan Opera was just down the block, and the ambience of the place appealed to him. But neither advertising nor continental service could keep the hotel afloat when Prohibition arrived, and Vincent Astor, the colonel's son, turned the Knickerbocker into an office building to salvage what he could in 1921.

Any doubts about the popularity of Times Square in its early days were dispelled by its number of theaters. By 1910, twenty-eight theaters stood within a five-block radius of Times Square and the number of seats came to 39,184, enough to accommodate the entire population of the suburban town of New Rochelle. With the ascendancy of Times Square came the waning of neighborhoods that had formerly been theater sections. In 1913, for instance, the valuation of Gilsey House, the hotel on Broadway at 29th Street, was lowered from over $1 million to less than $875,000. A judge ruled that the neighborhood had outlived its usefulness as a theater district, and the lowered valuation reflected its new incarnation as a loft district. Times Square reigned supreme.

112. *By the mid-1880s, the Vanderbilts had staked out their claim on Fifth Avenue. Mr. and Mrs. William H. Vanderbilt lived in the Italian Renaissance-style house on the northwest corner of 51st Street (on the extreme left in the post card); two daughters, Emily (Mrs. William D. Sloane) and Margaret (Mrs. Elliot F. Shepard), shared the twin mansion next door; son William Kissam Vanderbilt lived in the neo-Loire Valley chateau on the northwest corner of 52nd Street; two more daughters, Lila (Mrs. William Seward Webb) and Florence (Mrs. Hamilton McKown Twombly), lived at 54th Street; and son Cornelius Vanderbilt II lived between 57th and 58th streets. This was* their *Fifth Avenue, and they intended to keep it that way.*

7

The Vanderbilts'
Fifth Avenue

The Vanderbilts who built Grand Central Terminal made their fortune from transportation, one of the nineteenth century's greatest growth industries. The dynasty was started by Commodore Cornelius Vanderbilt, who accumulated an estate estimated at $100 million. The bulk of the fortune was left to his eldest son, William H. Vanderbilt, who started life as a black sheep but who proved as resolute as his father.

Cornelius Vanderbilt had moved from rural Staten Island to Manhattan's fashionable Washington Place and in 1863 William H. Vanderbilt made the move to sophisticated Fifth Avenue. By the 1880s, second and third generation Vanderbilts occupied seven buildings on Fifth Avenue, six of them on the west side of the avenue between 51st and 58th Streets. By the turn of the twentieth century, Vanderbilts occupied even more sites, both on and off the avenue, and they tried to control others to ward off the glacier-like persistence of commerce.

The first Vanderbilt house on Fifth Avenue was 453, a four-story brownstone on the east side of the avenue between 39th and 40th streets. In 1878, William H. Vanderbilt

decided to move to the west side of the avenue between 51st and 52nd streets. Across the avenue was the Roman Catholic Boys Orphanage; diagonally across stood St. Patrick's Cathedral. St. Thomas's Church was up the block on 53rd Street, and John D. Rockefeller lived on the south side of 54th Street between Fifth and Sixth avenues, with St. Luke's Hospital across the street from him. It was a transitional neighborhood of old institutions and new houses for the industrial aristocracy. On this foundation Vanderbilt began his family compound.

The mansion designed for William H. Vanderbilt and his wife, the former Louise Kissam, was Number 640, on the northwest corner of 51st Street. The building next door was ostensibly a twin, but it was really a two-family house that had one entrance at 642 Fifth Avenue and a second entrance around the corner at 2 West 52nd Street, and it was built for two of the daughters. Six-forty-two Fifth, which was linked to the senior Vanderbilt house by a portico and a common entrance, was a gift to the former Emily T. Vanderbilt and her husband, William Douglas Sloane, a director in his family's carpet, fabric, and furniture business, W. & J. Sloane. Two West 52nd was built for the former Margaret

Louise Vanderbilt and her husband, Colonel Elliot F. Shepard, a lawyer who owned and edited the *Mail and Express.* Four years passed before the completion of the twin mansions, but by all accounts the wait was worth it.

New York had nothing to compare with 640 Fifth Avenue in size, elegance, and cost, and descriptions went so far as to compare it with the Doge's Palace. Vanderbilt's mansion was 74 by 115 feet, and, although only four stories, it stood 76 feet high. A pair of bronze doors swung open to reveal the main hallway, where there were three stained-glass windows by John LaFarge. One window was an allegory depicting the foundation of the Vanderbilt fortune, with the Commodore as a young man at the bow of a barge that was being greeted on the shore by either a goddess of Commerce or a symbol of New York City, nobody seemed quite sure which. Around a central well, marble-covered iron columns supported the enormous weight of the building, whose walls were 32 inches thick in some places. The dining room ceilings, with scenes from Greek Mythology, were painted by Paul Baudry, known for his frescoes in the foyer of the Paris Opera. There were two picture galleries, the largest measuring 32 by 48 feet. Both galleries had two-story high walls that came to be completely covered by paintings. Construction of both Vanderbilt buildings was entrusted to J. B. Snook, who had designed Grand Central Depot, but the design was left to the Herter Brothers, who were more famous as interior decorators than as architects. They chose a heavy form of the Italian Renaissance, creating great boxes of brownstone with architectural appliqué.

Little dampened the enthusiasm of the 2,000-or-so guests who were invited to the unveiling of 640 in 1882. Even before the house was finished, its fame was so great that neither its address nor its owner had to be identified—"the great house lately built near the cathedral" sufficed. The little criticism that was voiced was that for all the profligate use of space, there were hardly any gardens to speak of. However, rumor had Vanderbilt about to buy the orphanage property across the avenue so that his own town square could be laid out in front of the house. Vanderbilt's descendants would rue its only being a rumor.

While the twin mansions were going up, two of William H. Vanderbilt's sons were erecting other great mansions along the avenue. At 660 Fifth, on the northwest corner of 52nd Street, arose the home of William Kissam Vanderbilt and his wife, the former Alva Smith. This Mrs. Vanderbilt, reports Andrew Tully, gave architect Richard Morris Hunt a free hand in selecting any style he liked—Norman, Italian, or Spanish. She didn't care what it was, so long as it was Medieval. What she got was the first neo-Loire Valley chateau in town. Its inspiration was the architecture of Francis I, when the Gothic was giving way to the Renaissance. Hunt's design spawned imitations for firehouses and apartment houses and mansions galore, but none was ever quite so fine. Critics said that at worst it was a flawed masterpiece, at best, the finest town house in America. It

would have been better if William K. Vanderbilt had taken Hunt's advice and bought the entire block front, but even for Vanderbilt, the land was too expensive. It was another decision the family would rue.

The house was given a facade of limestone to distinguish it from the sea of chocolate brown, and it had turrets and oriel windows and a moat surrounding the place. The Herter Brothers' interiors were straight out of Chambord, including a two-story-high dining room called the Banqueting Hall, which had walls paneled in quartered oak and a double fireplace at one end. The skill and care that went into 660 Fifth were not lost on other architects. "Charles Follen McKim would often walk up the avenue in the evening to admire it, saying that he slept better for the sight of it, and, having gazed on it, he was ready to go home for another cigar before retiring," relates architectural historian Henry Hope Reed.

Six-sixty launched the socially ambitious Mrs. William K. Vanderbilt, who drew up a list of 1,200 of New York's bluest-blooded socialites, excluding only Mrs. William Astor, *the* Mrs. Astor. It was no oversight, explained Mrs. Vanderbilt, it was just that she and Mrs. Astor had never been formally introduced and one simply could not invite someone unless one had. Introductions were arranged, and the upstart Vanderbilts breached society's highest wall.

But the house was not a good home. In 1895, the authoritarian Alva married off daughter Consuelo to the Ninth Duke of Marlborough against the seventeen-year-old's wishes. Alva then divorced Vanderbilt to marry Oliver Hazard Perry Belmont, August Belmont II's brother, who was five years her junior, a scandalous affair. She wound up with two Newport "cottages" and a Hunt-designed mansion at 477 Madison Avenue. Upon Belmont's death, she continued the theme that had been begun on 52nd Street. She hired the sons of Richard Morris Hunt to design a mortuary chapel at Woodlawn Cemetery in the style of St. Hubert's Chapel at Amboise in the Loire Valley.

The fourth great Vanderbilt mansion was built by Cornelius Vanderbilt II and his wife, the former Alice Gwynne. This ersatz chateau, with features of Blois, was erected on the northwest corner of 57th Street and originally backed on the plaza at 58th Street. It was designed by George B. Post, who assembled some of the greatest artists of the day for the interiors, including John LaFarge and sculptors Philip Martiny and the St. Gaudens brothers. Their efforts resulted in an inlaid mosaic mantelpiece supported by gigantic caryatids and a 45-foot-long dining room whose ceiling's oak beams were inlaid with mother of pearl. Work on the mansion began in 1880, and by 1885 Cornelius Vanderbilt II knew that he could afford to enlarge it—father William H. had parlayed his legacy into the greatest fortune in America, leaving Cornelius the lion's share of the $200 million. By 1895, he had almost doubled the size of his red-brick and limestone apparition from the French Renaissance. A new porte cochere was built in the garden to allow the house to front on the plaza, and the decoration that had done for the dining room would do for the new billiard room, et cetera.

There were other Vanderbilt offspring for the paterfamilias to care for. William H.'s son Frederick was given the former family brownstone on 39th Street, and ground was broken in 1882 for gifts to the two other daughters, Lila Osgood Vanderbilt and Florence Adele Vanderbilt. Lila had married Dr. William Seward Webb, a Columbia-educated M.D. who wound up in the parlor-car business. Florence had married Hamilton McKown Twombly, a Harvard-educated and very proper Bostonian lawyer who had met his bride at Newport. The Webbs were given a house next door to St. Thomas's church at 680 Fifth, and the Twomblys moved into 684, on the southwest corner of 54th Street. Together, the houses were worth about $320,000. They were both designed by J. B. Snook, William H. Vanderbilt's favorite architect. The Webb house, adjoining St. Thomas's, was appropriately designed in the Gothic style and almost filled the entire 52-by-143-foot lot. The Renaissance-style Twombly house had a 48-foot frontage and filled less than the 143-foot lot on 54th Street. Both were four stories high, steam heated, and equipped with hydraulic elevators, and both had billiard rooms in, of all places, the basements. The Twomblys got a 76-foot-high tower whose winding staircase took stargazers to what was dubbed the conservatory. The Webbs were given a tower too, but theirs was ornamental. As expected, the rooms were spacious. Mrs. Webb's dressing room, for instance, was 18 by 20 feet. Her husband's oak-beamed study, whose plans he drew himself, was 18 by 22.

By 1884, when the Webb and Twombly houses were completed, the Vanderbilts' first orgy of building on Fifth Avenue came to a halt. How much they had spent on their enclave is anyone's guess, but estimates went as high as $15 million.

With the rich following the lead of the super rich, neighboring lots filled up with people who shared a commonality of interest. Speculator Jay Gould lived at 579 Fifth, real-estate investors Robert and Ogden Goelet lived at 591 and 608 respectively, banker Darius Ogden Mills lived at 634, and traction magnate William C. Whitney lived at 2 West 57th Street. But only one of all the mansions on Fifth Avenue was an architectural pacesetter, and that was William K. Vanderbilt's.

---

113. The six houses built by railroad stock speculator Henry Villard are grouped around an open courtyard and appear as one palace. The idea for the courtyard is ascribed to Villard, but it took McKim, Mead & White to execute the plan so brilliantly.

114. Five of the houses were built speculatively, and the sixth, more than twice the size of the next largest in the group, was built for Villard himself. The plan shows Villard's house on the right.

The Villard Houses

451 to 457 Madison Avenue, between 50th and 51st Streets
1883 to 1886
BUILDER: Henry Villard
ARCHITECTS: McKim, Mead & White

113

One building that was certainly in the architectural vanguard was built for railroad-man Henry Villard, whose name in the 1880s and 1890s was on the lips of many irate Northern Pacific stockholders. Born Heinreich Hillgard in Bavaria in 1835, he took the name Villard when he came to the United States in 1854. This brilliant immigrant began American life as a newspaperman. After the Civil War he became an agent for several German railroad investors, and his talent for being at the right place with the right backing allowed him to take over the receivership of the

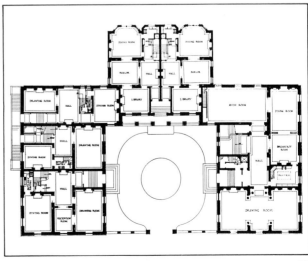

Oregon & Pacific and the Kansas Pacific railroads after the Panic of 1873. With these lines in his pocket, he raised $50 million and bought control of the not-yet completed Northern Pacific. Some of his financial shenanigans depended on borrowing against the assets of properties that he only intended to own and declaring dividends on earnings that were only projected. His financing schemes led to his undoing, but not before his estimated worth in the early 1880s had reached $10 million. It hardly put him in the same league with the Vanderbilts, but, then again, he did not move to Fifth Avenue.

In 1881, Villard bought the property on the east side of Madison Avenue between 50th and 51st streets. South of him was Columbia College, west was St. Patrick's, north was the Roman Catholic Orphan Asylum for Girls, and only a block east was the beginning of Vanderbilt's train yards on Park Avenue. Despite the institutional character of the neighborhood, Villard set about building a group of six houses around a central courtyard, with the house that occupied the entire southern wing set aside for himself. The five houses that Villard built speculatively cost about $33,000 apiece. His own cost about $595,000.

Villard had married Fanny Garrison, the daughter of abolitionist William Lloyd Garrison. Fanny's brother just happened to be married to Lucy McKim, the sister of Charles Follen McKim. Naturally, the firm of McKim, Mead & White was hired for the job. Their inspiration was Rome's Cancelleria, and the U-shaped grouping of the houses around an open-ended courtyard—which apparently was

Villard's idea—was the most urbane design in the city. The houses signaled the beginning of the neo-Italian Renaissance style that swept the country and had a longer lasting and far greater effect than Hunt's neo-Francis I style.

The six houses, with their sedate and unified brownstone facade, project themselves as one immense mansion. Four of the lots measured about 30 by 50 feet. The house that flanked Villard's had a 45-foot depth with a 50-foot frontage on Madison Avenue. Villard's house had the 50-foot frontage and extended the full depth of the 100-foot plot. His drawing room on the parlor floor occupied the

---

115. Through the Villard Houses' loggia were the entrances to two of the six houses. The talk of Renaissance precedents in the building often focuses on this arcade, which is compared with the cortile of Rome's Palazzo della Cancelleria.

116. The door and fenestration in Henry Villard's house combine elements from the Cancelleria's facade, and it is one of the grandest evocations of the Italian Renaissance in the city. McKim, Mead & White's reputation was made, and the revival of the Italian Renaissance took root.

117. This Saint-Gaudens mantelpiece is modest in scale compared with the one he designed for the mansion of Cornelius Vanderbilt II, but it is glorious. Today's caretaker-owner, the Palace Hotel, has restored many of the decorative materials that McKim, Mead & White specified, which were as grand as any used during the Age of Elegance.

118

119

118. The grand stairway in the Villard mansion has marble floors and walls, a mosaic ceiling, and a zodiac clock by White and Saint-Gaudens. It also had a price that only a railroad speculator would not blanch at. Ironically, Villard went broke almost on the very day he moved into his palatial home.

119. Villard sold his mansion to Darius Ogden Mills, who presented it as a wedding gift to his daughter and son-in-law, the Whitelaw Reids. They had John LaFarge paint the lunette above the musicians' gallery and had Stanford White decorate the ceiling of the music room, which is now used by the Palace Hotel as a lounge.

120. Villard's house was described as "chaste," with no "attempt at ostentation." The Reids, however, did over the front parlor and had it transformed into something more suited to a neoclassical palace.

entire Madison Avenue frontage, and throughout his house were ceiling mosaics and bas-reliefs over mantels, Tiffany-made glass and St. Gaudens-designed clocks.

Inscribed over Villard's dining-room mantel was "Per Adua Ad Alia," roughly "Through Hardship to Higher Things," which backfired. He and his family moved into their new home on Monday, December 17, 1883. The next day, Villard did not go to his office but stayed home to "get settled." There was a flurry of speculation that he was about to resign as president of the Northern Pacific. Rumor had it that he had falsely represented 30,000 acres of coal land in an application to the stock exchange. His house of cards collapsed in 1884, bringing down the securities firm of Decker, Howell & Company with it. Matthew Josephson later wrote that "the popular press pointed bitterly to the luxurious palace on Madison Avenue in which he still continued to live after his reverses. Here Villard dwelt amid so much costly and empty splendor because he had 'no other city home' and 'for reasons of economy,' while pondering new magic for the future." Villard got back on his

financial feet by 1889, but not before he was forced to sell his house in 1886 to Darius Ogden Mills, who presented it to his daughter Elizabeth when she married Whitelaw Reid, editor of the *Tribune* and future ambassador to the Court of St. James.

Villard would have been helped to a degree financially if he had been able to sell his speculatively built houses, but two factors hindered that possibility. One was how slowly the contractors were progressing on the courtyard, which precipitated a sharp word from Villard's lawyers to McKim, Mead & White, who were told that the "salable quality and its actual value would be greatly increased if the courtyard was more sightly. The long delay is . . . unpardonable." The other problem was that there were liens on his property and Villard could not sell anything until his indebtedness had been liquidated, which took until 1886. Banker and railroad man Harris C. Fahnestock bought the house that flanked Villard's for $168,750, which more than covered Villard's cost for all five of the speculatively built houses, so the proceeds for the remaining four houses was gravy.

The University Club

1 West 54th Street, northwest corner of
Fifth Avenue
1899
BUILDER: The University Club
ARCHITECTS: McKim, Mead & White

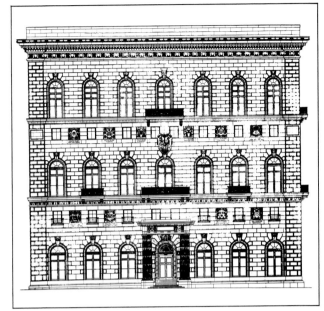

The Vanderbilts were in for a minor shock when the trustees of St. Luke's Hospital announced in 1893 that the hospital was moving to Morningside Heights from its 200-by-400-foot site on the west side of Fifth Avenue between 54th and 55th streets. Despite the Panic of 1893, an unidentified real-estate speculator believed that he could acquire the property with a short-term mortgage and sell the 32 lots individually, making a quick profit for himself. Lured by the notion of a single deal, and buoyed by the sales pitch that even in hard times real estate was a solid investment, the hospital's trustees accepted the speculator's offer. Their price for the package was $2.4 million, or about $70,000 a lot.

The prestigious Union Club bypassed the speculator and went straight to the trustees with an offer of $750,000 for the eight lots at the 54th Street corner. The trustees spurned the offer, although it meant turning down $93,750 a lot. To have accepted would have meant destroying the package deal. The Union Club raised its offer to $800,000, or $30,000 more per lot than the asking price, but the hospital would not see it. If the plot was to be broken up, the trustees wanted $125,000 a lot, or $1 million for the site. This time it was the Union Club that spurned the offer. The hospital sat tight until the speculator backed out. He was wrong about being able to sell the lots quickly, but he was right about the value of real estate in the ultimate scheme of things. By 1896, real estate was on the rise again. Individual sales were made to the likes of William Rockefeller, and another prestigious club was interested in the corner.

The University Club was renting the Leonard Jerome mansion on Madison Avenue at 27th Street, which was then owned by Jerome's daughter Jennie, Lady Randolph Churchill. The club was considering two Fifth Avenue sites that were being offered on a $35,000-a-year lease, but the idea of renting was anathema to the clubmen. They wanted a permanent home and were willing to pay the price for it. Three years after the Union Club had refused the 54th Street corner at $125,000 a lot, the University Club bought five lots at $135,000 each. The club then bought the neighboring 25-by-200-foot street-to-street plot from Rockefeller for $130,000 so that a more "suitable" clubhouse could be built, bringing the total price of the land to $805,000.

University Club members could well afford it. The club had been incorporated in 1865 and attracted New York's power elite, including John Taylor Johnston, who was the

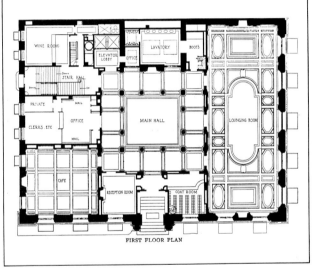

FIRST FLOOR PLAN

123

121. Charles Follen McKim knew his ancient and Renaissance precedents, and he used them as his inspiration for the facade of the University Club. He convinced the doubters that seals were appropriate, but he could not convince Princetonians that their shield should be rounded for the occasion.

122. The University Club paid the trustees of St. Luke's Hospital $675,000 for five lots on the corner of Fifth Avenue and 54th Street. Then, to accommodate a "suitable" clubhouse, the club bought the neighboring block-through lot from William Rockefeller for $130,000.

123. The University Club's lounging room overlooks Fifth Avenue. At about one hundred feet long, it is the main floor's largest room. It is not, however, the club's largest.

first president of the Metropolitan Museum of Art; jurist Joseph H. Choate, who would become Roosevelt's Secretary of State and a New York senator; traction magnate William C. Whitney; all three principals of McKim, Mead & White; and Chauncey Depew, who cut as wide a swath in the worlds of railroads and politics as he did in clubdom, with eleven memberships locally and honorary or non-resident memberships in about a dozen more clubs throughout the country. One of the University Club's qualifications was residence at a college or university for at least three years, but an honorary degree also passed muster. It meant that Vanderbilt employees like Depew could become members, as could some men who had married into the clan, but the Vanderbilt family's sole lineal descendant in the University club in the 1890s was Frederick W. Vanderbilt (Yale, 1876).

The clubhouse would be given the usual clubby amenities, such as dining rooms and lounging rooms and guest rooms and billiard rooms and a basement swimming pool, but with the advancement of art and literature the avowed objective of the club, Hugh D. Auchincloss said that one of the requirements was a fireproof library. Established in 1880, the collection had grown to 13,000 volumes, more than any club in the country. Only about six clubs in the city had good libraries, and it was claimed that some of them, like the Union and the Union League, maintained their collections for little more than appearance.

Clubmember Charles Follen McKim (Harvard, 1870) was chosen as the architect, and by the spring of 1897 builder Charles T. Wills was told to start construction on the building, whose anticipated cost was $760,000. If there were any prophets of financial doom, their fears were drowned out by the chorus of optimistic club members who believed the good life could continue without increasing the $60-a-year dues, despite the final tally that—including furnishings—came to over $2 million. With no fewer than 500 names on the waiting list at any time and with only about a dozen vacancies to fill a year, the admissions committee was sure that new members could always be recruited. And if the rolls were expanded while the standards were maintained, the club could have its clubhouse and pay for it too, which seemed a sensible solution. Despite the enlarged membership, the dues went up to $75 the year the clubhouse opened.

The increased dues were still less than those of many other first-class clubs, and the members of the University could boast of a clubhouse without peer in New York. McKim made the library the focal point. He specified En-

124. The lounging room's paneled walls and decorated ceiling, the carefully placed browsing materials, and the comfortably stuffed furniture all contribute to the image of an upper-class men's club.

glish oak with Alp-green marble trim to line the walls, and he asked H. Siddons Mowbray to paint the ceilings. McKim had the Borgia apartments in mind, with "its perfect unity, its glory of color and masterly detail.... The decoration ... should whisper and not shout." Despite the club's goal of encouraging art and literature, McKim's dreams for creating the perfect library were originally thwarted by costs. The clubmembers simply were not willing to pay the additional expense for decorated ceilings, so McKim had the ceilings painted white. The lack of color was so glaring that banker Charles T. Barney, who was overseeing the construction of the clubhouse and whose own house on Park Avenue was being refurbished by McKim, Mead & White, personally guaranteed the expenses for a finished ceiling. Mowbray went ahead, and when the ceiling was almost

125. McKim designed the University Club library to be the focal point of the clubhouse, but funds had not been allocated to decorate the ceiling. To accentuate the void, McKim had the ceiling painted white, whereupon the money for H. Siddons Mowbray's paintings was quickly forthcoming.

126. The University Club's dining room is 135 feet long and occupies the entire 54th Street side of the seventh floor. The English oak paneling is in the same richly decorated Renaissance style that is found in all the club's public rooms.

127. Paneled in French walnut, the council room has a predominantly blue coved ceiling with gilded ribs and architectural elements. The oval painting is by H. Siddons Mowbray, who also oversaw the ceiling's color coordination. This room is often used for private dinners.

completed, McKim had J. Pierpont Morgan view the work. While the scaffold was being removed, "there was nothing to do but wait," reported Mowbray. "The silence was a little painful. McKim, to break it, remarked that 'White was crazy over the work,' to which Mr. Morgan responded that 'He was always crazy.' I was relieved when the last plank came down. There was another silence. Mr. Morgan looked at the ceiling for a long time and simply said: 'Magnificent —Superb,'" accolades Morgan surely meant, since he hired the same team for his library a few years later. Money to pay for the ceiling was forthcoming, and, to share the new library with non-members, the club opened its doors for three days and admitted visitors.

The University Club's nine stories were artfully masked to appear as three stories, closer in scale to a real Italian Renaissance palazzo. Its facade bears the seals of American colleges, which created the delicate problem of which colleges to include. Precedence was given to the colleges with the largest numerical representation in the club. Annapolis had no seal, so one was created. A Princeton graduate complained that sculptor Daniel Chester French, who had prepared the designs for carving, had rounded the Princeton shield to follow the lines of the ornamentation, whereas the Princeton shield was pointed. And many members complained that any seals were inappropriate. McKim responded by mounting a virtuoso dissertation with photographs of shield-bearing precedents, including Rome's Porta del Populo and Palazzo Spada, which convinced even the most dubious members. Arnold Bennett unhesitatingly called the University Club a masterpiece, the finest building in New York. When asked which building appealed to him the most in the world, he said the Strozzi.

The W. E. D. Stokes House

4 East 54th Street, between Fifth and Madison Avenues
1900
BUILDER: William Earl Dodge Stokes
ARCHITECTS: McKim, Mead & White

Fifth Avenue in the 50s was filling up with mansions and clubs at the turn of the century that reminded discerning observers of Europe. In the classic pattern of urban life, smaller buildings lined the side streets, where the elegance of the avenue was reflected on a somewhat less grand scale. William Earl Dodge Stokes, for instance, paid $100,000 for a pair of rowhouses at 4 and 6 East 54th Street in June 1898, had them torn down, and asked McKim, Mead & White to design a five-story brick house trimmed in limestone for the 36-by-100-foot site. A month later, Stokes changed his mind and opted for a house with a complete limestone facade.

This was the capricious W. E. D. Stokes who had inherited about $6 million and was probably worth far more as a result of speculating in West Side real estate. Stokes had fallen in love with noted beauty Rita Hernandez de Alba Acosta from her picture in a photographer's window on Fifth Avenue. He chased her and won her, and in 1895 they were married in the bride's home, which was transformed into a bower of flowers for the occasion. Florist Thorley, of Times Square real-estate doings, excelled himself, selecting orange blossoms imported from Florida and violets by the thousands amid orchids and American beauty roses. The couple moved into 262 West 72nd Street, one of the bridegroom's many West Side houses, where their son was born. Three years later they were planning their East Side home.

When the Stokes house was built, the neighboring building to the west did not abut the property, allowing windows to fill the west wall. The New York tradition of entering a rowhouse by way of a high stoop off to one side was replaced by a more classically correct doorway in the center of the building, which came to be known as the American-style basement. As one entered the house as it was planned, an office was on the right of the vestibule and a reception room on the left. Ahead was a marble-floored hall with walls that had marble pilasters and columns. The kitchen was in the rear. Just as the first floor was designed for receiving, the second floor was designed for entertaining. The drawing room filled the full width of the front and was set off from the dining room in the rear by a hall and a conservatory. The floors were quartered oak laid in a herringbone pattern, except in the conservatory, where the floors were marble. The library filled the front of the third floor. In the rear were the master bedroom and bathroom,

128

128. The opening of the St. Luke's property to real-estate development had a spillover effect on the side streets east of the avenue, where William Earl Dodge Stokes ordered a home with a brick facade and limestone trim for his site at 4 East 54th Street. On second thought, he ordered architects McKim, Mead & White to make the facade marble.

129. Stokes got his marble facade, but he and Mrs. Stokes were divorced before the family could move into the new house. It was sold to Mr. and Mrs. William Moore.

complete with built-in shelves of Italian marble. On the fourth floor were more bedrooms, with Weddy's nursery planned for the rear. The Stokeses, however, were divorced in 1900 and never moved into their dream house.

William H. Moore paid Stokes $325,000 for the uncompleted house and took occupancy in 1900. Moore, the son and grandson of bankers and merchants, was a corporate lawyer. He promoted the Diamond Match Company, assembled the National Biscuit Company, and helped form some of the steel companies that went on to become the United States Steel Corporation. In addition to creating business monopolies, he held a virtual monopoly as a breeder and exhibitor of thoroughbred horses. An early promoter of the American hackney horse, Moore was an accomplished four-in-hand driver who usually took a "blue" at the Madison Square Garden Horse Show.

Moore was the grandfather of the Right Reverend Paul Moore, Jr., the Episcopal Bishop of New York, who fondly remembers visiting the house while his grandmother still lived there. "The house was decorated in the style of those days, with Persian rugs, Victorian furniture, etc.," he said. "The bottom floor had a dressing room for men on one side and women on the other, . . . and sort of a marble fountain affair in the middle of the hall as you entered. Then, going up the stairs to the second floor you found . . . a small drawing room with French furniture and many glass cases with collections around the walls." There were portraits of the bishop's grandparents, "plus a Corot, a Renoir, etc. . . . And on the floor above that were guest rooms. . . . Before entering these bedrooms, however, the stairs gave onto a large billiard room where there was a pool table and where my grandfather's cups, which he had won with his horses, stood against the wall." The neighborhood changed, as they will, and the bishop recounts an anecdote from later years: "The Stork Club established itself behind my grandmother's house, and I'm told that every month or so, Higgs, the butler, would call Sherman Billingsly and tell him that the Stork Club was making too much noise."

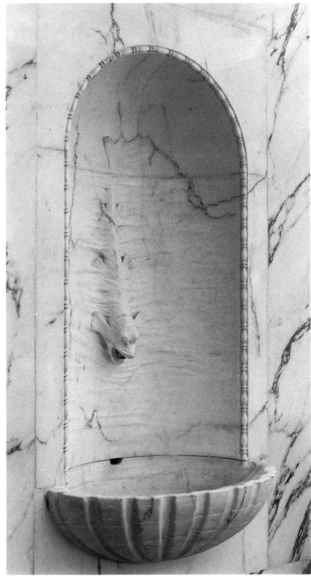

130. The dining room of the Stokes house had a sideboard built in amidst paneling and mirrors (the flanking curtains are reflections from the far wall). Today, the sideboard is an integral part of a shoe salon.

131. Because the neighboring houses on Fifth Avenue were not built to the lot line, the sun streamed into the Stokes house from the west when it was first built. A leaded-glass window is seen through the glass doors to the conservatory.

132. In the conservatory, a marble fountain added sparkle to the potted plants, ferns, and palms. Openness and lightness created the feeling of a very civilized terrace.

The St. Regis Hotel

**2 East 55th Street, on the southeast corner of
Fifth Avenue**
1904
BUILDER: Colonel John Jacob Astor
ARCHITECTS: Trowbridge & Livingston

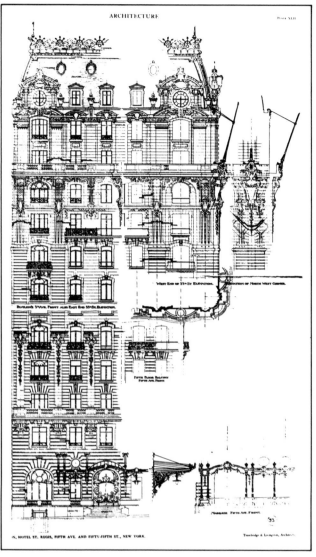

A potential maker or breaker of the neighborhood in the 1890s was the empty lot on the southeast corner of Fifth Avenue and 55th Street. It was owned by Lily Hamersley, the widow of Louis Carre Hamersley, and then wife of the dissolute eighth Duke of Marlborough, making her Lily Churchill, the Duchess of Marlborough. (Lily Churchill is not to be confused with another Duchess of Marlborough, Consuelo Vanderbilt, who married the ninth Duke of Marlborough; nor is she to be confused with Jennie Churchill, the former Jennie Jerome, who was married to Randolph Churchill, Lily's brother-in-law. It was Jennie's father, however, who introduced Lily to her Duke in the Newport home of Mrs. Paran Stevens in 1887. It was a tight little society.)

When Lily Hamersley married the duke in 1888, her fortune was estimated at $6 million. Soon the income was being used to fit up a London town house and to restore Blenheim, the ancestral home which, it seems, the profligate duke had despoiled of its choicest artistic and literary treasures to meet the most pressing demands of his creditors. In 1891, Lily Churchill raised $500,000 by selling the vacant lot on 55th Street to William Astor, from whom it passed to his widow, Caroline Schermerhorn Astor, and son, John Jacob Astor IV. The Astors, *mere et fils*, considered the 55th Street property as a site for their new mansion, but they decided to build on 65th Street. Their efforts to dispose of the property for residential purposes proved fruitless, and the conservative Astor managers were not about to invest in a major structure unless they were sure of the ultimate character of the neighborhood. In 1899, they announced the coming of a three-story, $70,000 studio building with stores on the main floor. There were gasps from the Vanderbilts, who feared that the Astor building would provide the wedge for further extension of business on Fifth Avenue.

Colonel Astor could afford to be a bit less conservative than his managers, and he had every inclination to be so. He was quixotic, a dreamer whose interests were less in conservative real-estate transactions than in scientific ideas and writings. In 1894, Appleton published his science fiction novel, *A Journey in Other Worlds*, in which he created a physical property called "apergy" that reversed gravity and allowed his protagonist to travel through space. He also dabbled with turbine engines and the vagaries of flight, and he said that suction cups should be fastened to the legs of deck chairs to keep them in place in high seas.

Colonel Astor believed that since the scientific method of constructing skyscrapers gave good results in office buildings, it should give equally good results in hotels. In 1901, the Colonel decided to build the eighteen-story St. Regis—the city's tallest hotel—on the vacant plot on 55th Street.

One of the subjects that Colonel Astor had written about was weather control. At the St. Regis, he set out to do something about it, equipping every room with an automatic thermostat so that guests could select the air they wanted. Heated, moistened, dried, or cooled, the air was pumped into the rooms through ducts powered by blowers on the third, seventh, and twelfth floors. Another innovation was the Kenney Vacuum Sweeping System, which allowed a maid to attach a flexible tube to an outlet in the room. When the machine was turned on, dust was sucked through the nozzle and down to the basement through a system of ducts.

The custom at the turn of the century was for managers to lease hotels from the owners, and any profits were his.

Rudolph H. Haan, of Haan's Restaurant in the Park Row Building, leased the St. Regis from Astor for a term of twenty years, with privileges of three renewals. The deal was a manager's dream, since Astor said that no expense was to be spared in the construction and furnishings of the hotel. Architects Trowbridge & Livingston spent three years working on the limestone-clad, steel-framed sky-scraper. Arnold Constable provided the furnishings for the suites and single rooms, and manager Haan spent two years in Europe seeking furniture and accoutrements for the public rooms. There was china by Royal Worcester and Royal Minton, and two sets of Royal Sevres, as well as a set of solid gold flatware service. For the musical guests there were 47 Steinway pianos; for the literary, a 3,000-volume library. The general contractor was Marc Eidlitz & Son, with the foundations, steel structure and masonry by the Thompson-Starrett Company. The elevators were by Otis, the fireproofing by Roebling, and the Hecla Iron Works provided the elevator grilles and the original marquise. All the stairways and corridors, as well as the engine and boiler rooms 60 feet below Fifth Avenue, were lined in marble.

When the final tab was presented to the colonel, the costs came to about $4 million for construction and $1.5 million for furnishings on ground that by then was valued at $700,000. Haan was proud that he had tried to make the St. Regis a temporary home for those who were used to the best of everything and could appreciate their surroundings. Astor assured him that he had succeeded, that the hotel was reminiscent of a fine, harmonious private house.

Not everyone in the neighborhood was ecstatic. Some neighbors lived there to flaunt their wealth, not to make it. William Rockefeller, who was the brother of John D. Rockefeller, lived on the northeast corner of Fifth Avenue and 54th Street, and he was as distressed about the eighteen-story St. Regis looming over his home as Mrs. Astor had been about the Waldorf looming over hers. To block the St. Regis from having a service entrance at the rear of its property and next door his, Rockefeller bought the lots at 3, 5, and 7 East 54th Street.

Another problem was the blue law that forbade selling liquor within 200 feet of a church. Haan was reluctant to go hat in hand to the Fifth Avenue Presbyterian Church to receive its dispensation, so he altered the plans for the hotel's entrance. By moving the entrance from the avenue to the side street, Haan effectively placed the entrance to the hotel beyond the 200-foot limit.

135

133. The St. Regis was built by Colonel John Jacob Astor, who believed that skyscraper hotels could be as practicable as skyscraper office towers. The details of the elevation show that architects Trowbridge & Livingston took the close-up view and the perspective view into account when they designed the world's tallest hotel.

134. Like all the hotel's public halls, the St. Regis lobby is marble-walled. The front desk, on the right, and the domed revolving door are products of the Hecla Iron Works.

135. There were run-of-the-mill Cutler letterboxes and there were others. Those in the Woolworth Building are in the Gothic style; the letterbox in Colonel Astor's St. Regis might be dubbed American Imperial.

136. Colonel Astor said that the St. Regis was as comfortable as a fine, harmonious home. The Louis XIV room would certainly have made the Sun King comfortable on a tour of the provinces.

137. The perspective through the St. Regis's Louis XIV room to the library and the music room is palatial. Sliding doors faced with the same paneling as the rooms can shut off any part of the suite for intimate gatherings.

The daily rate for the State Suite, which consisted of a salon, reception room, dining room, and two bedrooms with baths, was $125 a day. With food averaging $75 a day, a year's stay for a family of four would cost over $250,000. Haan tried to play down as many of the outlandish stories as possible, including the obviously excessive one that the chambermaids carried room keys on strings of pearls around their waists. Denials notwithstanding, this was New York's newest exlusive hotel and it was in the heart of the city's most exclusive residential district. The crowds gathered simply to gaze on it.

The Gotham Hotel

**Two West 55th Street, on the southwest corner of
Fifth Avenue**
1905
BUILDER: 55th Street Realty Company
ARCHITECTS: Hiss & Weekes

When Colonel Astor first considered the St. Regis, the
southwest corner of Fifth Avenue and 55th Street was still
in the hands of St. Luke's. The 100-by-125-foot lot was finally bought in 1901 for $575,000 by two speculators who
sold it to another pair for $700,000 the same year. With
prices rising so rapidly, the Rockefellers and Vanderbilts
began to brace themselves for another shock. A year later
came the announcement that the site was sold for
$3.5 million to the directors of the 55th Street Realty Com-
pany, which planned the eighteen-story, $2.25 million
Gotham Hotel. The principal backers were said to be Senators Mark A. Hanna and Thomas Fortune Ryan, an asso-
ciate of William C. Whitney, and they wasted no time—the
plans were already drawn up by architects Hiss & Weekes.

The Gotham was planned to have a residential character,
with a lobby of gray Caen stone big enough for the needs of
the hotel's guests but small enough to discourage loungers.
All 400 sleeping rooms had private baths, and each large
suite had a butler's pantry served by a heated dumbwaiter,
so food could be delivered from the serving room in the
basement and kept hot on the way.

The main dining room, which overlooked the avenue,
filled the first floor. The 22-foot-high ceiling was heavily
decorated in the style of the Italian Renaissance and was
supported by square columns with paired Corinthian pilasters of black walnut. Three of the walls had black walnut
wainscoting with maroon velvet panels. The Fifth Avenue
wall was lined by French windows that gave onto a ve-
randa screened by a high parapet wall to maintain privacy.
Off the main dining room was a room with potted palms
and a domed ceiling of leaded glass. This was the palm
room, where smoking was permitted at all hours and in all
company. Next door was the writing room, equipped with
private cabinets for making telephone calls and sending
telegrams.

The Gotham's lessee was Frank V. Bennett, who had
managed the Arlington Hotel in Washington, D.C., and
who soon discovered the hotel's one glaring defect, which
all the elaborate limestone carving could not mask. Unlike
the St. Regis, which fudged the facts, there was no way to
distort the obvious—the Gotham came within 200 feet of
the Fifth Avenue Presbyterian Church, and the church was
not granting a dispensation for selling liquor. Bennet, un-
daunted, established the Bottle Brigade, a group of "seraphic" boys who came and went with compartmentalized

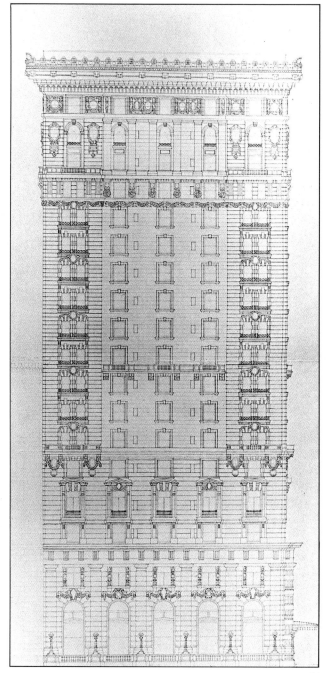

138

138. The Gotham Hotel was designed by Hiss & Weekes for a
consortium of speculators, and the plans were ready the day
the hotel was announced. The dining room occupied the
entire Fifth Avenue side of the main floor, but the hotel was
not permitted, by law, to serve liquor.

139. The Gotham was New York's only fashionable hotel of its
day to fail financially, which may have had something to do
with its name. According to Washington Irving, in an earlier
era Gothamites intentionally acted in a bizarre manner to
discourage people from staying.

139

Morton Plant's House

651 Fifth Avenue, southeast corner of 52nd Street
1905
BUILDER: Morton F. Plant
ARCHITECT: Robert W. Gibson

The Vanderbilts saw that Fifth Avenue in the 40s was becoming commercial, and when they learned that the residential Hotel Langham on the northeast corner of 52nd Street was up for sale in 1900, they took prompt united action to protect their enclave. William K. Vanderbilt and brother-in-law William D. Sloane commissioned the New York Realty Corporation to buy the 115-by-130-foot property for $1.3 million. The Langham property was cleared and put on the market with one restriction—only a private, single-family residence could be built on the site. No commerce was allowed, no apartment house, not even a first-class hotel. Nobody came forward.

Another rude shock came on the heels of the Langham. The Roman Catholic Orphanage between 51st and 52nd streets, across the avenue from the Vanderbilts' twin mansions, moved to the Bronx. Knickerbocker Trust company president, Charles T. Barney, headed the syndicate that bought the block. Residential builders scrambled for the side-street properties, and the Union Club, which had spurned St. Luke's offer, bought the 51st Street corner, with a 75-foot frontage on the avenue. In 1901, the 125 feet north of the club was bought by real-estate operators for $750,000 and resold practically overnight for $825,000 to Stewart H. Chisholm, whose partner in several ventures had been John "Bet-A-Million" Gates. Within a few weeks, plans were filed and blasting was begun for an eighteen-story hotel. The Vanderbilts only then awakened to the incursion into their enclave and again the New York Realty Corporation bought the property on their behalf, this purchase costing them $1 million. The Vanderbilt resale terms for the property were the same as they had set for the Langham site, and again, no buyers were found. Finally, George W. Vanderbilt announced that he would build two houses north of the Union Club at 645 and 647 Fifth Avenue to designs by Richard Howland Hunt and Joseph Howland Hunt. The marble-front dwellings were designed to be connected and easily converted into a double house, and the facade of each 37.5-foot house was created to reflect this unity. By 1904, Vanderbilt's niece, Mrs. William B. Osgood Field (nee Lillian Sloane) occupied 645 Fifth Avenue. The neighboring house at 647 was put on the market for $600,000, which made it the most expensive speculatively built house in the city at the time. No buyer was ever found and the Vanderbilts were forced to lease it out. (Number 647 remains today, but 645 was gobbled up by Olympic Tower.)

Even if it meant taking another financial beating, the Vanderbilts had to find someone who was willing to build a

wicker hampers between the hotel and a base of supplies just off Sixth Avenue. Everyone agreed that this flaunting of the law was silly, and the legislature passed a bill granting the Gotham a variance, which Governor Hughes vetoed. "Either the prohibition should be repealed or it should operate impartially," said Hughes.

The hotel was in trouble even before it opened. A succession of strikes had added about $250,000 to the final bill; the failure to obtain a liquor license hurt business, which not even the notoriety could ameliorate; and bad accounts, which often included fashionable but impecunious society leaders, compounded the difficulties. The first real hint of trouble was a paltry $741 butcher bill that went unpaid in the summer of 1908. Both the Metropolitan Life Insurance Company and the Knickerbocker Trust Company held mortgages that amounted to $1.7 million. It was Knickerbocker Trust that foreclosed, giving the Gotham a distinction of sorts—it was the only big, fashionable hotel of the period that was not financially successful in New York.

141

140. Struggling to maintain their enclave, the Vanderbilts sold their 52nd Street site to Morton Plant with the understanding that the property would remain residential for twenty-five years. Plant had Robert Gibson design this gem of an English Baroque-style house, which originally had its entrance through the center opening on the side street.

141. The wood-paneled salon on the second floor seems a haven from traffic noise, but the hustle and bustle of the neighborhood convinced Plant by 1916 that this residential bastion was crumbling. Since Vanderbilt had made the deal with Plant, Vanderbilt could get Plant out of the deal as well.

residence on 52nd Street's southeast corner, and they were lucky to find Morton F. Plant, a legatee in 1902 of $26 million. Plant's father had been the board chairman of the Southern Express Company and president of the Plant Line of Steamships. Young Plant was a director in a dozen-or-so companies, he owned the Eastern Baseball League's New London team and held interest in Philadelphia's National League team, and he founded Connecticut College for Women. He had the money and the will to spend it.

Morton F. Plant and William K. Vanderbilt struck a bargain. Plant could have the 50-by-100-foot corner property for $350,000, a loss of about $50,000 for the Vanderbilts, providing Plant built a first-class dwelling that would remain residential for 25 years. The five-story house that architect Robert W. Gibson designed had a florid marble and limestone facade in the English Palladian tradition. The building cost about $400,000 and was ready for occupancy by 1905, and it gave heart to the Vanderbilts in their struggle against encroaching commercialism.

By 1904, William K. Vanderbilt had extended the family control of the west side of the avenue as far as the Frederick Gallatin house on the 53rd Street corner. For his son and daughter-in-law, Mr. and Mrs. William K. Vanderbilt, Jr., Vanderbilt built a six-story, 50-foot-wide limestone house at 666 that was designed by McKim, Mead & White in a style closely conforming to the Hunt design that McKim had so admired, as if the firm were paying homage to Hunt. The family built only one more neighborhood building, at 49-51 East 52nd Street, a site that had housed Vanderbilt stables. The seven-story building was designed by Warren & Wetmore and represented a strange compromise for the Vanderbilts, who frowned upon apartment living. This was neither an apartment house nor a private house, but a pair of triplex apartments with a common entrance, reception hall, and billiard room on the first floor. In the basement was an automobile garage; on the roof, a summer garden. Only Vanderbilt family members ever occupied the apartments, and even they could not stem the tide.

In November 1909, the Gallatin house on the southwest corner of Fifth Avenue and 53rd Street—the one piece of property on that side of the block that the Vanderbilts did not control—was rented for $30,000 a year as showrooms to Brewster & Company, manufacturers of carriages and automobiles. And the Langham site was still empty. James Henry "Silent" Smith of Wall Street fame had bought the site but he never built on it; Edward H. Harriman consequently owned it, but he likewise never developed it. On December 31, 1909, came the announcement that the restric-

142. The entry hall to Plant's house was faced in plaster that was artfully crafted to simulate marble. The house became home to the New York branch of Cartier, and the jewelry firm has maintained as much of the original detailing as possible.

tions against business occupancy on the site had been lifted. Robert F. Dowling, president of the City Investing Company, paid $1.75 million for the site in July 1910, and up went an eight-story loft.

It was as if the prescient Louis XVI had come to Fifth Avenue in 1910 and said, "Apres moi le deluge." Early to go was Darius Ogden Mills's double-width house at 634 Fifth, which was replaced by an eight-story commercial structure. Then Columbia University lifted its restrictions against commerce on its Elgin Gardens property. A year later, Levi P. Morton, the former governor, vice-president, and founder of Morton Trust, decided that he was moving uptown to 998 Fifth. The fact that he was moving into an apartment was shocking enough, but he was also putting his seventeen-year-old McKim, Mead & White-designed home on the market. If he could not find a tenant for his residence at 681 Fifth for $40,000 a year, he would tear the house down and erect a thirteen-story commercial building on the site, which is just what he did in 1912. By the summer of 1911, the residences at the southeast corner of Fifth Avenue and 53rd Street were already torn down and about to be replaced by a C. P. H. Gilbert-designed building at 665 Fifth for Edward Holbrook, the president of Gorham.

Harry Payne Whitney had placed a billboard on his father's mansion on 57th Street, which he wanted to rent. To placate his neighbors, he offered to rent the house as a residence for about one-third the price he had been asking from "genteel" commercial tenants, but there were no takers. By spring 1913, a three-story tax-payer was about to rise on the site. At the same time, the Gallatin house with its Brewster showroom was being torn down, and John D. Rockefeller had bought the Webb house, which was to be replaced by a six-story business building, and rumor had him about to buy the neighboring Twombly house and tear it down as well.

By 1916, Morton Plant had had enough. He had put up with an empty lot across the street from his house, then a loft building with a dressmaking firm occupying most of it. Except for a few holdouts, Plant was surrounded on all sides by commerce, with unbearable traffic noises and the press of pedestrians, so he went to William K. Vanderbilt and asked to have their agreement nullified. Vanderbilt had made the restriction, and was empowered to lift it. He agreed to buy the house for $1 million, which was $75,000 above the assessed valuation. Vanderbilt then casually inquired what five percent of $1 million represented, and agreed to rent the house to the Cartier jewelry firm for the $50,000 a year, one of the highest rentals on the Avenue. This was 1917. Plant, in the meantime, built himself a new mansion far from the madding crowd on the northeast corner of Fifth Avenue and 86th Street.

Only eight years later, William K. Vanderbilt's mansion was demolished, to be followed by Cornelius Vanderbilt II's for Bergdorf Goodman's store in 1927. The longest surviving of the great Vanderbilt mansions was one of the twins, which had started it all. The year was 1947.

143. *Little more than an open space waiting to be filled in the 1890s, the plaza at 59th Street and Fifth Avenue still acted like a magnet for high-class development. Cornelius Vanderbilt II had his mansion at the south end of the plaza, the first Plaza Hotel dominated the west end, and bigger things were brewing.*

8

The Plaza's Plaza

he plaza west of Fifth Avenue between 58th and 60th streets was a poorly defined space in the 1890s that neither extended the verdure of Central Park into the city's built-up section nor clearly delineated the demarcation between the two. If architect Richard Morris Hunt had gotten his way, the plaza's northern half would have been different. Hunt designed a series of monumental gates for Central Park in 1865 that would have been the envy of Baron Haussmann. For 59th Street, he conceived a gateway with two major gateposts crowned by sculptural groups, and four smaller gateposts that were topped by single pieces of statuary. In front of the gateway was a pond, with a column rising from the center as a memorial to Henry Hudson. Water cascaded downhill to create still another pond, this one with a memorial to Christopher Columbus. Nothing came of Hunt's scheme,

partly because everything about it was contrary to the quest of park designers Frederick Law Olmsted and Calvert Vaux for a park in a natural setting.

Improved or barren, the open-ended square proved a magnet for high-class development, and by the 1890s several of the city's most prestigious hotels and private residences bordered the square. Dominating the western vista was the eight-story brick and terra cotta Plaza Hotel, which opened in 1890 and was described as "one of the most completely appointed and most artistically decorated hotel buildings ever devised for the entertainment of the shifting multitude," and its future seemed assured. The southern end of the plaza was the demesne of Cornelius Vanderbilt II, with his 60-room mansion. Dominating the east side of Fifth Avenue were the Savoy Hotel on the southeast corner of 59th and the Netherland Hotel on the northeast.

Carnegie Hall

154 West 57th Street, on the southeast corner of Seventh Avenue
1891
BUILDER: The Music Hall, Inc.
ARCHITECT: William B. Tuthill

Mansions, rowhouses, first-class hotels, clubs, and apartment houses were destined for the choice blocks on and off the park, and in the 1880s the neighborhood seemed far removed from the theater district, which huddled between Union and Herald squares. Nevertheless, it was in this seemingly remote residential outpost that Andrew Carnegie decided to build a concert hall in 1889. With a certain Scottish frankness, he called the hall The Music Hall, and it was incorporated by Carnegie with architect William B. Tuthill, Morris Reno, Stephen M. Knevals, and Walter Damrosch, whose peripatetic Oratorio Society had needed

144

145

144. Steelman Andrew Carnegie dropped out of the corporation that built Madison Square Garden to build the Music Hall, which was soon called Carnegie Hall. The new building's closest competition acoustically was Steinway Hall on 14th Street, which had been a center of culture and entertainment in the 1860s but was too far downtown by the 1890s.

145. Though never intended to compete with the glitter of the opera's Diamond Horseshoe, Carnegie Hall's boxes and galleries have wonderfully graceful lines.

a home since its creation in 1873. Carnegie put up all but $120,000 of the original $600,000, and by the time the undertaking was finished, he would put up $480,000 more and then some.

The Music Hall was to be more than a "shrine of the goddess of music," said Carnegie at the laying of its cornerstone in 1890. The hall was also to be a public meeting place that Carnegie hoped would be to New York what Faneuil Hall was to Boston. The hall was "not erected for gain. Its owners seek not to reap high profits from the community, but to perform a good for the community," said Carnegie. "It should not be closed if there remains one good cause desirous of using it, one effort to improve the community in any form which needs a meeting place. . . . If one price cannot be obtained for its use, then a lower, and a lower price should be accepted, and where the cause is wholly charitable or for the public good, then, if necessary, no price at all."

Carnegie's noble goals were thwarted from the outset. Where his dream had been for any reasonable offer to be taken, the speculators took him instead. They cornered the market on tickets for the opening festival, buying them by

147

the gross as soon as they were put on sale and selling them later at a dollar surcharge for a single ticket and a two-dollar surcharge on a block of four. The ushers realized that there was money to be made in charging standees a 25-cent surcharge. They then began extorting as much as $1.50 for seating reserved-seat ticket holders, and soon any seat that was vacant at the beginning of the concert was regarded as theirs to sell. To anger concertgoers more, late arrivals who were paying off the ushers were being seated in the midst of performances. Those who arrived on time, said one frustrated music fan, "had their peace disturbed and their tempers ruffled by the tramp of rustling and banging of persons less punctual."

Carnegie Hall, as The Music Hall was soon known, was six stories high with its roof ending in a blunt mansard. It was 150 feet wide on 57th Streer, while its Seventh Avenue wall was 25 feet short of 56th Street (within seven years of its opening, additions were made above it and on both sides of it). The hall's interior colors were rich but muted. The lobby's pilasters were gray marble, with the walls painted salmon, which was officially described as "old rose." The auditorium's predominant color was also "old rose," with yellow pilasters ornamented in white relief. The fronts of the boxes and balconies matched the proscenium's colors, and the seats, of course, were covered in red plush.

The Music Hall has been the scene of great concerts as well as the good causes that Carnegie hoped would be held there, and although he never expected to make money, nor did he expect to lose any. The hall, however, never broke even.

146. The massive abutments that support Carnegie Hall's proscenium arch are fittingly decorated with musical instruments.

147. Off to the right of the portrait-lined lobby, doors lead to Carnegie Hall's first-tier boxes; the view through the lunette windows shows the lobby.

The American Fine Arts Society

215 West 57th Street, between Seventh Avenue and Broadway
1892
BUILDER: American Fine Arts Society
ARCHITECT: Henry J. Hardenbergh

In a classic spillover of real-estate development, another cultural institution—the American Fine Arts Society—followed Carnegie Hall to 57th Street within the year. The society was the brainchild of Howard Russell Butler, who individually represented what the society set out to do collectively, which was to merge management with the arts. Butler was a Columbia-trained lawyer who gave up his law practice after three years to study art in Paris. Upon his return to New York he served as the president of the American Fine Arts Society from its founding in 1889 to 1906 and as the president of Carnegie Hall from 1896 to 1905.

The primary goal of the society was to provide space for the Society of American Artists, the Architectural League, and the Art Students League—a place where art courses could be given and artists' works could be exhibited. To raise money, stock was sold in the company. For a one-time $100 contribution, the patron was given a fellowship certificate, which meant a life membership. It entitled him to invitations to all private viewings, five tickets for each show, and a voice in management, as if the society were a club with all the concomitant privileges. By June 1890, the fellows included Vice-President Levi P. Morton, John Jacob Astor IV, Edwin Booth, Samuel P. Avery, George B. Post, Charles Scribner, Darius Ogden Mills, John D. Rockefeller, Robert Goelet, Cornelius Vanderbilt II, and brother George W. Vanderbilt, and the treasury stood at $30,000.

The six-lot site on 57th Street, which was 75 feet wide and a full block deep, was on the market in 1890. The size was right and the best part was that its 15,000 square feet cost only $154,000, or a little over ten dollars a square foot.

The original plan of having Architectural League members design the building was scrapped as unprofessional, and a competition, which attracted 31 entrants, was

148

held instead. The architectural committee included architectural critic Russell Sturgis, sculptor Daniel Chester French, and Metropolitan Museum of Art president Henry G. Marquand. The $160,000 commission was awarded to the society's own secretary, Henry J. Hardenbergh, with associates Walter C. Hunting and John C. Jacobsen, realizing the society's goal of matching members with patrons.

Hardenbergh designed a building that is more side-

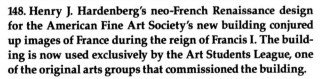

148. Henry J. Hardenberg's neo-French Renaissance design for the American Fine Art Society's new building conjured up images of France during the reign of Francis I. The building is now used exclusively by the Art Students League, one of the original arts groups that commissioned the building.

149. Plaques celebrating the domain of the American Fine Arts Society—painting, architecture, and sculpture—were set into the facade amidst neoclassical grandeur. Hardenbergh knew the proclivities of his patrons; he was one of them.

street clubhouse or mansion than art gallery and school, a picturesque evocation in pink granite and Indiana limestone of the Paris of Francis I. When the design was shown at the Architectural League's annual show, a *Times* reporter said that it "makes one think of brilliant dresses, rapiers, wigs, and sedan chairs." The deceptive front elevation shows three floors under a high, tiled attic roof, but a fourth floor is tucked into the building and a large skylight studio is on the fifth. The main building almost completely fills the depth of the front lots, and a one-story gallery behind was originally 75 feet wide and 40 feet deep. This was named the Vanderbilt Gallery from the outset, and at Christmas 1892, the reason was made clear. The gallery had been turned into a facsimile of a salon of the Musée de Cluny in Paris for the second annual dinner of the Architectural League, where the announcement was made that George W. Vanderbilt had contributed $100,000 to allow the gallery to be extended the 60 feet to 58th Street.

The Architectural League regularly held its shows in the Vanderbilt Gallery, giving the public the chance to view elevations of such important buildings as Hunt's plans for the Metropolitan Museum of Art and Gilbert's plans for the Custom House. The Gallery was the setting for many artists' first showings as well. Edwin Howland Blashfield, for instance, displayed his mural for the Waldorf-Astoria there before it was installed in the hotel, and C. Y. Turner showed his frieze in the gallery before it was installed in the hotel's restaurant. Clearly the building has proved a good home for at least one of its original tenants. The Art Students League is still there.

150

The Columbus Monument

Columbus Circle, Eighth Avenue at 59th Street
1892
BUILDER: The Italian-American Columbus
Monument Committee
SCULPTOR: Gaetano Russo

To celebrate the 400th anniversary of Columbus's discovery of America, Carlo Barsotti, the editor of *Il Progresso Italo-Americano*, assembled a group of Italian-American merchants in 1889 to raise funds for a monument that was worthy of the city and the event. Barsotti, who would be responsible for the erection of statues of Garibaldi, Verrazano, Verdi, and Dante, became adept at navigating the bureaucratic shoals of erecting public sculpture throughout the city, but before he could do anything, he knew he needed a design. He inveigled Italy's King Umberto into

appointing a committee to judge a competition, and the Royal Art Committee awarded the commission to the Roman sculptor Gaetano Russo, whose plan called for a 27-foot-high rostral column topped by a Carrara marble statue of Columbus in an admiral's uniform of the fifteenth century. Russo offered to waive his fee, which kept the proposal at a low $20,000, and the Italian government offered to transport the monument to New York in the hold of one of its warships.

To encourage contributions for the Russo statue, Barsotti displayed a ten-foot-high plaster model in a vacant store at Centre and Duane streets. Then he started a Committee of 1,000 with the idea that the drive would be half way to

150. After the big circle at 59th Street was offered as the site for the Columbus Monument and the rostral column topped by Gaetano Russo's statue of Columbus was installed, the name of the circle was changed to Columbus Circle.

solvency if each member raised just ten dollars. If cash could not be raised, contributions in the form of products would be accepted and sold later at a benefit auction. By July 1890, thanks in part to Barsotti's editorial prodding, about $12,000 in goods and cash had been raised.

The problem was that Barsotti had overlooked the fact that the discovery of America was not just an Italian affair. A Spanish-American committee had also been formed to erect a monument to the glory of Spain, the country that had underwritten Columbus's voyage. The Spanish-Amer-

151. On behalf of Carlo Barsotti's committee, Italy's King Umberto appointed a Royal Art Commission to choose the sculptor. One of the commissioners was Giuseppe Sacconi, the architect of Rome's Victor Emanuel Monument.

icans were offering a statue designed by Fernando Miranda that called for a stone basin 100 feet in diameter, from which fanciful fishes would send spouts of water into the air. A globe rising from the center of the pond was to be topped by three figures, one of them a sixteen-foot-high Columbus with one foot resting on Florida, the other on the West Indies. The site desired by the Spanish-American committee was the entrance to Central Park at Fifth Avenue and 59th Street.

The same site was being eyed by yet another committee, the Committee of 100, which was filled with names representing the New York establishment. To the dismay of some Italian-Americans, who thought that their respresentative should have been General Louis de Cesnola, the director of the Metropolitan Museum of Art, Barsotti had been voted to his place on the Committee of 100 by a "mass meeting" of the Italian-American community. His detractors pointed out that his "mass meeting" had only numbered 46 voters, but Barsotti stayed anyway. The Committee of 100 had its own art committee, with the likes of Richard Morris Hunt, John LaFarge, Augustus St. Gaudens, and Stanford White serving on it, and they gave the Barsotti project their stamp of approval and adopted it as one of their projects.

Although Barsotti had originally wanted the Battery as the site for the Columbus Monument, the step-fatherly Committee of 100 urged the same site as the Spanish-American committee was seeking. The parks commission refused both applications. The Spanish-Americans were informed they could use the entrance to the park at Fifth Avenue and 110th Street, which they spurned. The Italian-American committee was offered the Grand Circle at Eighth Avenue and 59th Street, which Barsotti graciously accepted on behalf of his committee with a sense of indebtedness to the municipal authorities.

By Columbus Day, 1892, the statue had been installed on its perch and a 10,000-seat amphitheater had been constructed around the memorial for the festivities, which the Committee of 100 had deemed would be nothing less than a five-day celebration, with parades and speeches and bunting everywhere. The route of the biggest parade was up Fifth Avenue, where some of the millionaires boxed up the more vulnerable lower portions of their mansions, pitching the tops of the boxes at angles to keep people from sitting atop them. If the estimates on crowds are correct, about 1.5 million spectators jammed the city for the parade, which had 51,400 marchers. Although the art commission had issued standards for decorations, the guidelines were joyfully ignored, with flags and bunting in gay disarray, except at the homes of the Vanderbilts and Whitneys and at clubs like the Manhattan, all of which remained aristocratically aloof. After the monument was unveiled, the celebration in the streets went on until after nightfall, with bands playing and crowds cheering the sculptor Russo, who had been wined and dined during his six-week visit and was the hero of the day.

The Sherman Statue

At the Plaza, Fifth Avenue between 59th and 60th Streets
1903
DONOR: The Chamber of Commerce of the State of New York
SCULPTOR: Augustus St. Gaudens
ARCHITECT: Charles Follen McKim

By the turn of the twentieth century, several proposals had been made for improving the plaza at Fifth Avenue and 59th Street, including the two Columbus memorials, a memorial to the soldiers and sailors of the Civil War, a Heine monument, and Hunt's gateway scheme. Sculptor Karl Bitter said in 1897 that the problem was that the plaza had never been treated as a whole, and he maintained that the plaza could become comparable to Paris's Place de la Concorde if only it were treated as a single, well-integrated composition. His idea was for a perfectly symmetrical ground plan with fountain-and-statuary groups placed opposite each other, and the whole unified by balustrades. A statue was, in fact, soon placed on the northern half of the plaza, but it was neither the type nor the site that Bitter had in mind.

The statue was of General William Tecumseh Sherman, who had marched through Georgia in the Civil War and then took New York by storm, where as a civilian he practiced law, advised railroad men, and negotiated such good business deals that he was made an honorary member of the Chamber of Commerce of the State of New York. At his death in 1891, a bank was named for him as well as the

triangular plot created by the intersection of today's Broadway and Amsterdam Avenue at 72nd Street. The Chamber of Commerce decided that a more fitting memorial would be a statue. The Chamber did not have to respond to political pressure, nor did it have to hold competitions. It only had to raise funds, hire a sculptor, and receive the city's blessing for an acceptable statue and a suitable site.

Money was no problem. William E. Dodge, who would donate the statue of John Jay for the facade of the Chamber's Liberty Street building, chaired the Sherman Fund Committee, which collected $44,786 by the end of 1891. The choice of Augustus St. Gaudens as sculptor was claimed by the Chamber to be unanimous, though General Howard Carroll, an associate editor of the *Times*, maintained that the selection was against the wishes of some members.

In the short run, many members no doubt regretted the selection of St. Gaudens. The contract for the statue was signed in March 1892 and gave St. Gaudens a little over two years in which to deliver. He planned to base Sherman's head on the bust he had modeled from life in 1888, which pleased the chamber, since it meant that part of the work was already done. St. Gaudens, however, was not to be content with just any statue. His *Sherman* had to transcend the usual portrayal of a sword-bearing military hero riding into battle. He imagined a bare-headed man reigning in his

---

152. Soon after General William Tecumseh Sherman's death in 1891, the New York Chamber of Commerce commissioned Augustus Saint-Gaudens to sculpt a memorial to the Civil War leader. To design the assemblage, Saint-Gaudens teamed up with Charles Follen McKim.

horse as he was being led by an angel of Victory, a subtle yet forceful idea.

Five years after the Sherman statue was due, a plaster model was accorded the place of honor at the Paris Salon of 1899. Although St. Gaudens said that it "looked bully and was smashingly fine," he was not yet content with it, and when the Chamber urged him to work a little faster, he wrote back, "I'm thinking about it—you'll be satisfied when it is finished." His rudeness was the result of his frustration, his real dissatisfaction with the quality of his work, but he kept refining it. In 1901, another plaster cast was exhibited, this one at the Pan-American Exposition in Buffalo, where St. Gaudens did not just win an ordinary gold medal, but an award "above and beyond all other awards." He was becoming more satisfied with his work, and all the publicity over the delays helped his cause in the long run, because there was still one hurdle to clear.

As early as 1893, *King's Handbook* said that the statue was to be placed at the newly named Sherman Square. St. Gaudens and architect Charles Follen McKim, who designed the base, both liked the spot in front of Grant's Tomb that had been designed for an equestrian statue of Grant. However, with three coats of solid gold leaf applied to Sherman's bronze skin, the colossal statue would have stolen some of the tomb's thunder, and the Grant family squelched the plan. By 1901, the southern end of Central Park's Mall was in the running. This was a site that Frederick Law Olmsted liked and St. Gaudens by then accepted, but other sculptors whose statues were on the mall feared that the *Sherman* would diminish the importance of their own works. Then others joined the fray. Some trees would have been cut down to make way for the statue, which led to further protests. *Architectural Record* rather grandly said that this sort of thing allows "horticulturists rather than sculptors the privilege of deciding negatively, at least, the position of a statue." A compromise suggestion was to place the statue at the north end of today's Times Square, where it would harm neither man-made objects nor the natural landscape.

The question was finally settled by William R. Wilcox, Mayor Seth Low's parks commissioner. Without the concurrence of the Art Commission, the Municipal Art Society, or the National Sculpture Society, Wilcox imperiously announced that the ideal place was the long-coveted site at the plaza on the northwest corner of Fifth Avenue and 59th Street. No complaints were heard from any of the watchdog groups.

Sherman was unveiled on Memorial Day, 1903, nine years after it was contracturally due. Cornelius N. Bliss, the Chamber's vice-president, made the presentation on behalf of the then-ailing William E. Dodge. Among the dignitaries were Alice Roosevelt, Mrs. Morgan Dix, the wife of Trinity's pastor, Secretary of War Elihu Root, and Bishop Potter. For those who participated in the exercises, luncheon was afterwards served at the Metropolitan Club.

The Plaza Hotel

On the Plaza, Fifth Avenue between 58th and 59th Streets
1907
BUILDER: The Plaza Hotel
ARCHITECT: Henry J. Hardenbergh

The financing for a new hotel was discussed one day in 1904 over lunch at the St. Regis. Dining together were Bernhard Beinecke, a wholesale butcher whose clientele included steamship lines and hotel chains; Harry S. Black, the president of the George A. Fuller Construction Company and the man who created the U.S. Realty & Improvement Company; and various associates. They had just bought The Plaza, the eight-story brick and brownstone hotel that had stood on the west side of the plaza since 1890, and they were wondering what to do with their $3 million investment.

An eavesdropping diner at the St. Regis said, "Get me Fred Sterry to manage the hotel and you can count me in for all you need. I'll wager my fortune on his hotel ability." The bettor was John "Bet-A-Million" Gates, who again was betting on a sure thing. Fred Sterry, while still in his thirties, was simultaneously managing the Poinciana and the Breakers in Palm Beach and the Homestead in Virginia, and he was making successes of them all. Black had already told Sterry that he belonged in New York, to which Sterry's response was, "Build me my kind of hotel and I'll come." The Plaza, although spacious and elegant, was not alluring enough for Sterry and it was not large enough for the new owners to earn a decent return on their $3 million investment. Since the frame of the building could not bear the weight of additional stories, the new owners soon began to regard the hotel as old-fashioned, out-of-date, and out of luck.

The Plaza's patrons were shocked. The Plaza was one of the best managed and most popular hotels in the city, and they questioned what kind of replacement could justify The Plaza's destruction. The syndicate's reply was something grander than anyone had ever dreamed, something that reflected all the glories of the Edwardian Age. It was the bait for Sterry and Sterry bit.

By the summer of 1905, the new owners were demolishing the building and selling everything, from bric-a-brac to the lace curtains with the emblematic lion's head woven

153. Henry J. Hardenbergh, the architect of Washington's Willard Hotel and New York's Waldorf-Astoria and Manhattan hotels, was asked by John "Bet-A-Million" Gates and his two partners to design the new Plaza Hotel. Gates was betting on a sure thing.

into the fabric. To design the new hotel, they hired Henry J. Hardenbergh, whose hotels included Washington's Willard and New York's Waldorf-Astoria on 34th Street and Manhattan on 42nd Street. Hardly had the architect and the contractors "got the work under way," said Managing Director Sterry, "before it was seen that the original sum [of $8 million] would fall far short of erecting such a hotel as the promoters desired, so it was decided to raise the additional sum necessary." There were two options—take out a second mortgage or ask the stockholders of record to subscribe to short-term notes. The triumverate of Black, Beinecke, and Gates, who together owned practically all the stock, put up the additional $4 million from their private resources.

Hardenbergh's design was loosely modeled after buildings of the French Renaissance, but at eighteen stories, some changes in scale were dictated. "Distance and mass are added to the consideration of the surroundings," said Hardenbergh. "In a skyscraper having an exposed situation, the distribution of masses counts far more than decorated details. But the surroundings are also a vital factor. In designing the Plaza Hotel, for instance, the situation on Central Park largely determined the simplicity of design." The Plaza was a skyscraper, so Hardenbergh distributed the ornament as though the building were a column with a base, a shaft, and a capital. To compensate for the height, he linked the building laterally by projecting the wings. To soften it, he rounded the corners, with oriel windows rising from the fourth floor to be topped by domes that stand free of the tiled roof, which he intentionally colored green to echo the trees in the park.

Sterry hired E. F. Pooley to design the interiors, and together Beinecke, Hardenbergh, Sterry, and Pooley went on a buying binge through Europe. All the furniture on the main floor was custom-made in France. The walls of the Louis XVI-style lobby were lined in French marble and topped by capitals of gilded bronze. In the center of the lobby floor was the Tea Room (now the Palm Court), which was topped by a dome of leaded glass through which natural light streamed by day. The Tea Room was finished in Caen stone and Breche Violette marble, with a floor of Istrian marble slabs joined in solid brass. An Italian palace supplied the four caryatids that represent the seasons, and greenhouses supplied the large palms, rubber trees, and tropical plants that created a cool garden-like effect. The Fifth Avenue corner at 59th Street was devoted to the men's cafe, which was permeated by the atmosphere of a men's club, with an Aubusson tapestry frieze above oak-paneled wainscoting (it is today's Edwardian Room). Two Louis XVI-style dining rooms—one reserved for permanent guests, the other accommodating transients—occupied the balance of the Fifth Avenue frontage. The barroom was paneled in antique-finished British oak, which gave rise to its present name, the Oak Room, where oil frescoes of German feudal castles on the Rhine show robber barons in

154

154. The caryatid in today's Palm Court, which was originally the Tea Room, was imported from an Italian palace. Its function is purely ornamental, since the George F. Fuller Company constructed a steel-framed skyscraper.

155. The Oak Room, so-called for its wood trim, is one of the period's few remaining hotel dining rooms that has remained pristine. Two of the Plaza's major dining rooms that overlooked the plaza are gone—one is used as an entrance, the other as a store.

156. The first Plaza Hotel had its lion's head insignia woven into the hotel's lace curtains, emblazoned on each piece of silver, even set into the mosaic floor that paved the lobby. Just as ubiquitous is the new hotel's insignia, here seen as a doorknob.

their original surroundings. Contemporary robber barons could be found in any of the six stock brokerage houses that occupied the west end of the main floor.

Every room in the hotel had a centrally controlled electric clock and telephone, and on the wall below each telephone were three buttons. They summoned the bellboy, maid, or waiter from the floor staff. Fred Sterry stipulated that there was to be no wallpaper on the walls of the bedrooms, so all were given plaster molding and wall paneling of pine, mahogany, or Circassian walnut. The same wood that was used for the paneling was also used for the room's front door and furnishings.

The $12.5 million construction costs included some extraordinary precautions. The fire that destroyed the Windsor Hotel in 1899 showed that not enough water pressure

could be generated to reach the upper floors of tall buildings, so the Fuller Company installed pumps in The Plaza's basement that developed 150 pounds of pressure—50 pounds greater than the fire department developed. Other precautions included the ten-time filtration of Croton water. Water for drinking and culinary purposes was filtered even more.

The Plaza's glittering glory was to the rich what light is to moths, and with about half of the suites rented on long-term leases, the super rich moved in. Mr. and Mrs. George Jay Gould checked into the hotel on opening day in 1907 for a two-year stay while their mansion at 857 Fifth Avenue was being built. The honor of being the first to sign the register went to Alfred Gwynne Vanderbilt, his wife, and their servant. With the rent at the St. Regis set at $125 a day for the State Apartments, the Vanderbilts got a bargain at $10,000 a year, a sum they could well afford—Alfred Gwynne Vanderbilt had inherited $44.5 million in 1900 upon the death of his father, Cornelius Vanderbilt II, whose mansion stood diagonally across the plaza. The price, of course, might have been a loss leader. Part-owner John Gates paid $15,000 a year for his suite.

158

157

The Alwyn Court Apartments

**182 West 58th Street, on the southeast corner of
Seventh Avenue**
1909
BUILDER: Hedden Construction Company
ARCHITECTS: Harde & Short

Rentals in prestigious apartment houses did not come
cheap, as the sign on the south wall of the Alwyn Court
Apartments attested. In large letters it proclaimed that rents
in the new apartment house started at $6,500 a year, or
more than $500 a month. In fact, the rents went as high as
$10,000 a year, and no lease was for less than three years.
For those who could afford the prices, the size of the apartments was said to be ideal. The Alwyn Court had two
apartments to a floor, and each apartment had fourteen
rooms and five baths. The tenants could live just as well
and entertain just as lavishly as in a house costing about the
same amount, and an apartment only required three to five
servants to run it, compared with twice that number to run
a comparable house.

According to the Alwyn Court's newspaper advertising,
the building was constructed "with the idea of affording
spacious homes of elegance possessing many advantages,
conveniences, unique features and special appointments
not duplicated in New York today—an up-to-date 'House of
Select Residences,' where the highest point of excellence in
apartment construction has been reached." The apartments

157. The Plaza's State Apartments are now used for functions,
but the glory of the suite, with its marble fireplace, mirrored
panels, and air of opulence, lives on. The only jarring note is
the fire-exit sign in compliance with fire regulations.

158. Rents as high as $10,000 a year for fourteen-room, sim-
plex apartments in the Alwyn Court bought more than physical luxuries; they paid for the privilege of living in "swell-
dom." The entrance used to be through the corner archway.

were designed so that only three rooms of every fourteen faced the courtyard (two of them were servants' rooms, the third a reception gallery). Some of the rooms had vast proportions. The living rooms, for instance, were 19 by 30 feet; the dining rooms were 19 by 22; and the galleries were 13 by 20. Including the music rooms, about 1,700 square feet of floorspace could be thrown open for entertaining. Architects Harde & Short were so proud of the arrangement that they cautioned other architects, owners, and builders not to plagiarize the floor plan under threat of lawsuit.

Despite all the hoopla about ideal size and shapes of apartments, one tenant did not find his prospective quarters big enough, and he prevailed upon the management to take two suites, one above the other, and combine them into a duplex, with the understanding that a ten-year lease at $16,000 a year would be signed. The undertaking was so successful that the management considered creating more duplexes and asking even higher rents than they were getting for the original duplex.

Most spectacular were the thirteen-by-seventeen-foot rooms at the 58th Street corner, distinguished from the outside by the bow windows. The interior finish was of white enameled woodwork with silken hangings. Off it was an L-shaped dressing room with mirrored closet doors. A millinery closet was arranged in boxlike compartments, with plate-glass shelves for a dozen hats. Another closet was designed exclusively for ball gowns.

The walls and ceilings of the bathrooms were mirrored, and the shelves were all plate glass. The dining rooms had parquet floors, mahogany doors, and paneled walls. Elsewhere, the woodwork was a composite material molded into a floral ornamentation. Every apartment had wood-burning fireplaces, a built-in vacuum-cleaning system, and an individual wine vault.

Practically every inch of the facade was ornamented with neo-French Renaissance detailing, with the symbolic salamander—a decorative motif that was used at Chambord, for instance—worked into the terra cotta. The apartment house's name, however, is not an allusion to French antecedents, but to Alwyn Ball, Jr., one of the building's five owners.

---

159. Every inch of Harde & Shot's terra-cotta facade at the Alwyn Court is decorated in the glossiest style of the French Renaissance. Here, a seraphic comedy and tragedy protect a fleur-de-lis encrusted escutcheon, all of which are protected by a canopy. Other symbols of French royalty include the salamander, which was adopted by Francis I.

The Maine Memorial

At the Entrance to Central Park, 59th Street and Central Park West (Columbus Circle)
1913
BUILDER: The National Maine Monument Committee
LANDSCAPE ARCHITECT: H. Van Buren Magonigle
SCULPTOR: Attilio Piccirilli

160

If the Spanish-American War that followed the sinking of the *Maine* was William Randolph Hearst's War, then the Maine Memorial was Hearst's Monument. To get the fund raising off to a good start, he contributed the first thousand dollars and he appealed to others through his *New York Journal* to join the cause. Former President Grover Cleveland said that Hearst's attempts were little more than a thinly masked advertising campaign to build circulation for the *Journal,* and he declined support. Many, however, went along with Hearst, including former Vice-President Levi P. Morton, Chauncey Depew, and Oliver Hazard Perry Belmont.

The north end of today's Times Square was selected as the site for the monument, and by 1901 enough money had been raised to warrant an architectural competition. The winner was H. Van Buren Magonigle, who had worked in the office of Olmsted & Vaux and was associated with sculptor Attilio Piccirilli for this design. With its shaft of about 60 feet high, their monument would have served as a bold exclamation point between Broadway and Seventh Avenue. It seems, though, that a clerk at the Municipal Art Commission had somehow neglected to record the site in the grant, and by the time Magonigle and Piccirilli arrived with their finished plans in 1908, it was too late. A comfort station had already been built on the site.

Over the wishes of Olmsted and Vaux to keep the park rustic and not subordinate its natural beauty to formal classicism, the site at Columbus Circle was pressed. To put the statue there would also have meant removing four trees, obstructing traffic and competing in height with the Columbus Monument. Magonigle was willing to revise his plans. He would design a broken arc, with the Maine Memorial placed in the center. On either side of the monument he would have two pathways and two roadways, which would be flanked by European-style garden houses, so that the whole would act as a true gateway. Sixteen feet would be lopped off the top of the shaft to minimize competition with the Columbus Monument, but then a sculptural group of *Columbia Triumphant,* which was an afterthought, brought the memorial almost back to its originally intended height. (The bronze group was cast by the Gorham Company from guns that were salvaged from the raised *Maine* and is hauntingly reminiscent of J. Q. A. Ward's quadriga for the Dewey Arch of 1899.)

The park's landscape architect, Samuel Parsons, was presented with the plans several times, and although he still believed that the design was out of harmony with the surroundings, he reluctantly assented. Everyone conveniently forgot the edict against monumental entrances, and in the summer of 1910, the Art Commission approved the revised plans for the *Maine Memorial* at Columbus Circle. The four offending trees were cut down, which led Parks Commissioner Stover to say in 1911 that he thought the vista through the park was improved. In the best Swiftian tradition, one letter writer inquired "why not cut down more trees and improve more vistas?"

The pink Milford granite memorial, with its pedestal and carved groups of Knoxville marble, was a gift to the city from Hearst's National Maine Monument Committee, which by 1902 had collected $102,000. By 1910, however, the price of the monument had increased to $175,000, and new fund-raising gimmicks included the presentation of a

160. William Randolph Hearst spearheaded the drive for the Maine Memorial and headed the fund-raising efforts for it. Since he owned property on the periphery of the circle, he was probably just as happy that H. Van Buren Magonigle's plans for the memorial were delayed and the original site at Times Square was forfeited.

moving picture at the Victoria Theater showing the raising of the *Maine* from Havana harbor. The money came into the coffers in dribs and drabs, with an estimated million individuals making contributions.

The day of the presentation, Memorial Day, 1913, called for a parade up Fifth Avenue and west on 59th Street to Columbus Circle. Hearst hosted a luncheon for the visiting dignitaries at The Plaza, after which they took seats in reviewing stands that had been set up for them on the avenue. At the end of the parade, the dignitaries followed the line of march by auto to the reviewing stands that had been set up at Columbus Circle for the ceremony itself. At the given moment, Hearst's little son, George, who was dressed in the white duck uniform of a navy enlisted man, pulled the silk cords that released the large American flag covering the monument, the band struck up the "Star Spangled Banner," and super-dreadnoughts in the Hudson River thundered out their simultaneous salute of 21 guns.

Hearst was delighted with the placement of the monument. He had held a vested interest in Columbus Circle for almost twenty years, and everything that contributed to improving its ambience contributed to his financial well-being. In 1895, Hearst had bought the Virginia Hotel, which stood on the irregular block on the south side of Columbus Circle between Broadway and Eighth Avenue. He wanted to erect the *Journal's* new headquarters on the site, but the plot was too small to accommodate the building he envisioned. He contracted to buy the block south of it in the expectation that the city would agree to close 58th Street and allow him to erect a massive 40-story building on the double plot. His attempt to have the street closed was a failure and his scheme went with it, but he did not give up on Columbus Circle. In 1911, Hearst bought the irregular block on the north side of the circle between Central Park West and Broadway where he wanted to build the second tallest building in Manhattan, and again the plan came to nought. In 1914, a three-story building was going up, with a foundation that was strong enough to support a 30-story tower in the future. Hearst's ultimate plans never developed, and Columbus Circle has never equaled the sum of its parts.

The Fountain of Abundance

The Plaza, Fifth Avenue between 58th and 59th Streets
1916
Bequest of Joseph Pulitzer
ARCHITECTS: Carrère & Hastings
SCULPTOR: Karl Bitter

The plaza at Fifth Avenue and 59th Street had become a great social center by the early 1900s, but it was sorely lacking in grace. A few years after Karl Bitter had designed a comprehensive architectural scheme for the plaza in 1897, G. T. Taylor had described his own vision for the southern circle, where he saw a "fountain on a noble scale, low in elevation, with perhaps a small flow of water, but with sculpture that would beguile our thoughts from the world . . . and prepare us for Pan." Few city planners paid much heed to Taylor's suggestion. There was still the dream of a comprehensive plan for the plaza, and newspaper publisher Joseph Pulitzer became a key figure in its potential realization.

Among his many bequests, Pulitzer left $50,000 to the city in 1911 for the erection of a fountain at the plaza. It was to be, as far as practicable, like those in the Place de la Concorde in Paris, the same grouping that Karl Bitter had singled out as his model. The possibility of merging the Pulitzer bequest with a competition to explore the broader possibilities attracted wide praise, but Pulitzer's son would commit no further funding for an overall scheme, obdurately standing by the stipulation that the $50,000 could only be used for the fountain that his father had imagined.

The city approved the overall concept of a plan for the site, which included the circle where *Sherman* stood, in 1912. The architectural competition was limited to John Russell Pope, Arnold W. Brunner, H. Van Buren Magonigle, McKim, Mead & White, and Carrère & Hastings, whose plans were displayed at the Main Branch of the New York Public Library. Judged by George B. Post on behalf of the executors, by Whitney Warren for the Park Commission, and by Paul P. Cret, Charles A. Platt, and Herbert Adams, the unanimous decision went to Carrère & Hastings. All the competitors provided for the improvement of the entire plaza, but Carrère & Hastings solved the twin problems of traffic and art, creating a fountain that could stand on its own without having to rearrange the rest of the plaza to make it work.

The fountain could have been described by Taylor eleven years earlier, and it is certainly reminiscent of Carrère & Hastings's fountain at Buffalo's Pan-American Exposition in 1901. The large, terraced structure, higher at the south to allow water to flow through basins to the north, is topped by a nude female figure of Abundance. And the symmetry

could have been described by Karl Bitter fourteen years before. It called for a loggia bordering the west end, with posts and chains defining the rest of the perimeter, and with *Sherman* and *Abundance* on the same axis. Since the site where *Sherman* stood was about to be plowed up to make way for an extension of the BMT subway, the shift of about fifteen feet posed no problem and could be easily effected.

There was no sculptor for *Abundance* until the National Sculpture Society held a competition, which was won in 1914 by Karl Bitter. It was Bitter, of course, who had figured out the whole scheme long before, and it did not take him long to create a two-foot-high plaster figure. Tragically, the forty-seven-year-old sculptor never had a chance to complete the statue. He was killed by an automobile in April 1915, and the work was completed by his student, Karl Gruppe.

Unlike Columbus Circle, the Plaza had a completely acceptable overall plan, but to implement it required a benefactor to come forward, and none ever has.

---

161. The Plaza was transformed into a gracious space by Joseph Pulitzer's $50,000 bequest. Unfortunately, the sum did not pay for Carrère & Hastings' entire plan, which included a fence and a loggia to define the perimeter, and the scheme never approached the Place de la Concorde in Paris, which was Pulitzer's avowed goal.

Fifth Avenue, New York,

Copyright by A. Loeffler, Tompkinsville, N.Y.

25873

162. *The Astor Mansion at 65th Street and Fifth Avenue, which is in the extreme right of the post card, was designed by Richard Morris Hunt as a two-family house for Caroline Schermerhorn Astor and her son, John Jacob III. By virtue of Mrs. Astor's social standing—she was* the *Mrs. Astor—Upper Fifth Avenue was established as the demesne of the very rich.*

9

The Astors' Fifth Avenue

An appeal of real estate is its permanency—what is built on the land might come and go, but the land remains, a fact that John Jacob Astor appreciated. Astor, who acquired so much New York real estate that at his death in 1848 he was called the "landlord of New York," established a trust that was managed in part by his heirs, in part by professional managers. Neither had to be particularly imaginative, since the land did the work for them.

One of the Astors' most prescient speculators was neither an Astor by blood nor a manager by training. She was Caroline Schermerhorn Astor, who married William Astor, the grandson of the founding father. This was the doughty Caroline who convinced her husband to leave the then-fashionable Lafayette Place in the 1850s for the southwest corner of Fifth Avenue and 34th Street, and this was the Mrs. Astor who by the 1890s had become *the* Mrs. Astor, to the anger of cousin William Waldorf Astor. With the death of her husband in 1892 and the coming of the Waldorf Hotel next door, Mrs. Astor decided that it was time to move from 34th Street. She conferred with her son and daughter-in-law, the John Jacob Astor IVs, and considered the southeast corner of Fifth Avenue and 55th Street as a possible site for

the new family house, but the neighborhood was considered perilously close to the edge of commercial development. William had bought the vacant 75-by-100-foot lot on the northeast corner of Fifth Avenue and 65th Street from Standard Oil's James Stillman for $215,000 in 1891, which, with an additional 50 feet of frontage, Mrs. Astor decided would be the site for the next great Astor mansion. What the farsighted Mrs. Astor viscerally understood was that upper Fifth Avenue, with Central Park at its doorstep, was ripe for development.

Mrs. Astor knew the successes of architect Richard Morris Hunt, and during one of his visits to Newport she proffered the chance to design the double mansion she envisioned as a worthy successor to her 34th Street home. Hunt took the plum and designed a four-story, Indiana limestone-clad house with a slate-and-copper mansard roof in a style that was part country chateau from the banks of the Loire, part city mansion from the banks of the Seine. The plan for the Astor mansion was determined by its being a two-family house with a single entrance, with Mrs. Astor ensconced in the sunnier southern half and her son and his family in the northern half. Some rooms were common to both sides of the house, and they could be thrown open for large parties. The only disparity was that Mrs. Astor's rooms were all somewhat larger. The projected cost of the house was $300,000, but with baubles such as a two-ton bathtub that was cut from a solid marble block, the final tally was no doubt higher.

The new Astor mansion was finally ready in January 1896, and Mrs. Astor was able to invite a few guests one afternoon for tea. She had the drawing rooms, libraries, dining rooms, and breakfast rooms all thrown open *en suite* and decorated with cut flowers and potted palms from the Astor conservatory at Rhinebeck, New York. The great hall, with its monumental double staircase, was filled with music by a band under the direction of Nathan Franko, the Metropolitan Opera's conductor. About 1,000 invitations were sent out, and "judging by the throng," said the *Times,* "there were few regrets." If, indeed, 1,000 guests did come for tea that afternoon, Mrs. Astor had to greet eighteen guests a minute between the hours of four and seven, a breathless pace even for this hostess of hostesses.

A week later, Mrs. Astor reentered the social fray with another of her social events of the season. For this occasion, the art gallery was transformed into a ballroom, and although it could accommodate 600 guests comfortably, it did not give rise to a new standard for society. The guests began to arrive after the Metropolitan Opera's performance of *Carmen,* and since the dancing would continue far into the night, supper was served at midnight. The menu for the consecration-of-the-house ball called for five hot entrées, including sweetbreads, steak, and wild duck, followed by six cold courses, including squab, pâté de foie-gras, a gallantine of pheasant with truffles, and "sandwiches assortis," topped by a choice of nine desserts. Among the choice of potables were claret and champagne. The guests came and ate and danced, and with the Astors' new northern outpost, the impetus was provided for yet another northward migration of fashion.

In 1890, there was hardly a fashionable house on Fifth Avenue north of 59th Street, but twenty years later Fifth Avenue was lined by millionaires' mansions with hardly a break from Elbridge T. Gerry's house on 61st Street to Andrew Carnegie's on 91st. This mile and a half held about sixteen acres of building sites facing Central Park, and the tax assessments on the property in 1910, including the few vacant lots, were set at $60,814,000, or $10,135 a foot front.

Just as property on the Vanderbilts' stretch of Fifth Avenue had become fair game for speculation, so it did on the Astors'. In 1902, August Heckscher sold his house at 835 Fifth Avenue to a syndicate for $300,000. When the announcement was made that a sixteen-story apartment-hotel was scheduled for the site between 64th and 65th streets, a shudder ran through the neighborhood. It meant that Frank Jay Gould would have a towering structure to the north of his $500,000 mansion and that again Mrs. Astor would have her property thrown into shadow. Within six weeks a consortium of neighbors had bought

back the property, which they said would only be used for purposes in keeping with the residential character of the avenue. Who paid how much to buy back the property was never revealed.

Defensive real estate continued. In 1906, the Astors bought the house at 844 Fifth Avenue that stood between them and stockbroker Grant B. Schley, whose house was on the southeast corner of 66th Street. The Astors completely rebuilt 844 Fifth on the American basement plan and rented it on a long-term lease to Paul Morton, the president of Equitable Life.

In the meantime, *the* Mrs. Astor, senile to the point that she was receiving nonexistent guests to nonexistent balls, died. Her son inherited the house and hired Carrère & Hastings to convert the double house into a single mansion. Mrs. Astor's dining room became the library, and one of the colonel's two salons became a drawing room, the other a morning room. The new dining room in the northeast corner of the house was finished in Vermont marble. The central hall was turned into a 40-foot court with a fountain in the center and a vaulted ceiling of decorated glass and bronze above. A colonnade created a loggia that led to the ballroom-picture gallery. The predominant colors were still white and gold, the predominant style was Louis XVI, and the estimated remodeling costs came to $125,000. The celebration of the consecration of the refurbished house in 1910 had a familiar ring to it. A dinner dance was hosted by Colonel and Mrs. John Jacob Astor IV for 250 guests.

The Metropolitan Club

1 East 60th Street, northeast corner of Fifth Avenue
1894
BUILDERS: The Metropolitan Club
ARCHITECTS: McKim, Mead & White

The Metropolitan Club was created in 1891 to rectify injustices that were allegedly suffered by two perfectly acceptable clubmen at the hands of the Union Club. J. Pierpont Morgan had proposed membership for John King, president of the Erie Railroad, whose "career and character have won him the universal respect of all who know him," according to the club reporter of the *Times.* But gossip had it that King's table manners were not up to Union Club standards, that he "ate with his knife," and his membership was denied. Then came the blackballing of Dr. Seward W. Webb, a son-in-law of William H. Vanderbilt and the president of the Wagner Palace Car Company. The story was that as an undergraduate, Webb had joined one secret society. When

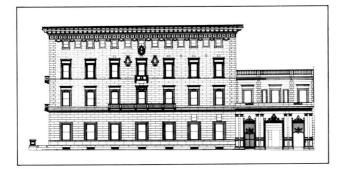

163

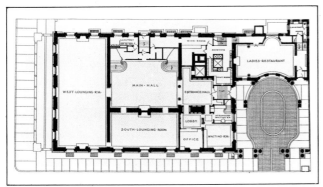

164

165

he changed colleges, he joined another. The Union Club said it was bad form.

With a certain righteous indignation, W. Watts Sherman gathered about 25 clubmen to create a new club that they said would be "the club of clubs." The charter members decided to buy the vacant property on the northeast corner of 60th Street that was owned by the same Lily Churchill who had sold her 55th Street property to William Astor. On behalf of the yet unnamed club, Cornelius Vanderbilt II, Charles Lanier, and William C. Whitney offered Lily Churchill $480,000 for the property. She took it.

The Metropolitan Club's initials instantly gave rise to being dubbed the Millionaires' Club, even Morgan's Club—with good reason. A score of its members were worth over $100 million each, and J. Pierpont Morgan was one of its guiding lights and its first president. The role of club secretary required endless time devoted to the club's correspondence, and being treasurer was a full-time job. Morgan's

163. Stanford White said that the Metropolitan Club manifested the severest and simplest character of the Italian Renaissance. It was designed to be the club of clubs.

164. A potent lure to new Metropolitan members was a dining room that was sequestered from the all-male enclave and set aside for the use of female guests. The Ladies' Restaurant overlooked the courtyard.

165. The Metropolitan Club, established in 1891, had the temerity to challenge the Union Club. The building committee decided that only a facade of marble would do.

role as president was more ceremonial and advisory than executive. He presided at functions and regularly scheduled committee meetings, and since he commanded universal respect by virtue of his unquestioned social, professional, and ethical standing, he set the right tone for the place. By extension, since Morgan had himself been spurned by the Union Club through its refusal to accept a Morgan nominee, this was sweet revenge.

"The club of clubs" was designed to wrest leadership away from the Union Club, which was no easy task. The Union was the club that 99 percent of clubmen who were not in wanted to be in, and anyone who was willing to pay the membership fees for the Metropolitan Club was right to expect the standards of the Union. To improve its position, the Metropolitan Club was considering the creation of quarters for the wives, daughters, and mothers of its members. Every woman in town whose husband had the social standing was expected to exert all her powers of persuasion to make him join. The clubmen were fast to say that the scheme did not mean that women were going to have the run of the place. However, a dining room would be fitted up for distaff use in the eastern end, distinct from the club proper. And if the experiment failed, the rooms could easily be rearranged for males-only purposes.

Initiation fees were set at $300, and by the summer of 1891, less than six months after the club's creation, there were already 600 members. With the membership that the club wanted for "the club of clubs" came McKim, Mead & White, the "architects of architects," with Stanford White in charge. "The clubhouse will stand unrivaled in its size," said White, "and although the style will be of the severest and simplest character of the Italian Renaissance and the feeling of severity and stolidity will be carried through the interiors, the scale of the building and the nature of its materials will give it an appearance unlike that of any building in New York." At first, the members could not decide whether the facade should be stone, marble, or brick, but after White's plans were presented to the building committee, there was no question—the clubhouse would have a marble facade. On top of that splurge, the members treated themselves to a 35-by-60-foot courtyard set off by a gateway of paired Doric columns and wrought-iron gates. The courtyard represented an exuberant act of conspicuous consumption, especially since the courtyard was reserved exclusively for private carriages.

Later clubs might be bigger, but the Metropolitan in its time was indeed unrivaled in size. The main building measures 90 feet on Fifth Avenue by 150 feet on 60th Street; the annex, housing the ladies' dining room on the main floor, measures 55 by 40 feet. The building is 104 feet high, but it contains only four stories. The lowest ceilings are on the fourth floor, which houses the residential quarters. There

were 35 bedrooms, each with its own bath and all capable of being turned into suites. Most of the public rooms are finished in woods of oak, cherry, and mahogany. The main vestibules and halls are lined in Numidian marble, with ceilings trimmed in gold. The stairways and galleries have handrails of forged iron, and bronze electrified sconces jut out from the walls. White even provided tor-chère-like lampposts for the sidewalks outside the club.

A 30-by-60-foot billiard room overlooks 60th Street from the second floor. The adjoining 20-by-30-foot billiard room had only one table in it and was reserved for demonstration games and championship tournaments. The small lounging room on the first floor overlooks the side street and measures 30 by 50 feet. The main lounge overlooking the avenue measures 40 by 85 feet and was decorated in the style of Louis XIII. One female guest who was shown the grandeur of the place during the opening-week ceremonies said that she felt as if she "were lost in space. The rooms are not cozy, but they are palatial in every respect, which is all a man wants, I suppose."

Women clearly wanted their annex. By 1898, so many women were dining at the club that warnings were going out to Delmonico's and Sherry's and even to the Waldorf-Astoria to look to their laurels in the near future. The Metropolitan Club was fast becoming an uptown rival of the fashionable midtown restaurants.

166. Wrought-iron gates and paired Doric columns set off the Metropolitan's driveway, whose use by anything except private carriages was precluded by club edict.

The Fabbri House

11 East 62nd Street, between Fifth and Madison Avenues
1900
BUILDER: Mrs. Elliott F. Shepard
ARCHITECTS: Haydel & Shepard

The Vanderbilts still controlled their stretch of Fifth Avenue in the 50s in 1898 when Mrs. Elliott F. Shepard, one of William H. Vanderbilt's daughters, announced that she was giving her half of the twin house on Fifth Avenue to her sister, Mrs. William D. Sloane. Mrs. Shepard's husband was dead, her children were already married or living on their own, and she wanted to spend the rest of her time at her country estate in Scarborough, New York. A few days after the announcement, the *Tribune* trumpeted the news that "Mrs. Elliott F. Shepard will have a town house after all." She had bought the two dwellings at 11 and 13 East 62nd Street with the idea of remodeling them into one house.

Mrs. Shepard did not remodel the houses; she tore them down and, continuing the family tradition of building homes for their children, presented a new house on the 45-by-100-foot plot to her daughter, Edith, who was married to Ernesto G. Fabbri, who while at Princeton traveled in the kinds of circles that attracted nubile Vanderbilt women.

Edith Shepard and Ernesto G. Fabbri were married in the Scarborough chapel that Mrs. Shepard had built as a memorial to her husband, Colonel Elliott Fitch Shepard. The carefully worded statement on the future of the newlyweds said that no decision had been made on where the Fabbris would permanently reside. Probably, after a short trip abroad, they would take a house in New York. The house they took was 11 East 62nd Street.

To design the house, Mrs. Shepard hired Haydel & Shepard, the same firm she had commissioned to design the Shepard Memorial Chapel. These two commissions appear to be the only two that Haydel & Shepard ever had, and little is known about the firm. Abner J. Haydel studied architecture at both Cornell and the Ecole des Beaux-Arts. August Dennis Shepard, Jr., graduated from the Lawrenceville School and studied in the United States and abroad, although, it seems, never formally. He just happened to be the nephew of his patron. Shepard went on to specialize in country estates and mountain lodges, where simplicity was the keynote of his designs "and where there wasn't a classical line or any molding except the round of a log and a pole in my camp structures," he said proudly. No doubt the Beaux-Arts extravaganza at 11 East 62nd Street was the inspiration of Abner Haydel.

Haydel & Shepard turned the space into a lavish stage whose pageantry would have pleased a dauphin. The *rez-de-chaussée* (ground floor) has about 3,500 square feet of

167

floor space. Aside from the elevator and the servants' stairs, it only contains two reception rooms, a great central hall, and the dining room, which occupies practically the entire rear of the house. A bay window overlooking the backyard

167. Mrs. Elliot F. Shepard's father, William H. Vanderbilt, gave her the house in which she lived, and she continued the family tradition of providing offspring with houses of their own. This house was a gift to her daughter Edith, who was married to Ernesto Fabbri. Mrs. Shepard also liked to keep things within the family, and the Shepard of the firm of Haydel & Shepard, who designed this rich Beaux-Arts facade at 11 East 62nd Street, was her nephew.

170

169

has a domed, stained-glass ceiling, the wood paneling on the wall is subtly detailed, and coved corners diminish the harshness of right angles. What seems to be an ordinary wall panel masks a door that swings out to reveal a built-in, walk-in, steel-encased Sargent & Greenleaf wall safe.

The second floor has only the salon in the rear and the music room overlooking 62nd Street. Against the west wall of the music room is a baronial fireplace, with the Fabbri

168. The second-floor bannister in the Fabbri house supports a pair of Louis XVI-style bronze and bronze *doré* candelabra supported by cornucopias borne by cupids. Each group is seventy inches high.

169. The coved dining room occupies the rear of the first floor of the Fabbri house. Artfully masked behind the wood paneling on the right is a walk-in safe.

170. The music room occupied the front of the second floor of the Fabbri house, and a Votey organ occupies its east wall. The organ's larger pipes are two stories high and fill the entire house with sound, since they open onto the stairway. This grand house is now the Johnson–O'Connor Research Foundation.

crest emblazoned on it, and filling the entire east wall is a Votey organ, with pipes that are built into the wall and extending two stories high. Upstairs are bedrooms, dressing rooms, guest rooms, and a library, with servants' quarters on the top floor. As in most houses, the ceilings are lower on the higher floors, but the fourth floor has ceilings about twelve feet high. Here is the nursery, where ingenious use of space was made by double-decking a walk-in closet above a fully equipped bathroom, with all the fixtures in lilliputian scale.

The highest quality was achieved in the wrought-iron entrance gates, in the perfectly balanced doors that close at the gentlest touch, and in a Palladian marble floor on the first floor. There is only a modicum of sham. The Baroque-like ceiling in the east reception hall, for instance, might look carved, but it was made of plaster.

The Fabbris did not occupy their house long. By 1907, Fabbri was working for Morgan, Harjes & Company, the Paris branch of his uncle's bank, and railroad man Edward Henry Harriman was living in the house while his own was being finished at 874 Fifth Avenue. Cousin Alfred Gwynne Vanderbilt then leased the house from the Fabbris in 1910 as a "bachelor's hall" for the season.

The year 1910 was a good time to live on 62nd Street between Fifth and Madison avenues. In 1901, the tabulators of the New York Social Register had declared that the city's social center was drifting north and east at the rate of about a block a year. By 1905, ground zero was Fifth Avenue at 58th Street, which meant that as many New York City residents in the social register lived north of the line as lived south, as many lived west as lived east. And in 1910, the social center reached 62nd Street between Fifth and Madison avenues, where it stalled for one season before inching north and east again.

171

172

The Schiefflin House

5 East 66th Street, between Fifth and Madison
1900
BUILDER: Mrs. Elliott F. Shepard
ARCHITECT: Richard Howland Hunt

In 1898, the same year that Mrs. Elliott F. Shepard gave the Fabbris their house, she gave a house to another of her daughters, Maria Louisa. The gift was specifically to Maria L. Shepard, Mrs. Shepard's daughter and wife of William J. Schiefflin, but if Mrs. Shepard's concern was gold digging, she did not have to worry much about Schiefflin. He was the heir to the Schiefflin family wholesale drug business, which had been founded in 1793. He was also the great grandson of John Jay, the nation's first chief justice. He was a graduate of Columbia's School of Mines and held a doctorate from the University of Munich. He was a civil rights activist, a founder of the City Club, and the president of the Citizen's Union. His *Times* obituary in 1955 said quite simply

that he was married to the daughter of Col. Elliott F. Shepard, "descendant of another old American family," blandly ignoring the crass Vanderbilt link. The Schiefflins were American aristocracy. The Vanderbilts just had more money.

The Shepard-Schiefflin wedding ranked with the best of the social events of 1891. After the wedding service at the Fifth Avenue Presbyterian Church, the Shepards and the Sloanes joined forces and threw open the picture galleries of their double house on Fifth Avenue for a sit-down wedding breakfast for 600 or more guests. Among the 300 gifts on display was a complete silver dinner service for 24 from the bride's grandmother, Mrs. William H. Vanderbilt. Not displayed was the gift from the bride's mother, a completely furnished, four-story, 25-foot-wide house at 35 West 57th Street that cost $93,000.

The Schiefflins lived in the 57th Street house during the 1890s, but the hustle and bustle of the busy crosstown street wearied them. Again Mrs. Shepard intervened. This time she bought the rowhouse at 5 East 66th Street for $45,000 and the neighboring house at 7 East 66th Street for an undisclosed sum. In 1898, she ordered them demolished.

This time she did not use the services of her nephew, young August Dennis Shepard. Instead, she hired Richard Howland Hunt to design the house for the 47-by-100-foot lot. Hunt and builder D. C. Weeks estimated $150,000 for construction costs, a handsome price to pay for a five-story, 84-foot-high building with a brick and limestone facade. The French style is typical of the work of the Hunts, father and son, from the rustication on the lower floor to the mansard crown. Of course, it is all a bit overblown, as are the interiors, which include a stair balcony supported by a bracket in the form of a shell and a fireplace in the dining room with a mantel supported by colossal caryatids, which are ascribed to Karl Bitter. The house was fireproof, thanks in part to hollow clay arches. Its steel I-beams allowed the floors to sustain 70 pounds a square foot, which is today's requirement for office buildings.

The house was the scene of Mrs. Elliott F. Shepard's last public appearance. When her granddaughter, Louise Vanderbilt Schiefflin, married Abram S. Hewitt in 1924, the wedding reception was held at home. Afterwards, Mrs. Shepard retired to her apartment at 998 Fifth Avenue, where she collapsed and died. The same year, the Schief-flins joined the swelling ranks of millionaire apartment dwellers and moved to 620 Park Avenue.

---

171. The Schiefflin house continued the Vanderbilts' predilections—it was given by Mrs. Elliot F. Shepard to her daughter Maria Louisa, wife of William J. Schiefflin. The architect was the son of Richard Morris Hunt, who was a favorite architect for the older Vanderbilt and Astor generation.

172. The Schiefflin's formal staircase, with a shell motif under the overhanging balcony, leads to the second floor, where the wood-paneled library overlooks 66th Street; at the rear is the ballroom, which, when converted into a banquet hall in today's configuration for the Lotos Club, can accommodate 130 for dinner.

173. Karl Bitter is credited with sculpting the fireplace in the Schiefflin home. Bitter was Richard Morris Hunt's protégé, and after Hunt's death the work continued under the aegis of Hunt's son Richard Howland Hunt. Other Vanderbilt houses where Bitter sculpture was found include William K. Vanderbilt's Marble House at Newport, George W. Vanderbilt's Biltmore at Asheville, and the extension to the mansion of Cornelius Vanderbilt II on 57th Street.

The East 66th Street Studio Building

131–135 East 66th Street, northeast corner of Lexington Avenue
1906
BUILDER: William J. Taylor
ARCHITECT: Charles A. Platt

Artists in the Age of Elegance seldom lived in Vanderastor luxury, but some successful ones managed to live close to it. In 1905, builder William J. Taylor created the East 66th Street Studio Building Company for a group of artists who wanted a building that combined good working space with comfortable living quarters. Taylor bought the 100-by-170-foot lot on Lexington Avenue and 66th Street from the trustees of Mount Sinai Hospital for over $150,000, and for the site he planned a $700,000 building.

New York's first studio building was designed by Richard Morris Hunt in 1857. Despite its popularity, the 10th Street building was not emulated until the turn of the century, when landscape painter Henry W. Ranger began a new cooperative venture. Although the banks were not impressed, builder William J. Taylor was intrigued enough to participate, and ten artists, including Childe Hassam, gathered together to raise the capital for the studio-apartment house at 27 West 67th Street. The artists occupied half the building and rented out the other half, which produced a 23 percent return on their investment. For artists who had been renting both an apartment and a studio, the scheme was a dream, and its success made the banks think twice and encouraged Taylor to build more.

The general rule for studio-apartment houses was for modest facades belying sumptuous quarters. Taylor asked architects Pollard & Steinman, who had designed the West 67th Street building, to follow the rule for the East 66th Street house. The founding participants in the cooperative, however, wanted both grand interiors and a facade to match, and they saw to the hiring of Charles A. Platt, whose fame rested on his designs for private residences. For

174. The Studio Building was an enormously successful cooperative venture initiated by builder William J. Taylor, who had been responsible for the artists' studio-apartments on West 67th Street.

175. The only simplex apartments in the Studio Building were the corner apartments. The others wrapped around the double-height studios, all of which faced north for the light and gave credence to the building's name.

174

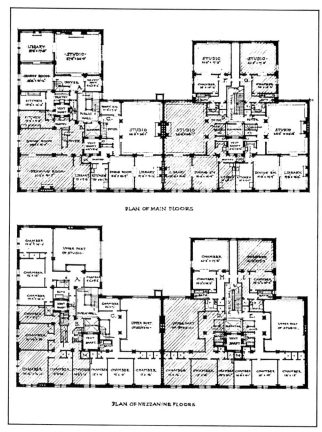

PLAN OF MAIN FLOORS

PLAN OF MEZZANINE FLOORS

the facade, Platt created an oversized neo-Italian Renaissance palazzo. Behind it he created seven duplex residences in each two-story expanse. The corner apartments were the traditional two-story configuration, but the other six apartments had double-height studios with northern exposures. Off the eighteen-foot-high studios were the living spaces. A typical apartment was spacious, with studios measuring 24 by 28 feet, dining rooms 15 feet square, libraries 15 by 16, kitchens 9 by 15, and bedrooms as large as 15 by 15.

The building was a success the day it opened. A founder's $20,000 share bought about the same space as $50,000 bought in a house, and the accommodations were considered better. All but one of the duplex rental apartments were taken within the first few months, despite the proximity of the Third Avenue elevated, a police station, a fire house, and other nonresidential institutions.

Several founders resold their apartments before the building was finished, many with profits of $2,000 or more. Taylor, too, made a quick profit. He had taken a $500,000 mortgage for one year at six percent. Since he received payments from the founders as work progressed, he could conduct the operation on a cash basis and hold finance charges to a minimum. In 1907, Taylor asked Platt to design an almost identical twin on the corner of Lexington Avenue and 67th Street. The layouts were improved and met with even greater succcess. Clearly artists and others who needed good light were attracted to the buildings. Architect Platt lived in the 66th Street building, as did Howard Russell Baker, the president of the American Fine Arts Society, and artist Kenyon Cox, who was one of the founders.

The Verona Apartments

32 East 64th Street, southeast corner of Madison Avenue
1909
BUILDER: Victor V. Kranich
ARCHITECT: William E. Mowbray

With society's epicenter on 62nd Street between Fifth and Madison avenues, the coming of an apartment house to the neighborhood might have thrown the Astors and Fabbris and Schiefflins into a panic, but the Verona Apartments hardly signified the beginning of the end. There had been a prestigious apartment house on the southeast corner of 62nd Street and Madison Avenue since 1902, and the neighborhood was suffering no ill effects. In fact, the neighborhood might have improved. In 1911, the social center was set on Madison Avenue between 62nd and 63rd streets.

176

The ten-story Verona is a great cube of a neo-Italian Renaissance palace, with massing, fenestration, and an outsized cornice that are strikingly reminiscent of Florence's Palazzo Strozzi. Unlike a true Renaissance palace, however, the Verona is built with a steel frame, with the rusticated limestone basement and the pressed brick and terra cotta acting as a curtain wall.

The fireproof building was in the vanguard of good apartment house planning. The kitchens, pantries, and service room were all grouped on the well-lit courtyard and served by their own elevator. Passenger elevators took the residents and their guests to private vestibules that connected with each apartment. One entered a 12-by-19-foot foyer, with the 18-by-25-foot salon ahead to one side, the 13-by-18-foot library directly ahead, and the 19-by-20-foot

176. The Verona Apartments, a great cube of a neo-Italian Renaissance palazzo, was built in the center of the neighborhood that was emerging as the new center of Society. The quality of the building allowed it to fit right in.

177

178

dining room next to it. Two 16-by-20-foot bedrooms over-looked 64th Street, and three more bedrooms, ranging in size from 12 by 13 feet to 19 by 20 feet, were in the rear.

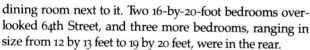

177. Tenants who leased their apartments before the Verona's interiors were finished were given their choice of interior trim. The neoclassical decoration for this salon's cornice is worked around a coved wall.

178. Needle showers, whose spray envelops the bather, were installed in the Verona. Freestanding models were installed at the Plaza Hotel, but they have all been removed.

179. True to the ideals of the revived Renaissance, neoclassical elements were used as decorative trim in the Verona Apartments, including the wavelike Vitruvian scroll in the stringcourse.

The Verona's construction costs were estimated at $800,000, or $40,000 an apartment, with annual rents ranging from $8,000 to $9,500. The tenants who leased apartments before the interiors were completed were offered their choice of decorations. Usually, the parlors were finished in white enameled woodwork with a tapestry frieze, the libraries in mahogany paneled walls and beamed ceilings, and the dining rooms in Flemish oak.

Madison Avenue was not a prime street for apartment houses, since the city had legislated against buildings that were taller than one-and-a-half times the width of the thoroughfare they faced. Madison Avenue, at only 80 feet wide north of 42nd Street, was restricted to apartment houses no taller than 120 feet, which explains why the Verona, with its ten-foot-high ceilings and thick floors, is only ten stories high.

The Colony Club II

564 Park Avenue, northwest corner of 62nd Street
1915
BUILDER: The Colony Club
ARCHITECTS: Delano & Aldrich

The women of the Colony Club announced in 1914 that they were abandoning their Madison Avenue clubhouse for a new one billed as "the finest clubhouse in the world." The warmth and charm of White and deWolfe were about to fall to the inflated grandeur of Delano & Aldrich and their brand of neocolonialism.

The building's estimated cost was $400,000, which not even this wealthy membership was willing to pay in cash, so a $500,000 loan was obtained for the building and land. The new clubhouse would have all the luxuries expected of a club that considered itself more exclusive than society itself; the stuffiness Mrs. Harriman had tried to keep out of the original clubhouse had descended.

At first glance, the red-brick and marble building appears to be a four-story residence with a mansard roof, but it is 130 feet high and it is filled with all the amenities, including a kennel where members could leave their dogs. The round entrance hall has walls of Caen stone; the one-and-a-half story high ballroom had walls with coral brocatelle hangings. The brass window fixtures were ordered from France and the chandeliers from Germany, though World War I hostilities had already begun in Europe. The delay in deliveries was so long that some members were said to be in favor of joining the peace expedition and going after their precious accessories.

The second floor holds two dining rooms, the library, a card room, and a 70-foot-long lounge paneled in American butternut, with lighting fixtures designed by the architects. In the basement is a 20-by-60-foot marble and tile swimming pool, and there are massage baths, mud baths, and sulphur baths similar to those at European spas. A special elevator links the basement with the fully equipped, oak-paneled gymnasium on the fifth floor, and the squash courts above. There are 40 bedrooms.

Clearly the club was a success. Life members included Mrs. Hugh Auchincloss, Mrs. James A. Burden, Mrs. Edward Harkness, Mrs. Moses Taylor Pyne, and Mrs. Herbert L. Satterlee. Its five honorary members were Mrs. Stanford White, Mrs. Charles T. Barney, Louise Lee Schuyler, Mrs. J. Pierpont Morgan, and Jane Addams.

Many of the houses that these women knew are gone, and *the* Mrs. Astor's was one of the earliest to fall. Fourteen years after the *Titanic* went down in 1912, with Colonel Astor aboard, the Astor mansion was slated to be torn down. The house had presumably been destined for a long life, but its usefulness had been outlived in a little over a generation. *Architectural Record* pointed out that the Astor residence "was originally designed not merely as a residence but as a building in which a leader of New York society could give balls and large dinners; but balls and large dinners [were] much less customary in [1926] than they were in 1890 and a house designed for such purposes might prove formidable and even a dreary place for comparatively quiet and more retiring people to live in. If in the course of years the land on which the house was built has increased sufficiently in value to take care of the original cost of the building, it's natural for its owner, who no longer relished such a palatial domicile, to sell it." John Jacob Astor would have understood.

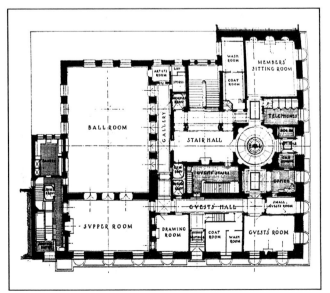

181

180. The Colony Club chose the grandeur of Delano & Aldrich when the members had grown restless with their downtown club and decided to move to the neighborhood that was emerging as New York's answer to London's Mayfair.

181. The Guests' Room (in the bottom right-hand corner of the floorplan) was the scene, no doubt, of many a frustrated hope at the Colony Club. This was where aspirant members were interviewed for membership.

182. *Richard Morris Hunt was the architect for James Lenox's library, which was built on part of the thirty-acre farm that Lenox had inherited. The library later merged with the Astor Library and the Tilden Trust to form the Main Branch of the New York Public Library; the site was sold to Henry Clay Frick for his mansion.*

10

James Lenox's Hill

I n 1839, James Lenox inherited a 30-acre farm at the five-mile stone from City Hall. The farm had cost his father more than he thought it was worth, but he was convinced that its value would increase until it would be the "site of a village at no distant day." James Lenox was no wastrel, but devoted himself "largely to pious objects," according to the *Sun*. In 1868, he gave the block bounded by Madison and Park avenues between 70th and 71st streets to the Presbyterian Hospital. Combined with a cash contribution, the gift came to about $1 million. Two years later, James Lenox announced that he was building a library and art gallery on his Fifth Avenue property between 70th and 71st streets that would be open free to the public. He would bear the costs of construction and maintenance, and he would donate the contents as well. He then hired Richard Morris Hunt, who designed a U-shaped building 101 feet high, 192 feet long, and 114 feet deep.

Visitors entered the library by way of the courtyard. The vestibule was faced in white marble, with dove-colored marble skirting the walls. The two first-floor reading rooms measured 30 by 108 feet and had ceilings 24 feet high. The reading rooms on the second floor had the same square footage, but with 40-foot-high ceilings. And the top

floor had a skylit 40-by-50-foot picture gallery. The building cost Lenox $648,000 by its completion in 1875. Nobody knows how much he paid for his collection of books and art.

The first gallery opening attracted over 15,000 visitors, "a number which indicates extraordinary public curiosity and interest," said Lenox, "especially in view of the distance of the library from the present center of population." The visitors saw paintings by Henry Inman, Frederic E. Church, Asher B. Durand, J. M. W. Turner, James and Rembrandt Peale, Gilbert Stuart, and others.

The Lenox Library was first and foremost a library, one of the three that merged to form the nucleus of the Main Branch of the New York Public Library. When the trustees of the Main Branch were looking for a site, the Lenox property was considered, but even in the 1890s it was deemed too far uptown. The site was finally bought by Henry Clay Frick, who agreed to await possession of the property until the library's contents had been transferred.

Since the Lenox Library was considered one of Hunt's best works, Frick's architects, Carrère & Hastings, convinced Frick to preserve it, and in 1912 he made the city the offer of his disassembling the building and re-erecting it at his expense on the site of the Arsenal in Central Park, providing the city tore down the Arsenal at its expense. The proposal led to a furor over encroachment on park land, not to mention the impact that the formal library would have on the romantic landscape of the park. The city spurned the gift and Frick spurned alternate suggestions, which included re-erecting the building on Lexington Avenue at 23rd Street for the College of Commerce of the City of New York or for the National Academy of Design on Amsterdam Avenue at Cathedral Parkway, where its supporters said it would become another Tate Gallery. Frick was obdurate, and either his original offer was accepted or there was no deal. Down came Hunt's masterpiece.

The Richard Morris Hunt Memorial

West Side of Fifth Avenue at 70th Street
1898
BUILDERS: A consortium of arts groups
ARCHITECT: Bruce Price
SCULPTOR: Daniel Chester French

The memorial to Richard Morris Hunt was intentionally placed on Fifth Avenue at 70th Street because of its proximity to the Lenox Library, which made the library's destruction particularly ironic. Hunt was America's most fashion-able architect in the last half of the nineteenth century, with credits that included the Tribune Building, the Metropolitan Museum of Art, the base for the Statue of Liberty, and residences galore, including "the" Mrs. Astor's double house and William K. Vanderbilt's Fifth Avenue "chateau." His practice earned him enough money to become one of Newport's earliest "cottagers" and to be accepted by the Vanderbilts, which led to his undoing—he got caught in a rainstorm at the Sloane-Burden wedding, after which he developed a cold that was complicated by severe gout. He died in 1895 at his house in Newport.

Hunt had said that he was not terribly keen on a memorial, because so far as he was concerned his life works were monument enough. The Architectural League, however, took the suggestion of architectural historian Montgomery Schuyler to create a Hunt memorial, and fellow architectural historian Russel Sturgis chaired the committee. Sturgis maintained that the most appropriate memorial to an architect was a design by him that had never been executed, so he recommended the memorial gates that Hunt had designed for the entrance to Central Park at Fifth Avenue and 59th Street. Hunt's original design could be pared down by eliminating the Columbus and Hudson fountains, but the cost was still estimated at $190,000, which was too high, and there was no reason to suppose that the suggestion would not be voted down again by the city. The league realized that the gateway was an elusive goal, so a consortium of arts groups was formed under the aegis of the Municipal Art Society with the goal of creating a memorial that was generous but not profligate.

The new proposal was for a semicircular granite and marble bench adorned with a bust of Hunt, to which sculptor Daniel Chester French added a pair of statues. One statue bears a palette and a sculptor's mallet to represent the allied arts; to represent architecture, the second statue holds a model of the Administration Building that Hunt designed for Chicago's Columbian Exposition. Bruce Price, who had been one of Hunt's students, designed the excedra. On the walls between the columns, Price artfully incorporated the names of the participating organizations: the Architectural League (Hunt had helped to found it); the Municipal Art Society (Hunt was its first president); the Metropolitan Museum of Art (Hunt was a trustee and architect of its grand plan); the American Institute of Architects (Hunt was a president); the Society of Beaux-Arts Architects (Hunt was the first American-born Beaux-Arts graduate and introduced its atelier method of training to the United States); the Century Association (Hunt was a member); The New York Chapter, American Institute of Architects (AIA); the National Academy of Design; the Society of American Artists; the National Sculpture Society; and the New York Watercolor Society.

Hunt died in possession of what was considered the finest architectural library in the country, but he made no public benefactions and left everything to his wife. The odds were that one member of the consortium would be the recipient of Hunt's books at some future time. Ironically, the library did not go to the Architectural League, which had started the movement for the Hunt Memorial. It went to the AIA.

The Gertrude Rhinelander Waldo House

867 Madison Avenue, southeast corner of 72nd Street
1899
BUILDER: Gertrude Rhinelander Waldo
ARCHITECTS: Kimball & Thompson

Gertrude Rhinelander Waldo was a direct descendant of Philip Jacob Rhinelander, who settled in New Rochelle in 1696 and was the progenitor of one of the land-owningest families in Manhattan (an Upper East Side telephone exchange was RHinelander). Gertrude Rhinelander became a leader of society through breeding and inclination, and when she married Francis Waldo, she did the socially acceptable thing and took grand Continental tours. A chateau in the French countryside struck her fancy—Blois, Chambord, Chenonceaux, nobody reported which—and back in New York she hired architects Francis H. Kimball and George Kramer Thompson in 1894 to design one for her.

The plans called for a building that cost $65,000, a surprisingly low figure considering the five-story house almost completely fills the 40-by-102-foot plot, has a limestone facade with statuary, and was constructed with steel I-beams and cast-iron columns and spruce floor beams. *The Real Estate Record* described the mansion as "costly," Montgomery Schuyler called it "extensive," and the *Times* said that it was "erected . . . at great expense and decorated elaborately."

183. Daniel Chester French and Bruce Price teamed up to create the statuary and exedra for the Richard Morris Hunt Memorial, which was placed across the street from Hunt's Lenox Library. Observers pointed out that it was just like New York, with its adoration of grand architecture, to honor an architect as the subject of public sculpture before honoring any other artist (Samuel F. B. Morse had been so honored, but more for his talents as a scientist than as a painter).

184. Gertrude Rhinelander Waldo never moved into her home at 867 Madison Avenue, a neo-French Renaissance chateau designed by Francis Kimball. Mr. Waldo did not live to see it finished, and after his death Mrs. Waldo chose to live out her days with her sister across the street, from where she watched her sweet confection turn sour.

The entrance through the central bay led to a large, mahogany-lined hall. To the left was the billiard room, to the right, the library. The grand staircase had walls lined in mosaic. It led up to the second floor, where there were two salons, the main dining room, the breakfast room, two kitchens, and a pantry. The third floor contained bedrooms and boudoirs and dressing rooms. The greater part of the fourth floor was occupied by a ballroom where it was said that half of the house's 2,200 lights were installed. To run a house the magnitude of this one, according to the standards of the day, would have required as many as a dozen servants, but only two servants' bedrooms were provided, with no room for a manservant.

During its construction, the Waldos toured Europe again, where Mrs. Waldo purchased accessories for the house, but Mrs. Waldo never moved into her house, and most of the treasures she had collected in Europe remained in their cartons. By the time the house was finished, Francis Waldo was dead, and Mrs. Waldo chose to live with her sister, Miss Laura L. Rhinelander, whose house at 31 East 72nd Street overlooked Mrs. Waldo's dream turned sour. In 1908, a "For Sale" sign hung in front of the building, but there was no sale, as much because of Mrs. Waldo's price tag as her impetuosity. One broker had practically consummated a sale, but while the papers were being drawn up Mrs. Waldo calmly said, "I don't think I'll sell," and walked out.

By 1909, the Waldo mansion was dilapidated, its stonework discolored, its interior fittings damaged by the rain that leaked through the roof. Despite the ostensible protection of a high iron fence around the house, the $200,000 worth of bronzes, paintings, and tapestries that were stored in it became an easy mark, and four times within as many months the house was burglarized. Two years later, Mrs. Waldo died, with $9,221 owed in unpaid taxes and a $150,000 mortgage on the house. The Dime Savings Bank came into ownership by default and tried to sell the plot with the assurance that an apartment house could be erected on the site. A restrictive clause covered the block, but the bank claimed that an apartment house was tantamount to a series of private houses within a multifamily dwelling and was well within the definition of a private house. The restrictive clause held, and the house stood vacant until 1921, when the first floor was converted for stores and two apartments were created in the still luxurious quarters above. It was the first time that anyone had ever lived in the place.

185. Many of the sculpture niches in the Waldo house stand empty, but where the niches are filled the impression of a proud seat of French Renaissance kings is complete. Kimball had studied with England's great French Gothicist, William Burges, who always managed to work a figure in medieval costume into his designs.

The Isaac D. Fletcher House

2 East 79th Street, southeast corner of Fifth Avenue
1899
BUILDER: Isaac D. Fletcher
ARCHITECT: C. P. H. Gilbert

Blocks that were restricted might prove to be headaches to later generations, but they were reassuring to the original developers. The block bounded by Fifth and Madison avenues between 78th and 79th streets was part of the original Lenox farm. Robert Lenox had urged his descendants to keep the farm intact, but as prices advanced parcels were sold off. Marcellus Hartley bought the block in 1877 for $420,000 and sold it three years later to banker and railroad investor Henry H. Cook for $500,000. Cook built a mansion for himself on the northeast corner of 78th Street and Fifth Avenue and planned to build houses on each of the other three corners as a speculative venture. Instead, he sold the plots, with restrictions. The houses had to be built to a quality that he specified and they had to be occupied by the owners. It was as much to protect his investment as to ensure a residential block of high quality for others.

In 1897, Isaac D. Fletcher bought the 32-by-100-foot corner plot on 79th Street and Fifth Avenue for about $200,000, which Fletcher could easily afford. As a twenty-one-year-old, he left Bangor, Maine, for New York City, where he rose to become the president of the Barrett Manufacturing Company and the New York Coal Tar Company. Fletcher was living at the Astoria Hotel when he commissioned Gilbert to design a $200,000 house like William K. Vanderbilt's neo-Loire Valley chateau. Fletcher's house is ringed by a moat, and after the bridge has been crossed, the great Renaissance-style doors swing wide to reveal the foyer, with the requisite grand staircase in the tradition of Francis I and an elevator in the tradition of Gilbert, who maintained that any house that cost more than $25,000 deserved one. Overlooking Fifth Avenue and filling the entire west end of the 32-foot-wide house was the drawing room. In the east end was the dining room, with the butler's pantry conveniently off it (a dumbwaiter linked it with the kitchen in the basement). The conservatory overlooked 79th Street from its bowed window. There were three service sinks on the first floor, but, curiously, there was neither a water closet nor a washbasin for the use of guests. On the second floor, the library repeated the scale of the drawing room. The oval music room was in the center of the house, with Mrs. Fletcher's bedroom in the east end. Mr. Fletcher's was directly above hers on the third floor, where there were also a sewing room, a guest room, and, overlooking the park, the den.

187

The Fletchers were assembling a formidable collection of art that included paintings by Rembrandt, Rubens, Gainsborough, Reynolds, and David. Since they were particularly proud of their mansion, they commissioned Jean François Raffaelli to paint a portrait of it for them. The French Impressionist, whose forte was urban scenes, visited New York several times at the turn of the century and was as well known in America in his time as any of his contemporaries. If the Fletchers had been more vainglorious, they would have put some of their millions to work as an endowment and used the house as a splendid setting for the Fletcher Collection, but they believed that the public would benefit more with their collection in a museum. In 1917, after their deaths, the notable bequest of $3 million and 251 works of art, including the Raffaelli, moved up the block to the Metropolitan Museum of Art.

186. C. P. H. Gilbert's neo-Loire Valley chateau pleased Mr. and Mrs. Isaac Fletcher so much that they commissioned the French Impressionist Jean François Raffaelli to paint a portrait of the mansion. The painting is now in the collection of the Metropolitan Museum of Art.

187. Some of the spandrels in the Fletcher mansion are filled with grotesques, arabesques, and all the discreet charms of the transitional architecture of Francis I, when the French Gothic began to give way to the French Renaissance.

The Pulitzer Mansion

11 East 73rd Street, between Fifth and Madison Avenues
1903
BUILDER: Joseph Pulitzer
ARCHITECTS: McKim, Mead & White

A fireproof home was rare indeed at the turn of the century, but after Joseph Pulitzer's $200,000 house at 10 East 55th Street was partially destroyed by fire, the newspaper publisher decided that his family would never again occupy a house that was not fireproof. Only three months after the fire, Pulitzer paid $240,000 for a 76-by-100-foot plot on East 73rd Street, hired McKim, Mead & White to design a limestone and granite house, and specified that it had to be fireproof. He then went off to Aix and Wiesbaden to buy paintings and tapestries with which to stock it (the fire had consumed a Franz Hals and a Bouguereau as well as four Gobelin tapestries).

Pulitzer wanted "no ballroom, no music room or picture gallery under any disguise, [but] an American home for comfort and use, not for show or entertainment." Stanford White told Pulitzer that his house would be as fine a house

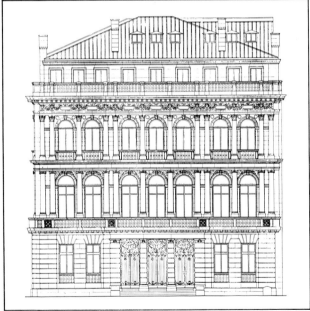

188

188. Joseph Pulitzer's eyesight was failing, but he so dreamed of his house during the planning stages that he had the architects build a plaster model of a detail so that he could study it by touch. He was told by Stanford White that the house would be as fine as any that the firm had designed.

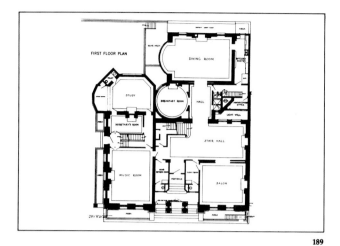

FIRST FLOOR PLAN

189

190

189. Pulitzer specified that he wanted a house for comfort, with "no ballroom, music room, or picture gallery under any disguise." He got a music room anyway.

190. The New York home of Joseph Pulitzer was hardly lived in by the publisher, who was suffering from an assortment of maladies—psychosomatic and otherwise. McKim, Mead & White's design is as Venetian as anything in New York, from the easily defensible canalside entrance to the open upper stories designed to catch the breezes off the Adriatic.

as any the firm had ever built, its design based on two seventeenth-century Venetian houses by Baldassare Longhena—the Palazzo Pesero and the Palazzo Tezzonico. The interiors, as the facade suggests, were hardly designed for anything but show and entertainment, and Pulitzer got a music room anyway. The intricate interiors included a round, glass-domed breakfast room, a hectagonal study with a glass-roofed conservatory at one end, a concave-walled dining room, and two salons, one on the first floor opposite the music room, the other on the second floor. In the basement was a swimming pool that apparently was never filled and remained dry. The bill for all this unused and presumably unwanted grandeur came to $369,310.

While Pulitzer continued his daily management of the *New York World* and the *St. Louis Post-Dispatch*, his eyesight was failing. But Pulitzer so loved the idea of the house during its planning stages that he asked the architects to provide a plaster model of a facade detail so that he could study it by touch. He wanted nothing to go awry, and when his Washington bureau chief began to poke fun at the idiosyncracies of McKim, Mead & White, who were re-modeling the White House, Pulitzer wired that "if you have no compassion for the architects, please have some for me. I am an old man and hope to pass my few remaining years in a house I am building. These architects are my architects and unless you allow me to show them more respect in my own paper they never will finish the house for me."

When the house finally was finished, Pulitzer hardly lived in it, even when he was officially in residence. His desire for silence bordered on mania, and so far as he was concerned his private quarters were not soundproofed, de-spite double-wall construction. Pulitzer felt, as much as heard, the vibrations of an electric pump that was under the house. "The pump was shifted under the sidewalk," related Pulitzer employee Donald C. Seitz, "but he aban-doned the room and built a single-story annex in the yard, with double walls packed with mineral wool. The win-dows were guarded by triple glass; ventilation was by the fireplace chimney. He was sure that the jar of early morning whistles found its ways to his ears by this opening. Silk threads were stretched across it to break the sound."

Like most millionaires, Pulitzer only resided in town a few months every year, so the whole exercise was almost academic. He spent summers at Chatwold, his country estate at Bar Harbor, Maine; winters at a "cottage" on Jekyl Island, Georgia, or at the Villa Arethusa on the Riviera; and whenever he became bored with any of them he could be found aboard *Liberty*, the 269-foot, $1.5-million yacht he built in 1907 that required a crew of 60. Despite his big spending, when Pulitzer is compared with other million-aires of the Gilded Age, he was not terribly profligate, and his philanthropies included the establishment of Columbia University's School of Journalism and the statue of *Abun-dance* at the Plaza.

191. The Pulitzer mansion has been turned into an apartment house, and many of the original features are gone. The organ pipes in the stairwell, however, have survived.

The Harkness Mansion

1 East 75th Street, northeast corner of Fifth Avenue
1908
BUILDER: Edward S. Harkness
ARCHITECT: James Gamble Rogers

Edward S. Harkness was almost in a league of philanthropy by himself. Harkness's father was Stephen V. Harkness, one of John D. Rockefeller's early partners in Standard Oil. Young Harkness inherited the bulk of his father's estate and proceeded to give it away almost as assiduously as his father had accumulated it. Harkness was educated at St. Paul's and Yale and became a young man of cultivated taste. In 1912, wealth and inclination earned him a place on the board of the Metropolitan Museum of Art—one of New York's most exclusive clubs. His interest in Egyptology became so great that he was present at the opening of the third tomb of King Tutankhamen in 1924, whereupon he bought the Earl of Carnarvon's collection of Egyptian antiquities, which he presented to the Metropolitan. He gave the land plus $4 million for the new Columbia-Presbyterian Hospital, and he gave $4 million to Columbia, $6 million to Yale, $11 million to Harvard, $7 million to Philips Exeter, $1 million to the New York Public Library, and $8 million to the Commonwealth Fund, which his mother had started in 1918 with a $30 million grant "to do something for the welfare of mankind."

Harkness was living in a rowhouse on the Cook block at 16 East 79th Street in 1907, but he wanted something more. He hired James Gamble Rogers, of the newly created firm of Hale & Rogers, to design a home for himself and his wife, the former Mary E. Stillman. Rogers, like Harkness, was a Yale graduate. He had come to New York only a year before by way of Paris, where he had studied at the Ecole des Beaux-Arts, and Chicago, where he had worked for three years. The commission for the Harkness house represented the first of several Harkness-related plums, including Columbia's Butler Library, the Columbia-Presbyterian Hospital, and the Yale Quadrangle.

Compared with Pulitzer's house, the Harkness house appears diminutive, almost dainty, reflecting the wish of the client and the aim of the architect, according to Donn Barber, to design a dignified house that would not in an ostentatious way indicate its costliness, originally estimated at $250,000. The exterior of the restrained, neo-Renaissance house is of Tennessee marble, with granite and terra-cotta trim. The facade is only a facade, a curtain wall covering a steel post-and-lintel system.

Rogers solved some problems in interesting ways. He secured privacy for the first floor by raising the window sills above eye level as seen from the street. He installed leaded windows to bring light into the east end and into the

192

193

192. Inherited Standard Oil money and an education at St. Paul's and Yale made Edward S. Harkness a gentleman. He commissioned a fellow Yale graduate, James Gamble Rogers, to design this dignified neo-Italian Renaissance house.

193. The building contractor for the Harkness house was Charles T. Wills, who was also responsible for constructing the University Club, the De Lamar mansion, and the Morgan Library. Nothing but the highest quality materials were used in all of them.

194. Through one arch and up the stairs from the Harkness mansion's first-floor hall are the dining room, the butler's pantry, and the gentlemen's dressing room, which is tucked under the grand staircase. Through the other arch is the elevator.

194

core of the building while blocking unsightly views. For more light, he put a leaded dome atop the stair balcony and one over the vestibule, installing electric lights in the plenums. And to help the Harkness family save on electric bills, he designed a refrigerator room in the basement that opened onto the moat. When the temperature dipped low enough, the door was opened and the power could be turned off.

Not all was economical. The walls of the entrance vestibule are wainscoted with Botticino marble, and underfoot is an intricate pattern of different marbles with a brass wreath set into the floor. The reception room fills the west

195. The steel-framed Harkness mansion has a facade of Tennessee marble with granite and terra-cotta trim. This restrained Tuscan portico belies the sumptuous interiors.

196. Architect Rogers artfully masked a blank wall yet allowed light to enter the Harkness dining room by incorporating leaded windows by Kenyon Cox. The portrait is of Mrs. Stephen V. Harkness, the builder's mother and the woman who started the Commonwealth Fund "to do something for the welfare of mankind."

197. In this small jewelbox of a ladies' dressing room in the Harkness mansion, arriving female guests could freshen up before making their grand entrance. The clothes' rack could be wheeled out for convenience; the WC is off to the right.

end of the house and overlooks the park; ladies' and gentle-men's dressing rooms are off the reception hall in the center; and the dining room fills the east end, with a butler's pantry next door that was outfitted with a warmer oven and a refrigerator. This was the dark end of the house, so Rogers had Kenyon Cox design leaded windows to rep-resent the *Abundance of the Sea* and the *Abundance of the Land*. The second floor had only three rooms. The music

room was above the dining room, and, like it, had leaded windows to light the east end. Overlooking the side street was the salon, with a recirculating fountain installed in a corner. And overlooking the park was the library, with a coffered wood ceiling painted in Italian arabesques in gold leaf. The third floor housed Edward Harkness's chamber, Mrs. Harkness's boudoir, his and her Mosler safes, a dres-sing room, a few bathrooms, and rooms for a maid and valet. The fourth floor was occupied by five chambers, a sewing room, and more servants' rooms.

Edward Harkness died in 1940, and his widow died ten years later. To Yale she had given a Gutenberg Bible. To the Commonwealth Fund she gave her home, whose scale was human, grand but not grandiose.

---

198. One of the richest ceilings in the city, a honeycomb of neoclassical arabesques and Italian motifs in gold leaf, is found in the Harkness library, which overlooks Fifth Avenue.

199

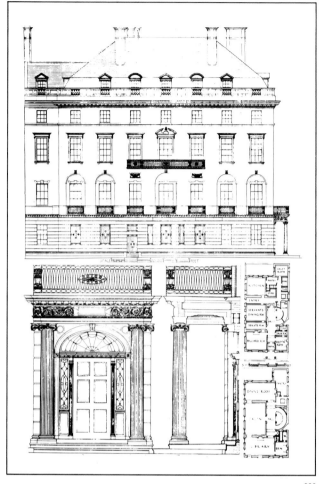

200

The Percy Pyne House

680 Park Avenue, northwest corner of 68th Street
1911
BUILDER: Percy Pyne
ARCHITECTS: McKim, Mead & White

By 1910, the New York Central tracks on Park Avenue were covered and the avenue was taking on the trappings of luxury between Grand Central Terminal and 96th Street. Between 68th and 72nd streets was quickly becoming the "Mayfair of New York," and development was spurred by the removal of both the Lenox Library and the Union Theological Seminary, which moved from the west side of Park Avenue between 69th and 70th streets in 1909. Good corners were becoming unobtainable, and prices were rising to $3,500 a foot for even run-of-the-mill property. One owner refused $125,000 for his twenty-foot-wide house on Park Avenue between 71st and 72nd streets in 1910, and prices were expected to go higher.

The house that anchored this newest development was built by Percy Pyne, a third generation banker. After Princeton, Pyne joined his father and maternal grandfather, Moses Taylor, at First National. Under their tutelage, he earned enough to fancy himself a country squire at his New Jersey estate, Upton Pyne, where he bred dogs, rode to hounds, and raised sheep and Guernsey cows. In town, Pyne lived at 36 East 36th Street, but in 1906 he purchased the 51-by-100-foot lot in what was emerging as the *new*

---

199. Percy Pyne was well acquainted with McKim, Mead & White's work, since the firm was remodeling his bank on Wall Street. He could afford to be profligate, so he used the lot next door as a garden, which also provided double exposures for some of the rear rooms.

200. When the plans for the Pyne house were being completed, Stanford White was already dead and Charles Follen McKim's health was failing. The primary design work fell to William M. Kendall, who was McKim's protégé and the firm's senior partner.

201

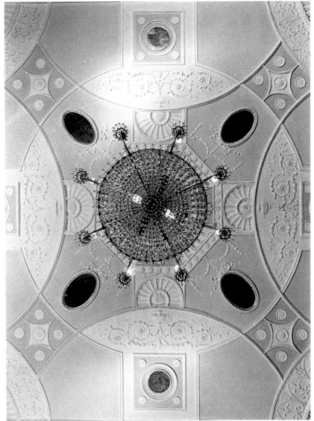

202

Murray Hill for about $150,000. Pyne knew McKim, Mead & White, who were remodeling First National's Wall Street headquarters, and he hired them to design the house. McKim and William M. Kendall chose a durable design from the Federal tradition, with a proper fanlight over the main entrance, proper Adams-like trim, and the proper classical portico, which was placed off center both to anchor the row and to allow space for a billiard room in the corner room of the main floor. The only other first-floor rooms that were not part of the servants' quarters were the reception room, a dressing room, a WC, and the hall leading to the stairs or the elevator. The second floor provided the salon overlooking the sidestreet, the dining room and pantry to the west, and the library and den overlooking Park Avenue in the east.

Instead of designing the house to fill the building line, the architects cut a notch into the sidestreet facade to provide light for the rooms in the west end, abrogating the need for an interior court for light. The light was superior from the street, and the square footage sacrificed was roughly the same. It was a simple idea, the kind that money can buy, and Pyne spent a lot of it—about three-and-a-half times the original estimate of $100,000.

201. The door between the salon and the dining room of the Pyne house was enlarged by the present tenant, the Center for Inter-American Relations, to improve the flow for receptions. Otherwise, these rooms are much as they were when Percy Pyne made his home here.

202. The ceiling in the salon of the Pyne house could have been designed by Robert Adam or John Soane. The panels were painted by the eighteenth-century British painter Angelica Kauffmann, who decorated London's Adelphi, Somerset House, and some of St. Paul's Cathedral.

203. The leaded-glass skylight atop the stairwell in the Pyne house echoes the fanlight above the front door. The interior stairs led to the servants' quarters.

203

The James B. Duke Mansion

1 East 78th Street, northeast corner of Fifth Avenue
1912
BUILDER: James B. Duke
ARCHITECT: Horace Trumbauer

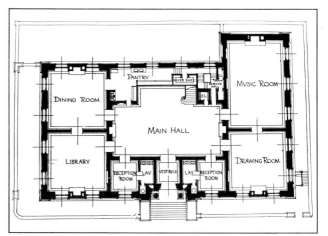

Percy Pyne graduated from Princeton, but James Buchanan
Duke probably would have proudly said that he graduated
from the school of hard knocks. He was born on a tobacco
farm near Durham, North Carolina, in 1857, the year that
his namesake (James Buchanan) assumed the presidency,

206

and he was described as one of America's last log-cabin success stories. In New York, where he represented his family tobacco farm, the young Duke lived in rented rooms and ate in Bowery restaurants. He saved every penny he could and reinvested his savings until he was able to create the American Tobacco Company. He was worth about

204. James B. Duke had Horace Trumbauer design a neoclassical *palais* for the site of the former Cook mansion, which Duke had bought for $1.25 million. Duke's freestanding limestone house, originally estimated at a cost of $365,000, has rear walls that are as finely detailed as the front facade.

205. Though the first floor of the Duke house appears to be profligate in its use of space, it does have some utilitarian features. The silver safe, for instance, is neatly tucked under the grand staircase.

206. The Duke mansion's library is wood-paneled in the grand manner of the French Renaissance as practiced by Trumbauer. Duke's only child, Doris, who was one of the "poor little rich girls" of the 1930s, took her first marriage vows in this room in 1935.

$50 million by the time he was forty-eight in 1905, at which time he confounded his friends. This ostensibly confirmed bachelor married, to be divorced less than a year later and remarried in 1907. His second bride was Nannie Lee Holt Inman of Atlanta, who bore him a daughter, Doris.

In the 1900s, Duke owned a 2,500-acre farm in Somerville, New Jersey, a former Vanderbilt "cottage" in Newport called Rough Point, and a winter retreat in Durham. He owned a five-story stone stable at 30 West 66th Street and he was living at 1009 Fifth Avenue. When Henry H. Cook died in 1905, Duke became interested in buying the house that had been in the vanguard of Upper Fifth Avenue's development and a conspicuous landmark since it was built in 1883. The construction of Cook's white marble and sandstone mansion had been done by "day's work," which meant that the work did not have to be finished either within a certain time or within a certain cost. If a feature did not please Cook, he ordered it ripped out or altered until it did.

Cook's executors put the house on the market at $1.5 million, and Elihu Root, acting for the heirs, accepted Duke's offer of $1.25 million in 1909. Duke took a $700,000 loan and commissioned C. P. H. Gilbert to prepare plans for remodeling the house, but then he changed his mind. Duke abandoned the expensive remodeling job and decided to tear down the Cook residence and build a new house. The fireplace and mantel that had been imported from Italy at $15,000 fetched $300; the oak panels that had cost $55 apiece were sold for three dollars each. The demolition company said that the Cook residence was the best-built house ever torn down in New York City, and the watchman on the job echoed the sentiment.

To design the new house, Duke commissioned Horace Trumbauer of Philadelphia, who had been doing very regal things, especially for the Wideners. For Duke, Trumbauer designed a 72-by-140-foot freestanding house with all four sides faced in limestone. The inspiration was a Bourdeaux mansion, and the plans for the 30-room house called for an estimated bill of $365,000. Flanking the entrance were reception rooms, each with a lavatory. Ahead was the grand staircase, with the silver safe sequestered within and accessible from the pantry. The library filled the southwest corner, the dining room filled the northwest corner (the butler's pantry off it was linked to the basement by two dumbwaiters), and off the east end of the main hall were the drawing room and the music room. There were eight chambers and as many full bathrooms on the second floor, with entire rooms dedicated to linens and clothes. The third floor contained twelve servants' rooms, a sewing room, and another linen room. The basement had still another linen room, a servants' dining room the size of the

208

library, a laundry the size of the music room, and rooms for the footman, the butler, the valet, the housekeeper, and the cellarman, plus amenities that no mansion could be without, including the wine storage room. Of course, there was an elevator.

When Duke died in 1925, his estate was estimated at $100 to $150 million. His daughter Doris inherited $50 million at age thirteen and became one of the poor little rich girls. She was married in a civil ceremony in the library in 1935, and her mother lived in the mansion until 1957, when she donated it to NYU's Institute of Fine Arts. The mansion was assessed at $1.6 million at the time of Duke's death, with furnishings valued at $600,000. Mrs. Duke gave it all up for the simpler life at the Stanhope Hotel.

207

207. Over five feet high, the music stand hints at the height of the ceiling in the Duke mansion's music room. The fireplace's marble is scarred by cigarette burns, no doubt made by such American Tobacco Company products as Pall Mall or Lucky Strike or Sweet Caporal—a fitting touch.

208. The Duke mansion appears to be only two stories high, but tucked behind the balustrade and out of sight from the street is a third floor, whose dormer windows peek out from a pitched roof.

209. Duke skimped as a young man and saved enough to launch the American Tobacco Company. Two years after his mansion was finished, he had made enough to retire in elegance.

The Frick Mansion

1 East 70th Street, northeast corner of Fifth Avenue
1914
BUILDER: Henry Clay Frick
ARCHITECTS: Carrère & Hastings

Henry Clay Frick was a self-made millionaire by his early thirties, when he began to buy an interest in the Carnegie, Phipps & Company steel works. He became its chairman, and by 1892 held absolute control over all of Carnegie's steel interests. "He is courteous," said the *Times*, "but he does not believe in wasting time."

By 1905, Frick believed that Pittsburgh was no place to show off the beginnings of his great art collection, and

there was a rumor that Frick, the man who had held firm against the Homestead strikers, wanted to enter politics on a national level. He decided that New York was the only place to launch himself properly into an art-loving society and, if he chose, into politics. And what better place to live than the William H. Vanderbilt brownstone mansion on the northwest corner of Fifth Avenue and 51st Street. The house had passed to George Vanderbilt, and by the terms of

---

210. Art dealer Joseph Duveen steered steelman Henry Clay Frick toward Carrère & Hastings, who designed a limestone palace in the style of Louis XVIII for Frick's $2.5-million property, former site of the Lenox Library. Frick had the property landscaped by Wadley & Smythe, but the thirteen chestnut trees that they planted on the curb were killed by a leaking gas main in 1915.

210

only one buyer with whom the trustees had to deal, there was only one transaction. Frick knew that the Lenox site was the last Fifth Avenue block-front that could be acquired in a single transaction, and the rest of the block was vacant. It would be divided into 25-by-100-foot building lots, with restrictions reserving the use of the land to first-class residential purposes until 1929. This development pleased Frick, who, like others of his ilk, liked to control his environment.

The $2.47 million that Frick paid for the 200-by-125-foot plot aroused the *Times* to editorialize that if Frick used every inch of the land for a residence, he would be paying "rent" on a sum that was not to be lightly contemplated. His $2.47 million would earn over $8,000 a month if invested at four percent, and he could doubtless get more for it. It was "more than one man and his family could really get the good of," concluded the *Times*.

Frick, however, was considering more than one man's family. His ultimate goal was to have his home metamorphosed into a museum upon the death of himself and his wife. Frick was one of the great collectors of his time, and his art dealer was Joseph Duveen, one of the great art dealers. Their respect for each other was enormous, Duveen for Frick because Frick was satisfied with only the very best, and Frick for Duveen because his taste was exemplary. Duveen did not want his client to squander $3 million on just any old mansion. It had to be a jewelbox, the proper foil for the objets d'art he sold to Frick. Duveen knew art and architecture, and it was Duveen who selected Carrère & Hastings to design the Frick mansion. To design its interiors, Duveen chose Sir Charles Allom, who went to the extent of creating full-scale mock-ups to ascertain whether all the components jelled. Frick gave Duveen and Elsie deWolfe a free hand to buy the furnishings and accoutrements that accompany art of the highest order—from mantelpieces to andirons, price was of no importance, only the best mattered. To complement Frick's already substantial art collection, which included Velázquez's portrait of Philip II of Spain and Rembrandt's *The Merchant*, Duveen provided eleven Fragonard panels he had bought from the J. Pierpont Morgan estate, some Boucher panels that had been commissioned by Mme. de Pompadour, and Gainsboroughs, Van Dycks, Vermeers, and Houdons.

To accommodate the irregularly shaped building, which measures 110 feet on 70th Street and 135 feet on 71st Street, Frick bought an additional 50-foot-wide parcel running the 200 feet from street to street. A driveway entered the property and served the east end of the house, where there is now a courtyard. The house has only three stories, yet it is 51 feet high. Its steel frame is masked by a limestone facade, whose neoclassicism is reinforced by pedimental sculpture within the pavilion by Attilio Piccirilli, the sculptor of the *Maine Memorial*, and pedimental sculpture over the 70th Street entrance by Sherry E. Fry, who had studied at the American Academy in Rome, one of Frick's philanthropies.

his father's will, although not allowed to sell it, he could rent it. Frick, whose income was said to be $2 million a year, could well afford the terms—$100,000 a year on a ten-year lease. Vanderbilt agreed to some basic alterations, after which the vintage Vanderbilt mansion was as up-to-date as the palace that Frick's former partner, Charles M. Schwab, was building on Riverside Drive. The difference was that Frick was only renting.

In December 1906, Frick bought the site of the Lenox Library for $2.47 million. The deal was right for both sides. The trustees of the New York Public Library had set a goal of purchasing any requested book that was not in the collection, no matter the cost or difficulty in acquiring it, and the proceeds of the Lenox sale would go to acquisitions. Also, Frick agreed not to take possession of the land until the Main Building was completed and the contents of the Lenox Library were transferred. And since there was

211. Behind this arcade, which forms the ell in the floor plan for the Frick mansion, was the largest private art gallery in the city. Frick planned for his house to become the home for the Frick Collection.

212

213

The style of the mansion is Louis XV and it was a palace in the true sense of the word. There were private apartments for the Fricks, and reception rooms in the ell of the north wing where art was displayed for the delectation of their friends. The one-and-a-half story high picture gallery was the main feature of the house, and at 35 by 100 feet, nobody could remember a larger private art gallery in the history of the city. But everything was impressive. There was a drawing room that was 26 by 32 feet, and a library that was 26 by 43. In the center of the house, a 41-by-50-foot living hall opened onto the inner garden. The landscape gardening was by Wadley & Smythe, who dumped tons of soil into the front and back gardens and planted thirteen mature chestnut trees along Fifth Avenue's curb line. And Frick was not to be outdone in the organ department. He bought a carved organ (vintage 1625), which was pulled from "The Rows," a house in Chester, England, and was designed by Christopher Wren. The cost: $100,000.

Mrs. Frick outlived her husband and died in 1931. According to plan, Duveen stepped in to oversee the renovation. He hired John Russell Pope, who would go on to design Washington's National Gallery, to remodel the interiors of Manhattan's last block-long mansion. Four years later, the Frick Collection opened its doors to the glories that were Henry Clay Frick's, and visitors can understand that this was indeed someone's home—the buttons that used to summon the pantry maid or the butler are still in the wood paneling in the main gallery.

Soon after the removal of the Lenox Library and before the completion of the Frick mansion, a prestigious group that included Otto Kahn and C. C. Auchincloss had already built houses on the block that only a few years before had been undeveloped. The Lenox block was restricted, but the neighboring block to the north was not, and a battle was raging over the future of the southeast corner of 72nd and Fifth Avenue. The James A. Burden house was coming down and a twelve-story, $1 million apartment house was planned for the site, to the dismay of neighbors. A lawyer for the real-estate speculators said that "if the Strozzi Palace, or any of the other seignorial houses of Florence or Rome that have never been equaled in architectural beauty were to be exactly repeated with the most beautiful part of Central Park as a background, the only possible modern adaptation for them would be to divide them—as they are today divided—into splendid apartments. Their civic value as monuments of beauty is no less or no more inharmonious." Despite their lawyer's dramatic sense, Burden and his associates gave up the project because of continued objections. But the neighbors' victory was short lived. By 1916, a twelve-story, neo-Italian Renaissance apartment house that was not quite the Strozzi was on the site.

212, 213. Sherry Fry, who sculpted the voluptuous reclining nude in the pediment above the entrance to the Frick Collection, obviously rejected his predilection for archaic Greek sculpture in this case. The building originally had a second entrance that was reached by a driveway to the right of the richly carved pillar.

New York. Metropolitan Museum of Art.

Copyright by Brown Bros. N.Y.

214. As more and more bequests came the way of the Metropolitan Museum of Art, conditions became so crowded that the museum was forced to store many of its benefactions in the basement. The wings by Theodore Weston hardly made a dent in the museum's need for more space in the 1890s.

11

Carnegie's Hill

The Metropolitan Museum of Art, which has become one of the great repositories of art in the twentieth century, opened its doors in 1872 to a modest collection that was housed in a Lower Fifth Avenue brownstone. Within a year the museum moved to larger quarters where it stayed for the rest of the decade, during which time Joseph H. Choate forged the relationship between the city and the museum that has remained virtually unchanged to this day. The city agreed to build and maintain a main building and additional wings as they were needed on eighteen-and-a-half acres of land in Central Park between 80th and 85th streets, which put the museum, with the Lenox Library, in the vanguard of the movement to Upper Fifth Avenue. The arrangement reflected an early use of park land for less than the pure purposes that its designers had intended. (Although both Frederick Law Olmsted and Calvert Vaux were founders of the museum, they found themselves in the awkward position of advocating the creation of the museum on the one hand while fending off its incursion, and others like it, in their park.) The city's argument, however, was irrefutable—

since the city already owned the land, no purchase was necessary and funds could be applied to labor-intensive undertakings.

The first offspring of the city-museum union was the Ruskinian-Gothic building designed by Calvert Vaux and Jacob Wrey Mould that opened in 1880. Despite the newly found capaciousness, a common plaint was soon heard—articles that should have been on display were stuck in storerooms and cellars for lack of display space. With a major bequest of sculpture casts and architectural models, the need for more space became acute. This time, $340,000 was appropriated, and Theodore Weston prepared the designs for a new wing with large, light-filled halls. The completion of the wing in 1888 heralded the first time that the museum could hold its annual reception and comfortably receive its guests under its own roof, but a few presents more and the trustees would hardly know where to turn for space. If the museum's display space was to keep pace with its growing collection, a new wing had to be built. By 1894, another version of Weston's design appeared as the north wing, and still the museum was cramped.

The East Wing of the Metropolitan Museum of Art

Fifth Avenue at 82nd Street
1902
BUILDER: The City of New York for the Trustees
ARCHITECT: Richard Morris Hunt
SUPERVISING ARCHITECT: Richard Howland Hunt

The trustees of the Metropolitan Museum of Art came to realize the folly of building higgledy-piggledy, with a new wing here and another there. They needed a master plan by a master architect, and they found one among their own number. Richard Morris Hunt, a board member since the museum's incorporation and flushed with triumph from Chicago's Columbian Exposition, was asked to design a grand plan. Hunt created a monumental Beaux-Arts plan whose new wings would completely surround and box in the Vaux and Weston buildings. It was understood that years would elapse before the scheme could be completed, and Hunt's plan in no way harmonized with Weston's designs, but neither did Weston's with Vaux's.

The trustees and the Parks Department, which would be responsible for construction, approved Hunt's plan. (Vaux, on behalf of the department, suggested only the addition of a carriage drive, a feature of Weston's first building that had proved enormously popular.) The city allocated $1 million to begin work on the central portion of the East Wing and authorized a series of $100,000 bonds to be sold as funds were required, which gave the trustees confidence that the city would build with dignity.

Although the East Wing held two-thirds as much space

215. The solution to the space problem at the Metropolitan Museum of Art was a rationalized building plan. The trustees asked one of their own to provide a plan, and Richard Morris Hunt obliged. Only one ninth of his design—the East Wing on Fifth Avenue—was completed to his specifications, and not even the four sculpture groups atop the paired columns were finished.

216. The Metropolitan Museum's Main Hall, which originally housed sculpture casts, is a series of domed spaces, elemental in form but grand in scope. Nobody could cite anything comparable in New York City.

217. The limestone walls and neoclassical trim of the Metropolitan's Main Hall were designed by Hunt as the perfect foil for the museum's treasures, which were increasing at an unprecedented rate by the turn of the century.

as the already-existing wings combined and was far grander, the contractor estimated in 1895 that only 400 work days would be required to complete the construction. By the fall of 1899, not even the roof had been raised, and two more years passed until the wing was ready to be equipped. Lingering dampness was the final delay that kept the exhibition cases from being installed.

When the East Wing finally opened in December 1902, it was a hit. Thanks to its position on the avenue, the wing acted as the natural entrance to the museum. Its design, like Grand Central Terminal's, is elemental: three Roman arches flanked by colossal Corinthian columns. True to Beaux-Arts principles, Hunt included plans for sculpture on the facade. He wanted members of the National Sculpture Society to be assigned the job of sculpting the four groups atop the attic story, but the society was slow to act. Hunt gave his protégé, Karl Bitter, the job of creating the medallions, keystones, and caryatids, the latter to represent painting, sculpture, architecture, and music.

Inside, the hall's massive neoclassical simplicity reflects the proportions of the facade, a scale that had never been seen in New York before. "Indeed," said the *Times*, "the great staircase and large hall are . . . as large, finely proportioned and elaborate in decoration as the great court of the Louvre and the staircase of the National Gallery in London."

The tragedy of Hunt's plan is that it was never extended —the wings on Fifth Avenue, for instance, are a more restrained neoclassical design by McKim, Mead & White— and even the East Wing was not finished. Before the National Sculpture Society got around to awarding the commissions for sculpting the piles of stones into allegorical groups illustrating civilization during the ancient, medieval, Renaissance, and modern periods, the million dollars ran out. Reports were circulated that the board had not wanted the sculpture in the first place. If it had, no doubt the members could have raised the money themselves, since this was the wealthiest, most powerful board serving any cultural institution in the city—J. Pierpont Morgan was the president, and members included Darius Ogden Mills, Samuel P. Avery, William E. Dodge, Elihu Root, Frederick W. Rhinelander, and two Villard House neighbors, Whitelaw Reid and Harris C. Fahnstock. Unfortunately, Richard Morris Hunt died before the city had even granted its final approvals in 1895; otherwise, events might have been different. Hunt wanted the museum to be his monument, and no doubt he would have fought for further allocations to have had the job completed the way he wanted it. To justify the money that had been spent, Parks Commissioner William R. Wilcox told the opening-day crowd that "art no longer ministers solely to the pride and luxury of the rich, but it has become to the people their best resource and most efficient educator. If . . . the real objects of government [are] to raise the standard of citizenship by furnishing educational advantages to the people, then no expenditure of the city could be more wise or profitable."

The Carnegie Mansion

Two East 91st Street, southeast corner of Fifth Avenue
1901
BUILDER: Andrew Carnegie
ARCHITECTS: Babb, Cook & Willard

By 1900, Millionaires' Row stretched solidly along Fifth Avenue from the 40s as far north as the Metropolitan Museum of Art, where development abruptly stopped. Side streets were cut through but not paved, and not even Fifth Avenue was asphalted until 1898. In the area north of 90th Street lived only one man of substance, Jacob Ruppert, whose house on 93rd Street was surrounded by raggle-taggle farms and shanties.

Fifth Avenue's highest point is at 91st Street. The area then presented a rocky and rugged landscape that seemed fit only for the few goats that foraged there, but in 1898 Andrew Carnegie bought 32 lots on and off the avenue between 90th and 92nd streets. The 63-year-old Carnegie was filled with intimations of his own mortality. "The little life that has come to us," the steelmaker said royally, "needs the park and sunshine, and it is for these reasons that we not only have concurred in the advice of our physician, but deemed it a duty to remove to the highest ground and where there is plenty of room."

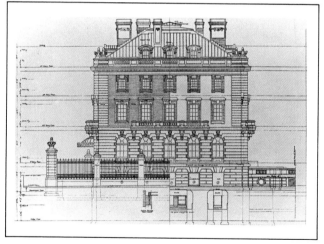

218

218. Babb, Cook & Willard's elevation for the Carnegie mansion shows the basement levels and a wall similar to the one that Bruce Price had designed for George Gould's estate at Lakewood, New Jersey—masonry columns every sixteen feet with a fifteen-foot-high wrought-iron fence.

Carnegie knew what he was doing. Because prices have a way of escalating at dizzying speeds when sellers sniff wealthy buyers, he employed a broker to secure options on the land. In the best Machiavellian tradition, the broker convinced each seller not to reveal to his neighbors that he had the prospect of closing a deal at what was ostensibly a big price. When all the options came due on the same day, property owners like Henry O. Havemeyer and Samuel Untermyer learned to their chagrin that Carnegie was the new owner and had succeeded in bamboozling them. The reported sale price was $900,000, a figure that Carnegie could well afford. He was already a wealthy man by the 1890s, but he was made a little richer by Henry Clay Frick, who bought an option on the Carnegie steel plant with the agreement that if he failed to raise the needed capital, he would forfeit $1.1 million. Frick's scheme fell through and Carnegie decided to build the house on 91st Street with the proceeds.

In the fall of 1899, Carnegie bought four more lots on the south side of 91st Street, bringing his side-street frontage to over 350 feet. His original purchase had extended the first-class residential section about ten blocks further north, and values had almost doubled in the ensuing year and a half, and despite agents' working on his behalf he paid dearly for the new lots. Trading north of Carnegie Hill was hectic, with speculators like Darius Ogden Mills, John S. Phipps, James A. Burden, Jr., and John H. Hammond buying and selling whole blocks at a time.

The house that anchored this paper boomtown was, according to Carnegie, "the most modest, plainest and most roomy house in New York. . . . As for building a grand palace, that is foreign to our tastes." Occupying a 73-foot frontage on the avenue and 184 feet on 91st Street and filled with 64 rooms, the house was, at least, roomy. Its estimated construction costs were $500,000, but the actual price tag was reportedly closer to $1 million. The *Times* said that

---

219. Steelman Andrew Carnegie said that building a grand palace was foreign to his tastes and he went on to describe his sixty-four-room neo-Georgian mansion as "modest." He made sure that his neighbors would build equally modest houses by refusing to sell the nearby lots to just anyone.

220. The conservatory in Andrew Carnegie's home is a sun- ▷ filled room that looks out on the verdure of the garden. Other residences of the period, such as Isaac Fletcher's house, had conservatories, but few had their own gardens land-scaped in the manner of Kensington.

222

architects Babb, Cook & Willard "eschewed the over-elaboration of detail which is such a marked fault of so many New York residences and have designed a quiet, picturesque but dignified edifice . . . which is similar in many essentials to the once villified but recently again popular style of the early Georgian period."

A driveway leads to a leaded-glass and bronze marquise, with bronze doors leading into the vestibule. You would expect the giver of libraries to give himself a monumental one; instead, he gave himself three room-sized libraries: a

---

221. The Carnegie mansion is now home to the Cooper-Hewitt Museum, the Smithsonian Institution's National Museum of Design. In that role, some of the mansion is sometimes closed off, which explains the screw eye in the wall of the grand staircase—the requisite red velvet cordon hooks into it.

222. This small car in the basement of the Carnegie mansion shuttled between the coal bin and the furnace, automatically picking up coal in the former and depositing it in the latter to keep the home fires burning evenly. All the basement walls were tiled for easy cleaning.

family library, a main library, and a working library (part of a suite that included its own lobby, reception room, and office in the southwest corner). In the northwest corner was the tea room; next door was the drawing room. Filling the northeast corner was a two-story billiard room that doubled as an art gallery. Overlooking the garden from the southeast were the dining room, the breakfast room, and the oval conservatory, a peninsular-like room whose glass walls brought in the verdure of the garden. And still the first floor had rooms for coats and lavatories, a butler's pantry, a walk-in safe, and the instrument that no proper house could be without, an organ.

The suite of rooms occupied by the Carnegies was in the west end of the second floor, with views across the park. Their boudoir, sitting room, bedrooms, bathrooms, and dressing rooms shared the floor with the valet's rooms and a maid's room, among others. The third floor contained their daughter's room, an apartment for Mrs. Carnegie's sister, and guest rooms. The fourth floor was for servants.

The Carnegie house has three below-ground levels with all the floors and walls covered in tile and with enough mechanical equipment for a grand hotel. The heating equipment cost $110,000, the plumbing about $55,000. The coal bin held 200 tons of coal and was linked to the furnace by a miniature railroad track upon which a small coal car operated. When the furnace ran low, the coal bin automatically dumped a quarter ton of coal into the car, which made its way to the furnace to deposit its load. The wine cellar had terra-cotta walls honeycombed with small openings, each the perfect size for one bottle. And instead of speaking tubes throughout the house, there were twenty telephones.

The southern side of the property was given over to a terraced garden whose design was similar to the fashionable gardens in London's Kensington. To avoid the kind of saplings that usually surround new houses, Carnegie had twelve sugar maples, five poplars, three elms, and one silver leaf maple uprooted from Westchester and Connecticut and hauled by truck to the site, where they were carefully transplanted. He saved the only tree that was indigenous to his property—a silver leaf poplar—by first encasing it in iron to protect it from the hazards of construction, then by digging a moat around it to ensure moisture, and finally by moving it to the east side of the building and out of harm's way. The workmen began to call the tree their pet, a nickname that Carnegie began to use himself.

When the building was nearing completion, Carnegie began to sell off his property to the north. He sold the 50-by-100-foot lot on the southeast corner of 92nd Street for $150,000 to I. Townsend Burden, "one of the ironworks Burdens" from Troy, New York. Burden asked Horace Trumbauer to design a 45-by-91-foot limestone and granite house for the site. Carnegie was reportedly reserving the 91st Street corner for a relative, and he sold the midblock property on the north side of 91st Street to Mr. and Mrs. William D. Sloane.

The Mrs. James A. Burden, Jr., House

7 East 91st Street, between Fifth and Madison Avenues
1902
BUILDERS: Mr. and Mrs. William D. Sloane
ARCHITECTS: Warren & Wetmore

The Mrs. John Henry Hammond House

9 East 91st Street, between Fifth and Madison Avenues
1906
BUILDERS: Mr. and Mrs. William D. Sloane
ARCHITECTS: Carrère & Hastings

Mr. and Mrs. William D. Sloane struck a bargain with Andrew Carnegie in 1901 for the midblock property that began 147 feet east of Fifth Avenue on the north side of 91st Street. The Sloanes bought the 135-by-100-foot site with the understanding that Carnegie would only sell the corner site as a single parcel and allow only a one-family residence to occupy the 130 feet from Fifth Avenue on 91st Street, leaving seventeen feet of undeveloped land to assure light and air for the Sloanes' property. Mrs. Sloane, who was the former Emily T. Vanderbilt, was continuing the family tradition of presenting Vanderbilt offspring with houses of their own. In this case, it meant houses for daughters Adele and Emily.

Adele Sloane, the eldest daughter, was considered a great beauty and sportswoman. In 1895, she married James A. Burden, Jr., heir to the Burden ironworks and a nephew of the Burden who had bought the 92nd Street corner. Young Burden, a graduate of Harvard, where he had been a member of the Porcellian Society, Harvard's oldest and most prestigious club, reputedly had a $1 million-a-year income at the time. At the Sloane-Burden wedding in Lenox, Massachusetts, reporters gushingly estimated that there were more society people than had ever been assembled in Lenox at one time before. After it all, the newlyweds took a 'round-the-world cruise. In 1902, they moved into 7 East 91st Street.

The house is freestanding, and a plain design in brick would not do for the exposed side walls. Architects Warren & Wetmore, the favored Vanderbilt architects of that generation, were told to use limestone for the flanks, whose design was almost as elaborate as the front. They created a 70-by-100-foot house in a severe Italian Renaissance style.

223

Inside, the house takes on a warmer formality around a monumental central staircase that ultimately leads to the formal dining rooms and a 65-foot-long ballroom on the top floor.

The house next door was built for the Sloane's second daughter, Emily, and her husband, John Henry Hammond, the son of General Sherman's chief of staff (young Hammond was educated at Yale and Columbia Law School). For the occasion of their marriage in 1899, the chancel of St. Bartholomew's Church was filled with palms and banked with pink azaleas and lilies. The wedding breakfast for 300

223. The freestanding Burden house by Warren & Wetmore was a gift to Mr. and Mrs. James A. Burden from her parents, Mr. and Mrs. William D. Sloane, who had bought the midblock property from Andrew Carnegie. Sloane's and Carnegie's mothers had been childhood playmates in Scotland, both fathers had been weavers, and the Sloanes were the only friends the Carnegies had in America when they immigrated. Carnegie liked the generational link and thought that everyone would be good neighbors.

guests was held in William H. Vanderbilt's mansion at 51st and Fifth, which had passed to George W. Vanderbilt, Emily's uncle. Gifts included a necklace and tiara of diamonds for the bride (from her parents), a ruby and diamond pendant for the bride (from her uncle and aunt, the Cornelius Vanderbilt IIs), and a complete set of table service (from her sister and brother-in-law, Mr. and Mrs. James A. Burden, Jr.). The couple moved into 14 East 72nd Street, where they lived until mother Sloane decided they deserved a house comparable to the one she had given the Burdens. When John Henry Hammond was shown the plans, he objected strongly. "Emily," he said to his wife, "I'm going to be considered a kept man."

The Hammonds were given 9 East 91st Street anyway, and plans for the neo-Italian Renaissance house were completed by Carrère & Hastings. In 1906, the couple moved into the house, over Hammond's "dead body," according to their son, the great musicologist John Hammond. The six-story house measures 65 by 100 feet, big enough for children to slip about unobtrusively and come and go as they please, which pleased young John enormously.

The house required an enormous staff. There were six-teen full-time servants in 1910, including the requisite butler, footman, cook and kitchen help, governesses and maids and chauffeurs, as well as various day workers. The male servants had quarters in the basement; sequestered at the decent distance of six floors were the female servants, who occupied eight rooms on the top floor. The top floor also contained an infirmary—with five children in the household, one always seemed to be in it. The fourth floor had a small suite for young John, a family room with a piano and Victrola, two bedrooms, and a small bedroom for one of the nurses. The third floor had five bedrooms and a suite with Mr. Hammond's second study and Mrs. Hammond's private bedroom, which was bigger than the

---

224. The Burden ballroom is where the Burdens held court. Mrs. Burden was seen at another extravagant Whitney Warren setting, photographed in a group portrait with Stanford White and James Henry "Silent" Smith, when Sherry's was turned into a miniature Versailles for the famous James Hazen Hyde Ball. The Burden house is now part of the Academy of the Sacred Heart, which explains the Madonna.

227

226

225. **The grand staircase in the Burden house seems to spiral its way to heaven. Warren & Wetmore reveled in the grand perspective and tried to achieve it in everything they designed.**

226. **Carrère & Hastings' plan for the Hammond house shows its perfect symmetry and balance. The fenestration has clear roots in Michelangelo, Vasari, and Bernini.**

227. **The Hammond house was another gift from the Sloanes to one of their children (Mrs. John Henry Hammond had been Emily Vanderbilt Sloane). The house has been the Consulate of the USSR since 1976.**

master bedroom. The second floor, with eighteen-foot ceilings, was the swellest. The ballroom could accommodate 250 guests, with another hundred comfortably ensconced in the adjoining music room, whose paneled doors could be opened to extend the ballroom.

It was in the music room that John Hammond was introduced to music by his mother, who religiously practiced the piano one hour every day. They would give musicales for his mother's friends, with him on the violin and her on the piano. In 1935, when John was about twenty-five, he joined forces with his mother for another type of musicale. Her concession to him was that Benny Goodman could play. His concession to her was that Goodman would play the Mozart Clarinet Quintet.

The floor housing the ballroom and music room was reached by a grand marble staircase from the lobby floor, where, in addition to the usual cloakrooms and waiting rooms, were found the dining and breakfast rooms in the north end of the house, as well as Mr. Hammond's private library, which had a vaulted ceiling and a marble fireplace with a pair of oversized caryatids supporting the mantel.

The interiors, said John Hammond, were decorated the same way that his mother handled the "conflict between living in opulence and the always nagging sin of ostentation, [which] was to furnish it as she accoutred herself, in a subdued and often tasteless fashion." The house was "furnished from the undistinguished but expensive stock of the family store," said Hammond, who did not remember a single rare antique or piece of real beauty in the house. The architects, nevertheless, managed to fill the interiors with the richest form of Louis XVI detailing, with sculptured paneling and plasterwork, with tapestry and fabric.

In the year that the Hammonds moved into their opulent house, Andrew Carnegie did what he had agreed not to do—he sold an inside 47-by-100-foot section of the corner plot. John Henry Hammond took the matter to court and the matter was quickly resolved to his satisfaction.

The Yorkville Branch, New York Public Library

222 East 79th Street, between Third and Second Avenues
1902
BUILDER: The Trustees of the New York Public Library
ARCHITECT: James Brown Lord

The city's first public lending libraries were started in the 1880s, when a group of philanthropists established the New York Free Circulating Library, but there was no lending-library system associated with the new New York Public Library. Out of the blue, Andrew Carnegie announced in 1901 that he had offered $5.2 million for a lending library system that would enlist the City of New York and the trustees of the nascent New York Public Library. Carnegie could well afford his largesse. In addition to all the money that Carnegie had been making in the 1880s and 1890s, the United States Steel Corporation was created in 1901, which gave Carnegie $492 million for his steel plant and an income that was conservatively estimated at $30 million a year.

Carnegie said that Dr. John S. Billings, the public library's director, had convinced him of the need for branch libraries "to reach the masses of people in every district." Billings was not describing a string of autonomous libraries, but a network of libraries established for loans between each other and the main branch. Carnegie arrived at the figure of $5.2 million quite grandly. He simply asked Billings if $80,000 was a good estimate for the construction of a branch library and whether 60 or 65 would do the job. To use Carnegie's phrase, this was "the day of big operations."

Carnegie's offer was simple—he would build the physical plants but the city had to buy the land and maintain the buildings. The trustees were reluctant to entrust the design of all the libraries to one firm, so they asked Carrère & Hastings, McKim, Mead & White, and Babb, Cook & Willard to form an advisory board to decide jointly on all matters concerning design and construction, with the understanding that the assignments would be divided equally among them. The libraries had to exhibit both uniformity and distinctiveness; and the results were buildings immediately identifiable as Carnegie libraries.

First came the Yorkville Branch, whose site on 79th Street began to be assembled only a month after the announcement of Carnegie's gift. The two 20-by-102-foot lots were not bought by the City of New York, as the agreement had stipulated, but by the library, and by October 1901, when the advisory board was being formed, James Brown Lord had already been assigned the job of designing the building. The construction contract was awarded in February 1902, and in March, Brown's plans for the 40-by-82-foot building were filed. Lord was known to have been suffering from cancer of the liver, which might explain the extraordinary rush to completion and the unique arrangement with the architect. In June 1902, before the Yorkville Branch was finished, the forty-three-year-old architect was dead.

One of Lord's legacies was the movement for the alliance of art and architecture. The Municipal Art Society picked up Lord's cue and urged that the Carnegie libraries incorporate paintings, mosaics, stained glass, and sculpture, suggesting that five percent of the libraries' building costs should be assigned to the decorative arts. The Board of Estimate said it cordially approved. But the board had no clout, since its responsibility was limited to providing the sites and maintaining the buildings, and the government was not even up to the task of assembling sites. The secretary of the New York Public Library had acknowledged that the city could not afford to pay for all the things that were needed as it was, and he wondered if the city would willingly undertake the financial obligations of a branch-library system. Sure enough, when the Palladian-style Yorkville Branch was finished, the city had bought only eight sites in all, and another six months was expected to pass before another branch library would open.

---

228. The Yorkville Branch was the city's only Carnegie-endowed library that was not designed by Carrère & Hastings, McKim, Mead & White, or Babb, Cook & Willard. James Brown Lord created his Palladio-like design before the emergence of the architectural triumvirate, whose goal was to divide the work among themselves and act as an advisory board for each other.

The Warburg House

1109 Fifth Avenue, northeast corner of 92nd Street
1908
BUILDERS: Mr. and Mrs. Felix Warburg
ARCHITECT: C. P. H. Gilbert

Frieda Warburg was the daughter of Jacob H. Schiff, a great philanthropist and patron of the arts, thanks to his role as Kuhn, Loeb's senior partner. For little Frieda, it meant Brearley School and French governesses and fencing classes. It also meant posing with her brother for Augustus St. Gaudens as the subjects of a marble relief sculpture their father commissioned and presented to the Metropolitan Museum of Art upon his induction as a trustee.

In 1895, Frieda Schiff and Felix Warburg were married, and he joined the house of Kuhn, Loeb. The Warburgs were living at 18 East 72nd Street in 1907 when Frieda Warburg purchased the vacant 100-by-100-foot plot on the northeast corner of Fifth Avenue and 92nd Street. The price was $400,000, and the seller was Perry Belmont, a brother of August Belmont II. The Warburgs wanted a six-story residence with a limestone facade that would occupy 50 by 74 feet of the site at the corner, leaving a 50-foot-wide garden next door. Architect C. P. H. Gilbert estimated that with the limestone facade the neo-Loire Valley chateau would come to about $260,000.

The youngest of the Warburg's five children, Edward Mortimer Morris Warburg, was born the year the house was finished. He recalls the front entrance as "terrifying in its formality, especially when the footman in livery answered the doorbell," and the young Warburgs made it a point to be at the door whenever any of their friends arrived, lest they flee in panic.

The first floor had two rooms that overlooked the park, where Felix Warburg mounted his collection of early German and Italian woodcuts and Rembrandt etchings. Some were on walls, some were in rotating pedestals with double-framed "pages," still others were placed in black boxes on a billiard table at the end of one of the rooms.

Overlooking the park on the second floor was the music room, with beamed ceilings and wrought-iron chandeliers, pieces of Gothic statuary on the mantelpiece, tapestries and paintings on the walls, and vitrines for Warburg's collection of especially rare books. The music room had a grand piano and an Aeolian pipe organ, which young Edward Warburg learned how to play, "that is to say," said he, "to operate, which required no music ability whatsoever. The pipe organ was adapted for pianola rolls." The neighboring sitting room was called the Red Room and held a collection of Italian paintings. "Few were of the first rank," said Edward Warburg. "Among the exceptions were four panels done by Pesellino for the base of an altarpiece. By a strange

229

trick of fate they turned out to be the predellas or base panels of the great Fra Filippo Lippi altarpiece which has been assembled in the National Gallery in London."

Next to the Red Room was the conservatory, where the small *Madonna and Child* attributed to Botticelli hung alone in its place of honor. The dining room, the floor's largest room, was used only on formal occasions. The tapestry-covered walls, the high-backed chairs with *gros point* needlework, the large mantel, all added up to a glorious room, and it was strategically placed. A dumbwaiter linked it with the kitchen and opened on both the tiled butler's pantry next door to the dining room and directly onto the dining room itself.

---

229. C. P. H. Gilbert's detailing in the Warburg house is masterful, an evocation of the Hotel de Cluny in Paris. Unfortunately, the retrofitted central air-conditioning system did not reach the upper floors, and the individual window units are a jarring but nevertheless accepted fact of late twentieth-century life.

230. The home of the Felix Warburgs, designed by Gilbert in the style of the early French Renaissance, now houses the Jewish Museum. In a picture within a picture, the museum's banner shows the Fifth Avenue elevation.

231

232

All the rooms on the second floor opened onto each other, creating a grand flow from the music room to the dining room. And there were marvelous touches. The neo-Gothicism of the conservatory, for instance, reflected the downstairs vestibule. The doors to the Red Room slid into the walls to be completely out of sight. And the hardware included window pulls that give when they are pulled to reduce the required effort.

The third floor, where the intimate family life took place, contained sitting and breakfast rooms, the Warburgs' bedroom, Mrs. Warburg's boudoir, and Mr. Warburg's dressing room. "The sitting room was built around two desks where my parents spent most of their free time maintaining their correspondences," relates Warburg. "The furniture was cut velvet, overstuffed, tufted, comfortable. . . . In this room, . . . tea was served and we were blessed every Friday night."

Life for the children was largely restricted to the fourth floor, where elaborate tracks for wind-up trains ran the length of the hall. The guest-room apartments were on the fifth floor, as was the squash court. The quarters for the large staff were on the sixth floor, where there was also a laundry room that was convenient to the roof for hanging out clothes to dry.

After the children had grown and moved out, and after Felix Warburg's death, Frieda Warburg gave the house to the Jewish Museum in 1944. "I confess the first time I entered 1109 after it had been transformed into the Jewish Museum was a very poignant moment," she wrote, "but I discovered to my joy that instead of depressing me, it gave me a wonderful feeling of happiness. I feel that the spirit of the house and the warmth and love it held for so many years still hover in the rooms."

231. The hardware in the Warburg house shows the care lavished on small things as well as large. This throwbolt opens and closes the French windows in the dining room.

232. The Warburg's organ harmonizes with the building's Francis I style. With a wonderful sense of self-mockery, Edward Warburg admits that his mastery over the instrument required little training and less musical skill, since the organ was adapted for electric pianola rolls.

998 Fifth Avenue

Northeast corner of 81st Street
1911
BUILDER: The Century Holding Company
ARCHITECTS: McKim, Mead & White

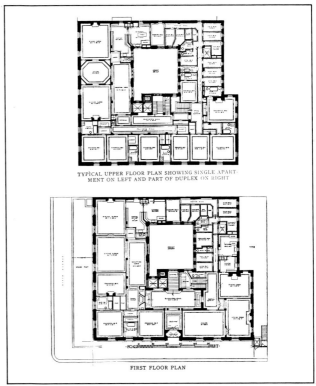

TYPICAL UPPER FLOOR PLAN SHOWING SINGLE APARTMENT ON LEFT AND PART OF DUPLEX ON RIGHT

FIRST FLOOR PLAN

233

August Belmont II bought the property at 998 Fifth Avenue in 1902, and having lost his first wife four years before and not yet having found Eleanor Robson, who was to become his second wife, he decided to sit on the property rather than build on it. By 1910, the 102-by-125-foot site was one of the few corners on upper Fifth Avenue that was not developed. More importantly, it was not restricted to single-family dwellings, and it had become the object of desire of James T. Lee and Charles R. Fleishmann, who were both Columbia-trained lawyers in their thirties. Lee had joined the millionaires' club by buying property along the proposed route of the subway that Belmont built. It tripled his investment.

After long negotiations, Belmont sold the property to Lee and Fleishmann's Century Holding Company for $590,000, or about $5,785 a front foot. McKim, Mead & White were commissioned to design an apartment house, for which the firm was given *carte blanche*. To help pay for it, Lee and Fleishmann then took a $1.35 million mortgage.

At 150 feet high, 998 is a huge neo-Italian Renaissance palazzo, its battered limestone and marble facade divided into three horizontal bands in the manner of the firm's University Club. In the core of the building is a 32-foot-square courtyard. Its walls are not common brick, as one would expect, but rusticated stone that is only visible to the tenants, their guests, and servants.

The apartment house was specifically intended to lure the wealthy from their private homes by offering all the advantages of a town house without the headaches of private maintenance. Each apartment was at least as large as the average Fifth Avenue residence and included all the latest amenities, and then some. The lobby was lined in Bottocino marble, the hallway and floors were Tennessee marble, and the elevators were paneled in French walnut. Doors throughout the apartments were framed in marble, and to prevent the spread of fire from the common hallway, the front doors were clad with galvanized sheet steel (kalomine) and painted to simulate wood. The ceilings average ten-and-a-half-feet high, except on the fifth floor, where they are a foot higher.

The interior design called for six duplexes in the southeast corner; the rest of the building was composed of seventeen-room simplexes. The reception rooms in the simplex apartments measured 14 by 36 feet and were usually copies of the Long Gallery in Haddon Hall, England. Their walls were paneled in English oak, and their ceilings were

often plastered in a Tudor motif. The walls of every apartment were given nine coats of paint, and the door knobs were made of cut crystal. Each apartment had three wall safes, all with combination locks. In the days when steam heat was either on or off, valves regulated the intake in each room. As at the St. Regis Hotel, a built-in vacuum-cleaning system allowed a maid to attach a nozzle to a hallway outlet and have the dirt sucked down to the basement. And as in all great hotels, there is a refrigerated wine cellar, where each tenant is provided his own locked storage space.

Although 998 was not scheduled for completion until July 1911, three apartments were reserved within the first week of the building's announcement in March 1910. One twenty-room apartment was rented as a loss leader to Senator Elihu Root for $15,000 a year. By September 1910, five of the seventeen-room apartments were rented, two of them for $18,000 a year and none with leases of less than five years. Murry Guggenheim was interested, but he feared that his family would be cramped in one of the ordinary seventeen-room simplex suites. Lee and Fleishmann agreed to rearrange the floor above and incorporate some of the upper floor for Guggenheim's use, giving him 24 rooms and nine baths. He signed a ten-year lease at the

---

233. Average simplex apartments in 998 Fifth were seventeen rooms and situated so that the spaces for entertaining overlooked Fifth Avenue; the duplex apartments overlooked 81st Street and the east.

234

235

heretofore unheard of sum of $25,000 a year. Guggenheim then installed a backlit, stained-glass ceiling that was suspended from the structural ceiling of his 15-by-34-foot conservatory. He also had all the hardware removed and sent to Tiffany & Co. to be gold plated. Since gold never tarnishes, it never has to be polished. After Guggenheim came former Governor Levi P. Morton, who was wearied of fending off trade on the Vanderbilts' Fifth Avenue, and Mrs. Elliott F. Shepard, who had decided that she needed an apartment in town.

The venture was a huge success, and in 1913 Lee and Fleishmann were made an offer of $3.5 million dollars. They had spent $807,000 on construction and $590,000 for the site, most of it borrowed, and they accepted the offer. Fleishmann retired from business five years later to occupy himself with a string of race horses. Lee went on to build the Shelton Hotel and enter the banking business. (One of his daughters, Janet, married John Vernon Bouvier III, making James T. Lee the grandfather of Jacqueline Bouvier Kennedy Onassis.)

When 998 was built, mused real-estate agent Douglas Elliman in the 1930s, 90 percent of New York society lived in private houses. Twenty-five years later, 90 percent lived in apartments. Most were lesser versions of 998 Fifth, which set a standard of excellence that was often aspired to but seldom achieved.

---

234. The trappings at 998 Fifth could lure some of the city's power elite out of their townhouses and into apartments. Mrs. Elliot F. Shepard, former Vice-President Levi Morton, and Murry Guggenheim were among the earliest tenants.

235. The dining room in a duplex apartment shows the attention to detail at 998 Fifth. The paneling changes scale to reflect the expanse of wall.

236. Durable Tennessee marble, which was used in Grand Central Terminal, also covers the floors in the foyers of 998 Fifth. The iron gate on this graceful staircase was added as a guard to prevent children from hurting themselves on the marble stairs.

237

The Otto Kahn Mansion

1 East 91st Street, northeast corner of Fifth Avenue
1918
BUILDER: Otto Kahn
**ARCHITECTS: C. P. H. Gilbert and J. Armstrong
Stenhouse**

Common sense told Andrew Carnegie that he could not keep the vacant 91st Street corner off the market forever, but he was forced to sell the property as a single package for a single-family house, which meant that he had to find somebody willing to make a huge investment. He found forty-six-year-old investment banker Otto Kahn, Kuhn, Loeb's most active partner, who preferred talking opera to discussing the finances of the opera, but who did both with equal proficiency.

Like Carnegie, but unlike so many of his contemporary business associates, Kahn believed that wealth in and of itself was not the chief aim of living. He was comfortable with the European custom of government support of the arts, and since he believed that the American government was shirking its share, he single-handedly tried to make up for the lack. The *Times* described Kahn as a "man of steel and velvet, because if he's winning, you're beaten gently; if he's losing, he retreats, looks for a weak flank, and attacks."

---

237. Carnegie sold the property that was directly across the street from his house to Otto Kahn, who, he felt, would build a house fitting to the area.

238. Kahn had C. P. H. Gilbert and J. Armstrong Stenhouse design a great neo-Italian Renaissance palace to suit his needs. In an understated act of conspicuous consumption, Kahn gave up first-class space for a porte cochère.

238

His favorite number for dinner was 60 and he liked to sport a black pearl stickpin, with a tiny orchid as a boutonniere.

Kahn was living at 6 East 68th Street in the early 1910s, but the thought of entering politics was luring the naturalized British subject back to England. However, perhaps the death of J. Pierpont Morgan in March 1913 led Kahn to speculate whether the time had come when Kuhn, Loeb could eclipse the House of Morgan, because he changed his mind and decided to stay in New York. "What little I may be able to contribute to the common weal, I can accomplish better in my present role than as a public official," he said.

Kahn bought the 91st Street site from Carnegie for $675,000 in June 1913. A year later, plans were filed for a twenty-bedroom mansion at an estimated cost of $375,000. The excavations for the house were finished in December 1913, but unexplained delays slowed progress until the next spring, and work did not begin again until October 1916. One explicable delay by then was that the building was being faced with a light stone imported from France, and there was a war on. The house was not finished until December 1918, and by then people were saying that it had cost close to $1 million.

The Kahn mansion was designed by C. P. H. Gilbert, who had designed Kahn's 68th Street house. In this venture, Gilbert was joined by J. Armstrong Stenhouse, who had designed furniture and interiors for such houses as the Blumenthal mansion on Park Avenue.

The Kahn mansion comes as close to a true Italian Renaissance-style house as there is in New York, complete with a drive-through porte cochere and an interior courtyard. The courtyard, which is open to Fifth Avenue above the second floor at the north end, is not just another rectangular space, and its complexity gives it grandeur. Kahn's library was partially housed in the second-floor loggia that rings the courtyard. His main library, which overlooks the avenue, had cupboards and drawers that housed his precious collections, all of which were kept under custom-made locks and keys. Kahn's private library was in the 91st Street corner, where a stone staircase spirals up to a sanctum sanctorum. Most of the windows on the second floor that overlook 91st Street look out from the banqueting hall, a room that easily accommodated the kind of dinner parties Kahn liked to give. Tucked into the northeast corner was the music room, where he often held premieres by composers whose music interested him.

The elements of the Kahn mansion, said *Architectural Record*, were "in all their traditional purity but subtly readjusted," making it a personal statement by the architects. This chaste building, this restrained palazzo with its exuberant use of space, had a quality worthy of a Medici prince, which was just the role that Kahn relished. It was the last of the great Fifth Avenue mansions, and of an era.

239

239. The second floor hall of the Kahn mansion is filled with the highest order of Renaissance-style detailing. The house is now part of the Academy of the Sacred Heart, whose students use Kahn's library, which is to the left, as their own.

240. This stunning evocation of Palladio and the Italian High Renaissance is fully appreciated only from within the Kahn mansion. From without, it is barely perceptible. The loggia housed some of this cultured man's library.

240

241. The Hotel Majestic was built in the early days of the Upper West Side's real-estate boom in the 1890s, when the neighborhood was beginning to outgrow its village roots. Advantages of the site included Central Park, fresh air, and an elevated railroad only a block away. An apartment house bearing the same name occupies the site today.

12

The Speculative West Side

The Upper West Side in the 1870s was at best a backwater. It only had a single horse car line and a few houses that were considered modern, which hardly deterred its boosters from saying that by the 1880s it would be the city's choicest residential quarter. The quarter never attracted high society the way the East Side did, but by the mid-1880s an elevated railroad and cable cars linked the neighborhood with the rest of the city, and buildings were going up.

To Jacob Rothschild, the blockfront on Central Park West between 71st and 72nd streets looked promising as a speculative venture. Despite the site's goats and chickens, the one-story frame houses and the vacant lots, the neighborhood was beginning to be developed, and Central Park provided a greensward in summer and a snow-filled wonderland in winter. In 1891, Rothschild began to buy parkfront lots for about $25,000 apiece, and by the time he had acquired the block frontage, he was ready to begin his dream of a twelve-story, 600-room hotel. He called it the Majestic and asked architect Alfred Zucker to design it.

Zucker estimated that construction costs would come to about $1 million, but the reality was probably twice the estimate. The building had load-bearing brick walls and iron supports, with a facade of stone and terra cotta. Advertisements claimed that the Majestic was the largest, most magnificent hotel in the world, with suites or single rooms that could be rented by the year or on a more transient basis. A few unfurnished suites were offered, but most were "elegantly furnished with all modern appointments," and every room had an outside view. The hotel offered the choice of American or European plans, and the hotel orchestra played every evening in the conservatory. Managing Director Richard H. Stearns offered special facilities for banquets and private dinners in rooms with such grandiloquent names as the Colonial Drawing Room or the Empire Room, both of which were thrown open for the occasion of the hotel's inaugural ball in December 1894. There were even bowling alleys.

Jacob Rothschild, the proprietor of the Majestic, was another nineteenth-century success story, a Horatio Alger character who made his fortune more by pluck than luck. After his father's death, the thirteen-year old Rothschild emigrated from Germany in the 1850s and went to work in a millinery shop on Grand Street. By twenty-three, Rothschild owned his own millinery shop, and soon after the Civil War he had a store on Ladies' Mile. By 1899, he had built several buildings, including his Zucker-designed home at 31 West 57th Street. Although he could have lived in pomp and splendor at the Majestic, he chose to stay in his home on 57th Street.

The Dakota Apartments

1 West 72nd Street, at Central Park West
1884
BUILDER: Edward Clark
ARCHITECT: Edward J. Hardenbergh

Speculator Edward Clark had confidence in the Upper West Side even before Rothschild. Despite the bleakness of the scene in 1877, Clark bought two acres of land with a 200-foot frontage on Central Park West between 72nd and 73rd streets from August Belmont and his wife, the former Caroline Slidell Perry. (Belmont represented the House of Rothschild in New York City, and his wife was Commodore Perry's niece.) The price was $200,000, but Edward Clark could afford it. He was a lawyer who had become the president of the Singer Sewing Machine Company by taking the litigious Isaac M. Singer as a client in exchange for half ownership in the company.

In 1880, Clark decided to build the most spectacular apartment house the city had ever seen, where persons of means could find a home with every comfort and luxury of a first-class town house but without the discomforts and inconveniences of the ordinary hotel. European capitals had been known for their luxurious apartment houses for years, but New York lagged. The city's first apartment house for respectable families was not built until 1869, when the Stuyvesant appeared on 18th Street. The Stuyvesant hardly had the luxury that Clark envisioned, and he was labeled a madman first for conceiving such a grandiose idea and then for attempting to carry it out in such a remote district. Although he began to call the building Clark's Apartments, others called it Clark's Folly, and one wag told him that West 72nd Street was as far from civilization as the Dakota Territory. The idea tickled Clark's fancy, and he dubbed the apartments The Dakota.

Clark asked Henry J. Hardenbergh to design the building, and the architect obliged with an eclectic design of Victorian massing. For detailing, he borrowed from the French and German Renaissance. For whimsy, and in honor of the apartment house's name, he incorporated an

242. The Dakota Apartments was a major real-estate gamble for Edward Clark, a lawyer who had assumed control of the Singer Sewing Machine Company. At 72nd Street and Central Park West, the apartment house was far removed from the mainstream in 1884 (as far from civilization as the Dakota Territory, it was said); in addition, the rents were high, and not many upper-class New Yorkers were prepared for apartment living.

243

occasional Western motif, including a relief statue of an Indian and a cluster of corn. The Dakota, which was completely fireproof and lavishly decorated, took almost four years to build. The walls were made of a distinctive buff brick, a process that was not perfected until 1883. For the production of light shades of brick, the clay must be free of iron, which produces the red coloring, and of sulphur, which produces a mottled effect. The foundation walls, constructed of bluestone laid in cement mortar, are three to four feet thick. The building's load-bearing walls diminish from a thickness of 28 inches on the lower floors to twelve inches on the upper floors. To add strength, six- to twelve-inch thick rolled-iron beams were set into the floors every three to four feet.

The Dakota is massive, and at 200 by 200 feet it was the biggest apartment house in the city. The porte cochere on 72nd Street leads to the central courtyard, where the entrances to the four passenger elevators were placed in the corners. The Dakota's 65 suites ranged in size from four to twenty rooms, and the rooms were large, with some parlors as big as 25 by 40 feet. The parlors, libraries, reception rooms, and dining rooms were all paneled and wainscoted in mahogany, oak, or some other hard wood. Conceived as a family hotel, tenants could follow the table d'hote plan and eat in the main-floor dining room, or they could be served "home-cooked" food by their servants in the privacy of their own dining rooms.

The idea that the higher you live the better you live had not yet caught on, and, despite the elevators, only the lower seven stories were fitted up as apartments. Servants' quarters had been traditionally ensconced on the top floor of private houses, so the two top floors of the Dakota, which offered spectacular views as far as the towers of the Brooklyn Bridge, supplemented the servants' quarters in the apartments. Under the mansard roof and gables were also laundries and drying rooms, dormitories for transient servants, and a play room and gymnasium for children.

Since the property extended 375 feet west of Central Park West, gardens, croquet lawns, and tennis courts were provided for the tenants. Under these pleasure grounds and

244

safely remote from the building itself were the boilers and dynamo that supplied the power for the building's own electricity.

Clark's scheme for the Dakota in particular and the improvement of the neighborhood in general included good stables, and although Clark died two years before the completion of the Dakota, his estate built the three-story Dakota Stables on the southeast corner of 75th Street and Broadway. The stables cost about $70,000, a drop in the bucket compared with the cost of the Dakota, which was

243. The Dakota was wired for electricity before the Upper West Side was. The building had its own power plant at a safe distance to the west.

244. Henry J. Hardenbergh designed the Dakota Apartments around a central courtyard and placed the entrances to the elevators in the four corners. Brickmakers Sayre & Fisher provided the cream-colored bricks.

245. Gracious details (seen in this view from an apartment's library to the foyer to the double-doored entranceway) made the Dakota popular enough by the 1890s for the management to institute a waiting list for apartments.

245

324 West 80th Street

At Riverside Drive
1898 (?)
BUILDER-ARCHITECT: Clarence True

If only for the salubrious breezes from the Hudson River, the Upper West Side was a desirable site for development, and the bluff overlooking the river had the greatest potential. Frederick Law Olmsted envisioned an avenue that maintained the natural topography of the bluff, and he submitted a plan that called for a winding road with thirteen changes of grade. The name of Eleventh Avenue was changed to Riverside Drive, the proposed Twelfth Avenue never materialized in the valley, and property owners on

246

set at $2 million. The investment, however, had instant returns. The Dakota was fully rented before it opened in 1884, and by 1890 the manager had a long waiting list. Applicants were often inveigled into taking houses or lesser apartments with the Clark Estate as their landlord until a vacancy came up in the Dakota.

The Dakota changed the living patterns of New Yorkers to the point where Mrs. Grundys could no longer make barbed remarks about proper families sharing common roofs with others, and it spurred imitations, even precipitating a trend in names. In the wake of the Dakota came the Nevada on Broadway at 69th Street, the Yosemite on Park Avenue at 62nd Street, the Montana on Park Avenue at 52nd Street, and the Wyoming on Seventh Avenue at 55th Street.

And after the Dakota came a building boom of vast proportions on the Upper West Side. In 1885 and 1886, about 1,500 private dwellings were built, and a thousand more were planned. The greatest activity took place between 70th and 95th streets, where block after block changed hands and prices advanced with unaccustomed rapidity. Lots that had been selling for $4,000 in 1884 were selling for $10,000 in 1886, and by the 1890s the speculators were still at it.

246. Architect-builder Clarence True dubbed his favorite style the Elizabethan Renaissance to encompass the loose framework in which he worked. Since he was building great swaths of the West Side at the same time, he also had the chance to change conditions that were usually immutable, such as the size of plots. The house at 324 West 80th Street, for instance, is thirty-nine feet wide and thirty-seven feet deep.

247. True designed houses with interchangeable parts, and since he built as many as eight neighboring rowhouses at a clip, the interior decoration for one house might be the same as another in the row. The fireplace in this dining room is gas-powered.

the drive were treated to unobstructed views, cool summer breezes, and different perspectives from just about every lot.

The drive was different from other New York City streets, and so were the houses that were built on it. For fifty years the New York tradition had been to encase middle- and upper-class homes in brownstone to prove the householder's wealth in the eye of the beholder. By the 1890s, the tradition was beginning to crumble, and the West Side's builders and architects were in the vanguard of the iconoclasm. The *Times* pointed out that "structures which satisfied the eye and fed the imagination" were found there, and architect-builder Clarence F. True was building some of the best of them.

True was so impressed with the possibilities of Riverside Drive and so intent on ensuring its future as *the* West Side residential district that he tried to secure all available property south of 84th Street and build beautiful dwellings on his holdings. By 1898 he had designed about 400 houses on the West Side, which the *Real Estate Record* said probably made him "the best known New York architect designing entirely residential structures."

True had studied architecture with Richard Upjohn, the great Gothic Revivalist, and his early houses were in the Gothic style. True also designed in a style dubbed the Flemish Renaissance, and in the neo-Italian Renaissance style, as shown in the working-class homes he built at 316 to 326 West 85th Street. His most cherished style, however, was what he called the Elizabethan Renaissance, because it offered him the freedom to adapt to the conditions of New York lots.

In 1897, True was building eight prefabricated houses on the southeast corner of Riverside Drive at 80th Street, which gave him the opportunity to divide the land sensibly. To provide light for the rear rooms and backyards, he staggered the depths of the houses on the drive, while he made the side-street houses shallower and wider. To facilitate construction, he kept openings in the party walls to allow wheelbarrows to shuttle between the hoist and the worksites. And to allow his clients who ordered houses in the planning stage to have their choice of decorative trim, he permitted them to pick and choose from his basic stock.

The house at 324 West 80th Street is a classic True house in its idiosyncrasies. It is 39 feet wide but only 37 feet deep, and a notch was cut out of its southwest corner for added light. Instead of having the staircase on one side of the house, which was the traditional place in a rowhouse, the staircase is in the rear of the center of the house, creating what is tantamount to three-room suites on every floor. As in many True houses, 324 could be adapted for both gas and electricity, and the wall sconces were equipped for both. Contact alarms were built into all the window frames on the first and second floors, as well as the top floors, and just to make sure that the servants were not stealing food, alarms were built into the kitchens as well as into the

248

iceboxes. The houses were constructed in accordance with a major revision of the building code, which called for cast-iron backs and tile-lined flues in the fireplaces, electrical wiring in metal conduits, steam pipes in raceways, and basement ceilings of metal lathe. (A hot-air duct system was built into the walls, but it was never hooked up to the boiler.) Just to make sure that supporting floor beams were not weakened by the heat from fireplaces, True designed frames that were cantilevered from the walls to support the floors around the fireplaces. The houses are not steel framed, but to avoid sagging at bay windows and staircases, True incorporated steel I-beams.

True could not suit everybody, of course. The *Times* fretted that houses were being erected on Riverside Drive that only "would be suitable on a narrow lot. . . . Some examples of the 'city' house have crept in already, and on one corner, where such a villa as the parklike character of the location demands might be erected, the owner advertises that he will build three 'city' houses. . . ."

---

248. A typical house had wall sconces "wired" for both gas and electricity. In the late 1890s, few people could say with any certainty which would prevail.

Villa Julia

**346 West 89th Street, on the southeast corner of
Riverside Drive**
1901
BUILDER: Isaac L. Rice
ARCHITECTS: Herts & Tallant

In 1899, Isaac L. Rice bought a 75-by-100-foot plot on the southeast corner of 88th Street and Riverside Drive from Egbert Viele. At the same time, real-estate developer William W. Hall bought an irregular piece of property on the southeast corner of 89th Street from merchant Benjamin Altman. The difference between the two sites was that Viele had sold his without restrictions, whereas Altman had restricted his property's use to a private, one-family house of not less than four stories. It was just what Hall did not want, but what Rice did want, so they arranged a swap. Since the 89th Steet property was 101 by 149 feet at its deepest, Rice made out well, and since Hall could develop the 88th Street property to the fullest, he was content.

The Rices were quite a couple. She was Julia Barnett Rice, M.D., president of the Society for the Suppression of Unnecessary Noise, the organization that lobbied for the creation of quiet Hospital Zones. Isaac Rice had graduated from Columbia Law School, where he remained on the faculty to teach law and political science. By the 1880s, the heyday of traction- and railroad-empire building, he was practicing railroad law. He founded the Electric Vehicle Company to build electric cabs, a product that was so successful that William C. Whitney and other venture capitalists wanted to buy him out. Rice set his price at an inflated $141 a share, and said, "Take it or leave it." They took it. In addition to his business acumen, Rice was a chess player of international repute, with an opening called the "Rice Gambit" to his credit.

Rice was a member of several clubs, including the Harmonie, which was refurbished in 1897 to plans by architects Herts & Tallant. Rice liked the firm's work and hired the young architects to design a freestanding house that would have placated the *Times*, for Rice would build a "villa as the parklike character of the location demands," complete with terraced gardens in the tradition of the Italian Renaissance. He dubbed it "Villa Julia," for his wife.

The 70-foot-deep house has a facade of brick with marble trim that combines elements of the Beaux-Arts, Georgian, and Northern Italian Renaissance. Among the house's many amenities was a wine cellar of the first rank and Otis push-button elevators. To make the building fireproof, Herts & Tallant used hollow terra-cotta blocks for the walls, with floors that are composed of metal sheets and steel beams embedded in cement. As late as 1906, Rice was making changes to the house, including the addition of a music room.

249

The Rices were granted permission to include a porte cochere within the stoop line in 1899, and in 1900 they were granted permission to build a terrace wall on the stoop line, which allowed their garden to occupy a share of the sidewalk. In 1907, however, the city declared that permission to build to the stoop line should not have been granted and reneged on its agreement. The Rices fought the decision and lost. The same year, Rice lost a fortune in the financial panic. Villa Julia was put up for sale, the Rices moved into the Ansonia, and Solomon Schinasi took title in 1908 for $600,000. Schinasi was in the cigarette manufacturing business with his brother, Morris, who only a few months before had bought the northeast corner of 107th Street and Riverside, where he planned a freestanding mansion. Solomon Schinasi hired C. P. H. Gilbert to make extensive renovations to Villa Julia, which, if they were anything like his brother Morris's mansion, included a room-long humidor. Of the roughly 30 free-standing mansions that lined Riverside Drive in the twentieth century, only the Schinasi brothers' mansions remain.

249. The freestanding home of Julia and Isaac Rice was designed by Herts & Tallant in the style of a country house in Tuscany. Dubbed "Villa Julia," it was just the kind of house that was deemed worthy of Riverside Drive, whose sweeping views of the Hudson had attracted about 30 freestanding mansions by the early 20th century.

The Ansonia Hotel

2107 Broadway, between 73rd and 74th Streets
1903
BUILDER: William Earl Dodge Stokes
ARCHITECTS: Stokes and Paul E. M. Duboy

250

Andrew Haswell Green, who in 1866 planned the development of the West Side between 59th and 160th streets, platted a sweeping 160-foot-wide parkway, which he called the Boulevard and which was renamed Broadway in 1899. It had a 30-foot-wide planted median flanked by 50-foot-wide carriageways and broad sidewalks for promenading. His vision called for the Champs-Élysées of New York, the domain of elaborate, freestanding private homes of a costly character. Landowners held out for the inflated prices that they were sure would come, but progress was slow. In 1891, the Boulevard was only paved as far as 92nd Street, and it was not until the coming of the subway in 1904 that Broadway's promise began to be realized. By then the private homes Green had wanted were not economically feasible, and the avenue became the scene of great apartment houses.

William Earl Dodge Stokes was one of the speculators who bought up large parcels of the West Side in the 1880s, and in the boom year of 1886, he was building about 50 houses west of the Boulevard. This was the same Stokes who had built and never occupied his dream house at 4 East 54th Street, but he could afford his foibles, thanks primarily to the earnings that Phelps, Dodge & Company had made for his father.

Stokes owned the blockfront on the west side of Broadway at a commanding bend between 73rd and 74th streets and he held onto the property until he felt the time was ripe, whereupon his dream of a great wedding cake of an apartment hotel began to take shape. Stokes made the original drawings of the Ansonia's floor plans in the basement-office of his home at 262 West 72nd Street, and he hired the French-trained Paul Duboy to draw them up. Stokes was not sure how many stories he wanted the Ansonia to rise. He considered taking it to twenty stories and topping it with a tower in the center, but when the building had reached sixteen stories, he decided that he wanted his apartment there and called it quits; the copper roof, which had already been designed with its cupolas, was added to bring the building to a logical conclusion. What resulted was the world's largest apartment hotel, an evocation of Paris's Belle Epoque blown out of all proportion.

Stokes oversaw every detail of construction, and some of the companies that he owned supplied materials. The terra cotta came from Stokes's plant in New Jersey, and the standard plunger elevators came from his company in Worces-

ter, Massachusetts. Stokes had the understandable eccentricity of disliking high fire-insurance premiums, and he wanted to make sure that the sixteen-story Ansonia was not only fireproof in fact, but was recognized and deemed so by the insurance underwriters. He got his wish, and never carried a dollar's worth of fire insurance on the building. The three-foot-thick terra-cotta partitions gave him the unexpected benefit of creating what is reputedly the best sound-proofed building in the city.

The construction of the mammoth, 2,500-room Ansonia created at least one superlative. The building's plumbing contract called for 400 fully-equipped bathrooms, in addition to an order for 600 toilets and wash basins. The total order came to over $350,000 for materials, which was considered the largest plumbing contract ever awarded. The appliances had few peers, and the selection was remark-

250. **William Earl Dodge Stokes, whose father had made a fortune from Phelps, Dodge & Company, took some of his patrimony and invested in West Side real estate. Stokes's major undertaking was the Ansonia Apartments, a great wedding cake of a building that was built on a commanding site at Broadway and 73rd Street.**

251

252

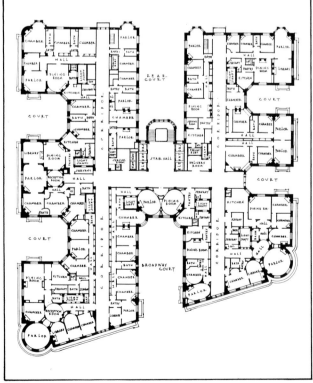

253

able. Tenants were offered the choice of an electric or the standard gas cooking range, and every apartment came equipped with a "chamber in which carafes and bottles may be immersed and frozen." Pneumatic tubes delivered messages to and from the manager's office, and every apartment was equipped with a house telephone con-

251. Stokes was not sure how high he wanted the Ansonia to go, and a drawing of the building only appeared after construction had stopped. The finials atop the cupolas were in place, but the tower was never built, despite the plans.

252. The Ansonia's terra cotta, which is almost rococo in its grandiosity, was manufactured by one of Stokes's companies. The cupolas were originally outfitted with finials rising from within the widows' walks.

253. Builder Stokes, who was concerned with bringing light and air into the Ansonia's apartments, designed the floor plans himself from models he had studied in France. He used his architect more as a factotum than as an architect.

254. Stokes was concerned with keeping his fire-insurance premiums to a minimum, and he built the Ansonia so that even the fire underwriters would deem it fireproof. Stokes never paid a penny in fire insurance.

nected with the public exchange. Filtered hot and cold water, in addition to ice water, was also provided, and filtered air was drawn from the sub-basement, where large electric blowers forced it over coils that were steam-heated in winter and cooled by freezing brine in summer. The temperature of the apartments was a uniform 70 degrees in winter.

Stokes used the roof as a minifarm where he raised chickens and goats—the chicken eggs he sold at discounted prices to tenants, the goat's milk he kept for himself to drink and make cheese. Another part of the roof was used as a garden where orchestras played on long summer nights. Two of the Ansonia's restaurants—the banquet hall and the English grille—were on the sixteenth floor. The main dining room, big enough for 550 diners, was on the lobby floor. The decor was Louis XIV, and its lighting was provided by electric chandeliers and wall sconces (ropes of cut crystal were festooned between them to create a huge tent-like effect). To make sure that everything ran smoothly,

Stokes lured Gurnsey E. Webb from The Plaza to manage the place.

The rents for all this luxury, including the Oriental carpets in the public halls, ranged from $600 a year for a one-room apartment with bath to $7,500 for an eighteen-room apartment with three bathrooms, and four toilets. Stokes and his son, Weddy, lived in a sprawling, sixteenth-floor apartment. In 1910, fourteen-year-old Weddy had a workroom that was a tangle of expensive radio apparatus. This was the club room and experimental station of Weddy's Junior Wireless Club. The boy had already been granted patents on several electrical devices, and he had just led a delegation to a Senate committee hearing to speak in opposition to the Depew Bill for the regulation of radio and communication, which Weddy maintained would have monopolized the air for professional wireless companies. During the interview with a *Times* reporter, Weddy was riding his bicycle through the hall, navigating between the gilt chairs and carved furniture.

The St. Urban Apartments

**285 Central Park West, southwest corner of
89th Street
1906**
BUILDER: Peter Banner
ARCHITECT: Robert L. Lyons

Real-estate speculators were usually either noted millionaires who could afford to tie up their capital while awaiting hoped-for returns, or professional operators who bought as a corporate body what they could not afford individually. Peter Banner was neither. An importer of linens, Banner lived in the Hotel Majestic, and no doubt his environs sparked the desire to build a luxurious apartment house. In 1903, he bought the key 125-by-100-foot lot on the southwest corner of Central Park West at 89th Street for $450,000 from

a real-estate company that had purchased the site about eighteen months before for only $180,000. Banner wanted to get in on the boom. He took a building loan of $850,000 from the Metropolitan Life Insurance Company and hired architect Robert L. Lyons to design a fireproof apartment house. The result was the 12-story St. Urban, which is distinguished on the Central Park West skyline by its single tower. At street level, it is distinguished by the city's grandest Beaux-Arts porte cochere.

Despite its name, the St. Urban is hardly filled with monastic cells. All 47 apartments contained eleven rooms and three baths, laid out so that the servants' rooms and kitchens were sequestered from the living quarters. By the spring of 1906, Banner had rented at least two apartments on long-term leases at good rates—$3,500 a year for a ninth-floor apartment, for instance—but neither his salesmanship nor his cash reserve was good enough. Banner had bought the southwest corner of 90th Street and Central Park West in 1904 for $150,000 as a speculation, and his finances were too thinly spread out. By the summer of 1906, he could not meet his mortgage payments on the St. Urban. Metropolitan Life foreclosed, and Banner disappeared as mysteriously as he had surfaced. The house was sold for $1,130,000 to Albert Forsch, who in turn sold it to the Barstum Realty Company.

Despite the claim that only a few apartments remained, Barstum went to the expense of publishing a two-color prospectus on coated stock to attract clients to the St. Urban. The landlord's inducements included electricity in the rent, artificial refrigeration in all apartments and full-length mirrors in all bathrooms. The rents were what Banner had been asking, ranging from $3,000 to $4,000 a year.

255

255. Speculator Peter Banner started the St. Urban Apartments on a weak financial foundation, and it gave way. Before the apartment house was finished, Banner was bankrupt and had to sell out.

256. Architect Robert T. Lyons designed the city's grandest Beaux-Arts porte cochère for the St. Urban. No doubt the driveway was capacious enough for hansom cabs, but today's automobiles have a tough time maneuvering in the tight spaces, and the driveway has been roped off.

256

The Apthorp Apartments

**390 West End Avenue, occupying the block to
Broadway between 78th and 79th Streets**
1908
BUILDER: The Astor Estate
ARCHITECTS: Clinton & Russell

Unlike the St. Urban, which was built by an almost anonymous speculator, the Apthorp Apartments were built by no less than the Astors, the city's premier family in real-estate affairs.

The 110 families in the Apthorp lived in fireproof splendor in a 12-story building on a site that measured 204 by 208 feet. The apartments were light and airy and large, with drawing rooms that measured 17 by 28 feet and dining rooms that were 16 by 24 feet, larger than the corresponding rooms in most twenty-foot-wide rowhouses. The decoration in the apartments showed great diversity, running the gamut from Elizabethan to Adams to Colonial, from Francis I to Louis XVI, with Louis XIV and XV thrown in for good measure. A design breakthrough included radiators behind wainscoting under windowsills, ice-making machines in kitchens, and mail chutes on landings so that tenants would not have to walk further than ten feet from their front door to mail a letter. If a tenant had more houseguests than his apartment could comfortably accommodate, guest rooms on the twelfth floor were provided (service was included, linens were not), and there was a rooftop pergola for spectacular views of the city.

Despite all the obvious luxury, the Apthorp was deemed a tenement house, which was defined as any multi-unit dwelling for three or more families, and it failed one of the conditions of the recently revised tenement house law—all tenement houses that extended from street to street had to have a twelve-foot-wide yard through the middle of the block. The Apthorp had an ample interior court whereby light and air were denied to no resident, but the architects had failed to provide the requisite twelve-foot opening. The tenement house commission acknowledged that the failure was a technicality, but the law was the law, and work on the building was held up for two years until the Astors could wrangle an amendment.

257. Great porte cochères in the Baroque manner lead to the interior courtyard of the Apthorp Apartments, designed by Clinton & Russell for the Astor Estate. Despite the luxuries that were scheduled for the twelve-story apartment house, the plans failed to comply with one of the provisions of the Tenement House Law.

PARLOR 15'-6"X19'-9" | DINING ROOM 14'-5"X19'-6" | KITCHEN 10'-6"X15'-3" | SERVANTS BEDROOM | SERVANTS BEDROOM | PARLOR 17'-8"X23'-9" | DINING-ROOM 17'-0"X23'-9" | SERVANTS BEDROOM | KITCHEN 10'-6"X15'-6" | SERVANTS BEDROOM | KITCHEN 10'-5"X15'-4" | DINING-ROOM 15'-0"X20'-0" | PARLOR 15'-6"X14'-0"

E FOYER 14'-5"X16'-3" | F FOYER 15'-9"X12'-9" | H FOYER 14'-9"X16'-4"

BEDROOM 15'-6"X14'-6" | BEDROOM 17'-9"X22'-5" | BEDROOM 15'-6"X22'-3" | BEDROOM 16'-3"X15'-9" | BEDROOM 15'-6"X22'-3" | BEDROOM 13'-9"X15'-0"

TOILET | MAIN-HALL | LIBRARY 11'-5"X15'-9" | MAIN-HALL | BEDROOM 16'-0"X14'-6"

BEDROOM 15'-6"X14'-3" | FOYER 10'-0"X22'-3" | BEDROOM 16'-0"X16'-0" | J FOYER 15'-6"X15'-6" | LIBRARY 15'-0"X16'-0" | BEDROOM 17'-5"X10'-9"

BEDROOM 17'-0"X9'-6"

DINING-ROOM 20'-0"X14'-9" | PARLOR 21'-0"X15'-0" | PARLOR 21'-0"X14'-9" | DINING-ROOM 21'-0"X16'-0"

THE APTHORP

BEDROOM 18'-0"X12'-6" | BEDROOM 16'-6"X16'-8" | BEDROOM 21'-0"X12'-3" | SERVANTS BEDROOM

TOILET | SERV ELEV | KITCHEN 16'-5"X11'-0" | KITCHEN 20'-3"X11'-9"

BEDROOM 14'-3"X11'-0" | SERVANTS BEDROOM | BEDROOM 19'-6"X10'-6" | SERVANTS BEDROOM

BEDROOM 14'-3"X11'-6" | SERVANT'S BEDROOM | 95' | SERVANT'S HALL

KITCHEN 20'-6"X10'-3" | SERV ELEV | LINEN | KITCHEN 15'-3"X16'-6"

BEDROOM 26'-0"X13'-0" | SERVANTS BEDROOM | BEDROOM 14'-0"X16'-9" | BEDROOM 21'-3"X16'-6" | BEDROOM 15'-3"X10'-3"

PARLOR 24'-0"X16'-6" | DINING-ROOM 18'-6"X16'-6" | PARLOR 20'-6"X15'-3" | DINING-ROOM 21'-0"X15'-3"

C FOYER 9'-6"X26'-6" | BEDROOM 16'-3"X16'-9" | BEDROOM 15'-0"X15'-0" | FOYER 11'-0"X21'-6" | BEDROOM 21'-0"X16'-3"

BEDROOM 11'-8"X15'-0" | K | BEDROOM 15'-0"X14'-0"

B FOYER 14'-6"X14'-6" | MAIN-HALL | LIBRARY 14'-3"X17'-0" | BEDROOM 15'-0"X21'-9" | BEDROOM 10'-6"X21'-9" | BEDROOM 16'-3"X15'-9" | BEDROOM 14'-6"X21'-9" | MAIN-HALL | FOYER 16'-0"X15'-6" | L

BEDROOM 15'-5"X16'-0" | A FOYER 15'-0"X14'-6" | LINEN | BEDROOM 15'-0"X15'-0"

PANTRY | SERVANTS HALL | PANTRY

PARLOR 15'-6"X20'-0" | DINING-ROOM 15'-5"X26'-6" | KITCHEN | SERVANTS BEDROOM | PARLOR 14'-3"X23'-9" | DINING-ROOM 16'-3"X23'-9" | SERVANTS BEDROOM | KITCHEN 16'-6"X21'-4" | SERVANTS BEDROOM | KITCHEN | SERVANTS BEDROOM | DINING-ROOM 15'-6"X22'-0" | PARLOR 15'-0"X21'-4"

259

260

Clinton & Russell's design merges the High Renaissance with the Early Baroque. A grand porte cochere leads to the courtyard, where the elevators are located in the four corners. Marble was used for the walls of the first-floor stair halls, and Caen stone was used for the corridors above. Limestone was used to surface all the outside walls, including the courtyard walls. It was said to be the city's largest apartment house, and with all its luxurious trappings and generous proportions, one of its most successful. Two months before the building was ready for occupancy, almost all of its seven duplexes were rented and two-thirds of its simplexes were taken, with rents up to $6,500 a year.

The Apthorp was built on a piece of property the Astor family had held since 1860, when William Backhouse Astor,

258. The floor plan for the Apthorp shows its imaginative design and the logical flow. Deluxe living quarters for families and generous spaces for servants met standards that more than satisfied the Tenement House Commission.

259. The logic of the design and the luxury of space contribute to make the apartments at the Apthorp simply splendid. Through the double doors from the parlor is seen this apartment's entrance foyer, which is laid in tile; the front door is glass, so natural light enters by way of the strategically placed window on the floor landing.

260. The passenger elevators were placed in the four corners of the Apthorp's courtyard and are reached by passing between the flanking torchères and under the marquise. Each elevator served fewer than thirty apartments.

261

John Jacob Astor's son, bought a farm for $16,875 that was in the then-village of Bloomingdale, the future Upper West Side. Astors did not like paying taxes on undeveloped property, but they did not mind holding onto property if they suspected its value would increase. In 1904, the IRT opened, which opened upper Broadway for development. And the Astors were ready. In 1905, Astor property included the west side of Broadway between 76th and 77th streets, the Apthorp block, the four blocks between West End and Amsterdam avenues from 90th to 91st streets and 92nd to 93rd streets, as well as the southwest corner of Broadway and 95th Street. The valuation of their property on the Upper West Side by then stood at about $10 million.

The Strathmore Apartments

404 Riverside Drive, on the southeast corner of 113th Street
1909
BUILDER: Akron Building Company
ARCHITECTS: Schwartz & Gross

In 1887, William Waldorf Astor joined other real-estate investors who were buying upper Riverside Drive property. C. P. Huntington had just bought the blockfront between 111th and 112th streets, and the Goelets had already purchased the blockfront between 114th and 115th streets when Astor bought thirteen Riverside lots that gave him a depth of 142 feet on 112th and 195 feet on 113th. Unlike his peers, he was considering the site for a mansion, but he settled on Fifth Avenue and 56th Street instead, and with his disillu-

sionment with all things American and his subsequent move to Great Britain, he never developed the property.

Steelman Charles M. Schwab became interested in the property when he was seeking a residential site at the turn of the century, but he could not come to terms with the Astor Estate. With the coming of the subway, however, the estate's inflated demands seemed justified to speculators, and in 1908, the 104-by-119-foot parcel on the southeast corner of 113th Street was sold for $95,000 to the Realty Equipment Company, who turned around and sold it to the Akron Building Company the same week. Architects Schwartz & Gross were then hired to design a $300,000, twelve-story apartment house that was given a swell-sounding name, The Strathmore.

Schwartz & Gross designed several apartment houses on the West Side, including the bow-fronted pair on the corners of 116th Street and Riverside. The firm's early apartment houses were ordinarily encumbered by heavy decoration in a style that was described as Renaissance. None of the designs had quite the style of The Strathmore, with its great marquee over the entrance, its torchères, and even its neoclassical cornice. The fireproof Strathmore consisted of only two apartments to a floor. Each one had ten rooms, three baths, fourteen closets, and separate servants' quarters. Rents ranged from $2,500 to $3,900 a year, with Bing & Bing acting as the managing agents. The Strathmore's south wall, which bore the remains of a painted sign advertising apartments until the early 1980s, attested to the rental agents' efforts.

Within a few years of the Strathmore's appearance, many sites that had been sitting idle were being developed to their maximum potential. In 1914, the *Times* reported that the oldest inhabitants of the West Side could hardly remember when the west side of Amsterdam Avenue between 92nd and 93rd street was not occupied by a half dozen of the "most diminutive suburban type of cheap wooden buildings." The site, whose value had skyrocketed, was being cleared for development. It was owned by absentee-landlord William Waldorf Astor.

---

261. Architects Clinton & Russell designed several apartment houses for the Astor Estate, including the Astor Apartments and the Clinton Court Apartments, but their detailings for the Apthorp reign supreme. These double doors, when swung open, dramatically link the parlor and foyer.

262. The Astor Estate seldom sold its property, but if it did, as in the case of 404 Riverside Drive, the reason was generally that some outside force had raised property values. On the Upper West Side the force was the coming of the subway, which opened the neighborhood for high-class development, as characterized by Schwartz & Gross's design for the Strathmore.

262

263. *The National Academy of Design planned to move to Morningside Heights in the 1890s and join the new Acropolis of New York. A competition was held for the proposed building on Amsterdam Avenue and 110th Street, which was won by Carrère & Hastings with this neoclassical design. The academy never raised enough funds and the building was never started.*

13

Seth Low's West Side

ities have their edges, places where vital functions are performed that might offend the sensibilities of the average citizen. The functions are not necessarily confined to industries that create noxious odors, like tanning, or unpleasant wastes, like abbatoirs. They can be reminders of failures within the social system, like the insane or the orphaned, people whom society feels a need to aid and succor, but not to flaunt. Through covenants or "gentlemen's agreements" or concern for basic economics, these functions are normally sequestered, shielding the citizenry from discomfort.

Morningside Heights was comfortably removed from the urban mainstream in the mid-nineteenth century. The Bloomingdale Insane Asylum was at Broadway and 116th Street, and the Leake & Watts Orphanage was on Amsterdam Avenue at 112th. By the 1890s, with the increasing crush of northbound population, these institutions began to be forced out, and institutions that were more easily socially integrated took their place. The Cathedral of St. John the Divine moved to the Leake & Watts property in 1891; in 1896, St. Luke's Hospital moved to Morningside Drive between 112th and 113th streets; and in 1897, Columbia University moved to the site of the Bloomingdale Asylum, which caused the neighborhood on the bluff overlooking the Harlem Valley to be dubbed the Acropolis of New York. In 1897, when the National Academy of Design announced its imminent arrival, the neighborhood was about to add one more feather to its cultural cap.

The National Academy of Design was founded in 1825 by a group of painters that included Samuel F. B. Morse, Henry Inman, Asher B. Durand, and Thomas Cole. Their goal was to establish an art school and to hold exhibitions of contemporary work. By the end of the nineteenth century, the Academy had become the American answer to the Royal Academy, the Paris Salon, and the Ecole des Beaux-Arts.

In 1896, Columbia proposed the merger of the academy into Professor William R. Ware's nascent School of Architecture. The academy declined the offer because it wanted to retain its identity, but it liked the idea of being near to Columbia, so the academy bought the site on the east side of Amsterdam Avenue between 109th and 110th streets for $245,000. It was hardly a fashionable spot. One hundred and tenth Street between Amsterdam Avenue and Broadway was filled with old wooden houses, groggeries, and summer beer gardens, earning the stretch the name "Little Coney Island."

Despite the unprepossessing site, an architectural competition attracted Ernest Flagg, Edward P. Casey, and Babb, Cook & Willard in 1898. All their proposals lived up to the Beaux-Arts ideal of incorporating statuary as an integral element in neoclassical design, as did the winning plan by Carrère & Hastings (both John Carrère and Thomas Hastings had been elected members of the academy, which entitled them to add "N. A." after their names).

A year later, plans for construction were postponed because the academy had less than $300,000 for a building that was scheduled to cost about $400,000. As a stopgap, Carrère & Hastings designed a $22,000, two-story building that was only big enough to hold art classes. Since the academy had already sold its site on Fourth Avenue and 23rd Street to Metropolitan Life, it had no place left for exhibitions, forcing it to use outside galleries such as the American Fine Arts Society. The winning design by Carrère & Hastings never was built, nor was the Lenox Library re-erected for the academy's use, despite the best intentions of some (see Chapter X). Classes were given in the "temporary" building until 1940, when the academy moved to its present home at 1083 Fifth Avenue, the gift of Archer M. Huntington.

The General Grant National Memorial

Riverside Drive at 122nd Street
1897
Builder: Grant Monument Association
Architect: John H. Duncan

The death of Ulysses S. Grant in 1885 set off a scramble among several states and the District of Columbia for the honor of erecting Grant's tomb within its borders. Ohio wanted its native son. Illinois wanted its adopted son. And the nation's capital wanted Grant's final resting place either in the district or on the slopes of Arlington. Grant himself had favored New York City, where he had retired after his presidency to write his memoirs. New Yorkers, he said, had befriended him in his need.

Within 24 hours of Grant's death, Mayor William R. Grace proffered the family a choice of two sites in Central Park or atop the bluff on Riverside Drive at 122nd Street. The mayor preferred the Riverside site, and if Mrs. Grant agreed to it he promised to have the name changed to Grant Park and have the Claremont Inn demolished, which would open the vista from the north.

The same day, Grace created a committee to collect funds for the proposed tomb, with former President Chester A.

Arthur as the committee's chairman, J. Pierpont Morgan as treasurer, and a whole host of politicians and socialites serving as members. The announced goal was $1 million, and within a month the energetic committee had $50,000. The flow of contributions that sprang so strongly in the summer slowed down to a trickle by the fall, and imaginative fund-raising gimmicks hardly made a dent in the apathy. In December 1886, the Republican magazine *Judge* announced a competition on word gaming, where as many words as possible were made from the letters of a sentence. Competitors were asked to send a 50-cent entry fee, half of which went to the fund, the other half to a pool for the prizes. The sentence was, "Who will be our next President?" In 1887, the Gilbert Manufacturing Company offered to change the name of one its best-selling lines of cloth to Grant Memorial Twill and donate the profits from its sales. If one woman in three bought enough material for a dress lining, the firm calculated that a million dollars would be raised. The Remington Standard Typewriter Company challenged all other typewriter manufacturers to a contest to determine who produced the superior machine. Each entrant would put $1,000 in the kitty with $500 going to the operators and the balance to the fund. One idea that did make some money was the removal of the collected funds from Morgan's bank, which did not pay interest on deposits, to banks that paid three percent.

One obstruction to donor enthusiasm was the lack of any concrete plans for the tomb. A design committee had been appointed as early as November 1885, but no competition was held until the summer of 1888, and it was open to anybody. The only guidelines were that the design combine sculpture with architecture, that ideally the monument be granite, and that it cost no more than $500,000, a figure that reflected the committee's despair of ever raising $1 million. The judges announced that three thousand artists, sculptors and architects had entered plans and that "commonplace" was the only word to describe the design of the grand-prize winner, Cluss & Schultze. Not one of the designs was worthy of execution, and the judges convinced the committee to pay off the winners and start all over again, this time with a field limited to professionals of high standing.

This was not to be another "open" competition with amateurs working for the glory of the cause, but strictly a cash deal with detailed plans for a set fee. A lay committee was selected to make the final selections from designs

264. If John Duncan's plans for the Grant Monument had been completed, there would have been a colossal equestrian statue of General Grant in front of it, four statues atop the portico, and a quadriga crowning the cone. The overall effect would have been more akin to the tomb of Mausolus at Halicarnassus, which was the architect's model.

submitted by Carrère & Hastings, Charles W. Clinton, Napoleon LeBrun, John H. Duncan, and little-known John Ord. All five submissions were considered worthy of execution, with four said to be based on either the Pantheon in Rome or Les Invalides in Paris. Winner John Duncan's submission was described as a variation on Les Invalides, but its roots were firmly planted in the tomb of Mausolus at Halicarnassus.

Duncan's design called for a cubic base supporting a cylinder surmounted by a cone. The bronze statuary would include an equestrian of Grant in front of the tomb, four equestrians representing the principal armies under Grant's command to crown the portico, a group atop the base, and a quadriga to top the cone. The bronze statues would provide depth and color to the tomb, and the equestrian statues explain why the wall above the portico is high and plain—it was merely a backdrop, a foil against which the statues would be displayed. Duncan placed the tomb facing south, so it commanded Riverside Drive. And because the tomb stood atop a bluff, with the Hudson River below, he designed a monumental stairway that adroitly bridged the exposed railroad tracks on the shoreline, creating a grand entrance from the river bank. The committee especially appreciated Duncan's pragmatism. He stipulated that his design could be built in stages, that for $150,000 the lower part of the tomb could be constructed and stand well enough on its own, that the cylinder and cone and statuary and riverfront stairway could be added as the money was raised.

The combination of a highly praised design in 1890 and the appointment of General Horace Porter as the president of the Grant Monument Association two years later saved the city from the disgrace of failing to provide the long-promised tomb. Porter, a West Point graduate, was a brigadier at twenty-seven, Grant's aide-de-camp in the Civil War, and his executive secretary at the White House. He became a vice-president of Pullman and president of the West Shore Railroad, then president of the Metropolitan Elevated Line in New York City, where he invented the ticket chopper used on the IRT's elevated and subway lines for years. He organized the official festivities for the Washington Centenary, was ranked as an after-dinner speaker with Chauncey Depew, whom he succeeded as Union Club president in 1893, and he was a formidable fund raiser. Porter created about 200 auxiliary committees, whose members passed subscription books. He arranged for contribution boxes to be placed throughout the city and in elevated stations. He gave souvenir certificates to contributors of 50 cents or more, having arranged with the Bureau of Printing and Engraving to produce a medallion head of Grant for use on the certificates. He inveigled Western Union into giving free use of its wires to anyone making a contribution to the fund. He wheedled money out of board rooms and club rooms, even out of lodging houses. In his first sixty days, Porter raised $350,000, enough for the tomb to be built to the cone.

In 1897, the Grant Monument Association was ready to present the mausoleum to the city, and Porter was prophesying that the dedicatory ceremonies would exceed in magnificence the ceremonies that attended the removal of the body of Napoleon from St. Helena to Les Invalides in Paris. An international parade of ships extended from Red Hook, Brooklyn, up the harbor and Hudson as far as the tomb, and nearly 60,000 soldiers and civilians paraded the city streets. Clubs, societies, and churches erected stands along the route, but the few stands that were open to the public fell into the hands of speculators, who charged as much as $25 for a seat near the tomb. One speculator rented vacant houses along the route of the parade and sublet them for the day for as much as $400 apiece.

President McKinley and Vice-President Hobart attended the ceremonies in the dignitaries' reviewing stand with fifteen governors, a host of mayors, generals, admirals, federal and state legislators, and anyone else who could wangle a seat. Tubs filled with long-stemmed American Beauty roses flanked the route by the tomb, and north of it was a temporary memorial arch. An estimated one million spectators were on hand.

When the official ceremonies were over, a dinner honoring Mrs. McKinley and the wives of several cabinet members was given at the Windsor Hotel. The dinner began at eight and ended at ten, and there were no postprandial speeches. The same evening, the Union League Club was host to about 1,000 gentlemen guests, including the president, the vice-president, the secretary of state, the secretary of war, twenty senators, eight governors, and three university presidents. Each guest of honor was escorted by a club member—President McKinley by club president Porter; the British Ambassador, Sir Julian Pauncefote, by former club president Chauncy Depew, and so on, while three bands played on.

The basic tomb had been built in its entirety, but, with the exception of the relief figures by J. Massey Rhind that flank the plaque on the portico, it was bereft of statuary. The Municipal Art Society pledged that it would raise the funds to complete the statuary and provide the panache and the symbolism of the original elevations. Ironically, the statuary was never set in place since sentiment had shifted to the belief that the monument should not portray Grant as a military man but as a statesman and that the statuary should signify a reconciliation betweeen North and South. Since the planned statuary was martial in spirit, the money was never raised and the tomb remains barren.

265. There is no escaping the chill produced by Duncan's hard-edged neoclassicism. The tomb's interior plan is similar to that of Les Invalides, where Napoleon is buried.

Columbia University in the City of New York

114th to 120th Streets, Broadway to Amsterdam Avenue
1897
BUILDER: Columbia University
ARCHITECTS: McKim, Mead & White

Six months after the dedication of Grant's Tomb, Morningside Heights's single-most important institution, Columbia University, moved to the neighborhood. In the 1850s, Columbia College's campus was in the heart of the built-up city, between Barclay and Murray streets west of Church Street. A new campus was proposed on the site of the former Elgin Gardens, a plot of land between Fifth and Sixth avenues from 47th to 51st streets that had come into Columbia's possession, and Richard Upjohn was asked to design the extensive project. As a temporary expedient, the college bought the neighboring Deaf and Dumb Asylum on the block bounded by Park and Madison avenues, 49th and 50th streets, and moved there in 1857. With the city's northward migration of population, the Elgin Garden site became so valuable that the college never developed Upjohn's plans for the property, but chose instead to rent the property.

In 1890, Columbia had a new president in Seth Low (Columbia class of 1870). By the time Low was forty, he had operated the family tea- and silk-importing business and had served two terms as mayor of the City of Brooklyn, once as an Independent and once as a Republican. At the time, the college was only beginning to develop its graduate departments, but Low was dreaming of a great urban university, which he called Columbia University in the City of New York, and at his instigation, a committee was formed to find a suitable site for his dream. They found a 17.5 acre site between Broadway and Amsterdam Avenue, from 114th to 120th streets. The price was $2 million, but the college only had $315,000.

Fortunately, the college was land rich. Some of the original campus in Lower Manhattan had been sold to finance the Madison Avenue campus, but the residual property of the quaintly named Lower Estate still brought annual rentals of $110,000 in 1892. The Upper Estate, or the Elgin Gardens, brought in $276,000. Low knew that Columbia had financed its growth and development by selling and leasing its land, and he understood that Columbia would be able to finance any future expansion by long-term corporate borrowing, using the estates and its midtown campus as security.

Low sent a letter to architects Charles Coolidge Haight, Richard Morris Hunt, and Charles Follen McKim asking them to work together on a comprehensive plan. Instead of a joint proposal, each architect submitted his own. Haight's design reflected the image of the simple, cloistered academic life. Hunt's had a courtyard and auxiliary wings in the tradition of a grand French plan. McKim conceived of a series of interconnected courtyards, and, taking the natural topography into account, he designed the campus on different planes, or platforms, with the main approach from the south and secondary approaches from the east and west. His style called for "pure classical forms expressing in the simplest and most monumental way the purposes to which the buildings are devoted."

Asked to comment on the plans were Columbia's professor William R. Ware and landscape architect Frederick Law Olmsted. McKim wrote to Ware that the design of the

265

campus was a glorious opportunity; the trick was to grasp it. Ware and Olmsted felt that he had, and Low concurred. They rejected both Haight's and Hunt's designs and suggested a classical style that was freer than McKim's recom-

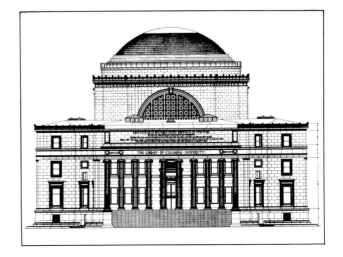

266. Columbia University's Low Library was clad entirely in limestone. The design is civic in nature, rather than institutional or even academic.

267. Real-estate holdings in Midtown and Lower Manhattan gave Columbia the collateral to move to Morningside Heights. President Seth Low knew that to raise more money required a show of financial strength, so he contributed the funds for the campus's focal building, the library.

269

mendation, because "a severe and classical style would require a greater uniformity and treatment." (Reading between the lines, donors might not be willing to contribute money for a building if one looked like every other.) "The creation of the platforms [is] a work of genius," Low wrote to McKim. "This will be seen to remove the plan out of the region of the commonplace, and to stamp the conception as one of those happy suggestions by which the artist makes whole communities his debtor." In 1894, a unanimous building committee approved McKim's recommendation and his image of "municipal classic."

The ambitious goal called for the college to occupy the site by 1897, which did not allow enough time to implement the grand plan. As a stopgap, some of the Bloomingdale Asylum buildings would be refurbished at a cost of $100,000. Guidelines for the buildings were laid out by McKim, Mead & White, but the firm did not design all of the first wave of Columbia's buildings. Howells & Stokes, for instance, designed St. Paul's Chapel, and Arnold Brunner designed the School of Mines. According to Low, the first building placed upon the new site would condition all that were to follow, first by its situation, second by its architecture. It would be the heart of the university and set

the tone of the buildings to follow, and it would be designed by McKim. It would be the library.

By holding the carrot of Columbia's future as a major university, Low was betting on attracting benefactors. The college had already been the recipient of enviable presents, from Trinity Church's gift of the first campus to the gift in 1890 of $30,000 and books on art and architecture from Samuel P. Avery, a collection that quickly grew to become the nation's premier architectural library. In 1892, contributions for the Morningside Heights campus included

---

268. The library is the heart of any university, but Seth Low wanted Low Library to be the symbolic heart as well. The floor of the rotunda was originally the main reading room, and there were tables set in concentric rings.

269. The floor plan for Low Library referred to the Trustees Room as the Business Office, which is probably closer to the mark, considering the business of trustees. This room has suffered some improvements—a few objects have been removed and portraits added, the chandelier is new and the table is not original—but otherwise it is pristine.

$5,000 apiece from Abram S. Hewitt, Samuel D. Babcock, Joseph Schiff, Oswald Ottendorfer, and Seth Low himself, $10,000 from R. Fulton Cutting, $200,000 for a building from Daniel B. Fayerweather, and $300,000 from William C. Schermerhorn for another building. The library, however, with a preliminary price tag of $750,000, was the main concern. To ensure that work on the university began properly, a contributor came forward with $1 million.

The donor was Seth Low, and this second gift was in memory of his father, Abiel Abbot Low, "a merchant who taught his son to value the things for which Columbia stands." The million dollars represented about a third of Low's personal fortune, no mean fraction to give away (only four American philanthropists—Peter Cooper, Daniel K. Pearsons, George Peabody, and Leland Stanford—had given away a like proportion while still alive).

The library became even more important than originally planned; its limestone facade stands out from the brick and stone-trimmed buildings, and its design conveys a civic rather than an academic image. It is flanked by urns and fountains and terraces, and is approached by a flight of stairs with a slight upward curve, giving it a virtually imperceptible bowed effect. McKim, who was the first to use Greek horizontal curves on a broad scale in modern design, said that the curves were "intended to counteract the apparent deflection in horizontal surfaces and lines of great extent." McKim considered the slight upward tendency beneficial above and beyond the physical, "conducing . . . to draw the eye towards the library, as the center of interest. . . . The intention [was] that the curvature should be felt rather than apprehended, as in the Parthenon and other classic buildings."

The plan for Low Library was a Greek cross. In the first arm were the grand entrance, the trustees' room, and the president's office. Two specialty libraries—Avery architectural and law—each had its own arm, and the catalog and delivery room were in the fourth arm. Under the dome on the main floor was the main reading room, as grand an interior space as the Library of Congress or the British Museum. And like those libraries, the reading tables were set in concentric rings. The second floor housed seminar rooms, the third floor held lecture halls, and everywhere there were books, even in the basement, where the rare books were housed in a vault.

Low's magnanimity might have been spurred by an ulterior motive. He was being courted to run for mayor in 1895, and the gift of the library was regarded as a means of establishing his public image and a start to a fund-raising campaign. (He won the mayorality on the Fusion ticket in 1901). Ironically, Low Library was considered a failure as a library and has been used for administration purposes since 1934, when Butler Library replaced it. Nevertheless, Low Library reigns supreme as the flagship building of Columbia University.

270

Alma Mater

On the Steps of Low Library, 116th Street between Broadway and Amsterdam Avenue
1903
DONOR: Mrs. Robert Goelet
SCULPTOR: Daniel Chester French
ARCHITECT: Charles Follen McKim

Classicist McKim naturally included plans for statuary in his grand scheme for Columbia, and in his mind's eye the most obvious place for a major statue was on the steps of Low Library. In 1900, Mrs. Robert Goelet, the sister of architect Whitney Warren, announced that she wanted to donate a sculpture group to Columbia in memory of her

270. Avery Hall houses Columbia's great architectural library. Its brick facade and limestone trim make it, like the university's other buildings, subordinate to the grandeur of Low Library.

271. Daniel Chester French's *Alma Mater* carries the crowned scepter as a symbol of Kings College, Columbia's pre-Revolutionary War name. The statue serves to animate McKim's grand scheme for Low Library, and has come to symbolize this great urban university.

husband, Robert, a Columbia alumnus. Her husband's estate was set at about $60 million in 1899, of which she was left the mansion at 591 Fifth Avenue and a $200,000 annuity. She was willing to spend about $25,000 on a statue, which prompted McKim to urge that a single figure on the site was more appropriate than a sculpture group, and he suggested that the job be given to Daniel Chester French, upon whom the establishment was showering commissions. McKim himself would design the plinth.

Mrs. Goelet was not convinced. McKim showed her a model of the statue that French had in mind, which was an idealization of the university's seal. McKim was sure that he had advocated the right thing, but he later confessed that he had been "in some fear and trembling, feeling that upon Mr. French depended the final making or marring of the whole composition of the court and the library. . . . I can only say that I was greatly delighted and relieved to find in Mr. French's creation a figure dignified, classic and stately." Mrs. Goelet agreed, Seth Low agreed, the Library Building Committee and the Committee on Art agreed, the trustees unanimously approved, and French went to work. The only dissenting voice was that of Fernando Miranda, the president of the American Sculpture Society (not to be confused with the National Sculpture Society), who complained about the principle of allowing architects to award contracts to the sculptors they favored.

After the gold-leaf-plated bronze was unveiled in 1903, it did not make a "ripple on the surface of New York," French wrote to his brother. "I have not seen a notice of any kind." What French had no way of knowing then is that *Alma Mater* caught the essence of what he was seeking, a gracious figure "with an attitude of welcome," and it has become the very symbol of Columbia University in the City of New York.

Congregation Shearith Israel

99 Central Park West, southwest corner of 70th Street
1897
BUILDER: Congregation Shearith Israel
ARCHITECT: Arnold W. Brunner

In 1893, Congregation Shearith Israel, the oldest Jewish congregation in America, was offered $170,000 for its 75-by-92-foot plot at 5 West 18th Street where its neo-Baroque synagogue had stood since 1860. Although the Panic of 1893 had forced down prices in general, they were on the rise in the increasingly commercial neighborhood. The congregation held out for $200,000, and in 1894 they got it.

For a new site, the congregation looked uptown, nearer

272

the homes of its congregants, among whom were poet Emma Lazarus and Justice Benjamin N. Cardozo. In 1895, a 100-by-125-foot site on Central Park West was bought for $140,000, and Arnold W. Brunner was asked to design a $250,000 limestone synagogue for the site. Brunner had recently designed Temple Beth El and Temple Shaaray Tefile in a style that combined elements of the Romanesque and Byzantine, which at least hinted at the Levant and ostensibly bore the patina of age. For the face of Shearith Israel, Brunner designed a great triumphal arch in the Corinthian order. The Sephardic congregation had a predilection for classical forms, and in 1907 Brunner stated his own preference for the style. The Palestine Exploration Fund had been investigating the remains of Greco-Roman synagogues in Galilee, and Brunner said that the classical form "perpetuates the best traditions of Jewish art and takes up a thread, which was broken by circumstances, of a vigorous and once healthy style." The neoclassicism of the Chicago World's Fair was also fresh in his mind, of course, and fresher still was McKim's neoclassicism at Columbia for which Brunner had designed the School of Mines.

272. Architect Arnold Brunner designed a synagogue for Congregation Shearith Israel that is reminiscent of a great Roman triumphal arch. The neoclassical form was perfectly appropriate, since synagogues built in Greco-Roman times were in the style of that day. Ten years after this synagogue was built, Brunner designed one for a Newark congregation that is remarkably similar.

273. Shearith Israel means "Remnant of Israel," and this Sephardic congregation took its name seriously and maintained its conservatism. The interior fittings of the synagogue are splendid, with ornamental windows and decorations supplied by the Tiffany Studios.

Soldiers' and Sailors' Monument

Riverside Drive at 89th Street
1902
BUILDER: The City of New York
ARCHITECTS: Arthur A. and Charles W. Stoughton
SCULPTOR: Paul E. Duboy

In 1869, with the Civil War still a vivid memory for New Yorkers, an attempt was made to erect a monument to honor New York's 12,215 war dead, but it took until 1893 before the state legislature appropriated $250,000, and no action was taken until one of the few good sites for a monument was threatened by a mediocre statue. The site was the Plaza at Fifth Avenue and 59th Street and the subject was the German poet Heinrich Heine. The sculptor, Ernst Herter, was hardly known, and architectural critic Russell Sturgis said that the $35,000 which was allocated "would buy a small and unnoticeable thing." With the exception of the city's few parks and squares and the open spaces created by Broadway, New York's right-angled grid system provided few sites where a monument could be placed advantageously, and Sturgis feared that the few good places would be filled with inferior work before the period's great sculptors had a chance at them. He said that the best thing for the Plaza was the proposed Soldiers' and Sailors' Monument.

In the interest of their membership, the National Sculpture Society and Architectural League set out to see that the appropriation was spent. A mayor's committee determined that the Plaza would be the site, and stipulated that the form was to be a granite shaft with suitable bronze figures adorning it. Of course, the municipality had to deal with the public. One hundred naval officers petitioned against the Plaza because it was not in sight of water. The Federation of Fine Arts claimed that any monument at the Plaza would be dwarfed by the tall buildings that were already there. Upper West Siders advocated Riverside Drive at 72nd Street, which would certainly placate the naval officers. More importantly, with Grant's Tomb at the northern end of the drive, the Soldiers' and Sailors' Monument would anchor the southern end and make Riverside Drive a parade ground commemorating the most memorable military event of the time. Mayor Strong, ignoring the brouhaha and acting on the suggestion of his advisors, reiterated his choice of the Plaza and asked architect Bruce Price to have seven teams of architects and sculptors submit plans by the fall of 1897, with the understanding that each would receive a $200 fee. Entries ranged from a replica of Rome's colosseum with a 125-foot shaft rising from its center to an L-shaped portal with three arches straddling roadways into the park and three more arches forming a pedestrian arcade, and with large groups of allegorical figures of Peace and War and Union and so forth atop it.

Judges Russell Sturgis, A. D. F. Hamlin, and Professor William R. Ware chose a terraced, 125-foot-high column designed by architects Arthur A. and Charles W. Stoughton; the column was to be capped by a heroic-sized statue of *Peace* by Frederick MacMonnies. Notably absent from the awards committee were J. Q. A. Ward, president of the National Sculpture Society, and Charles T. Barney, president of the Municipal Art Society, despite the 1896 law that stipulated that no work of art in the nature of a public monument or memorial could be erected on city property without the approval of both societies. The societies notified the city that any monument at the site had to be a component in the development of a comprehensive and artistic design for the approach to the park, and they vetoed the design at the Plaza. The sculpture society, however, liked the winning entry and would have approved it for a different site, such as Riverside Drive at 72nd Street.

Now the commission was stuck with an award-winning design that everyone liked, but nobody knew where to put it. Suggestions included Riverside Drive at 106th Street because the veterans were getting on, and the fifteen blocks from Grant's tomb was an easy march. The site of the Claremont Inn, a few hundred feet north of Grant's Tomb, was quickly vetoed by the National Sculpture Society because the effect of each monument would have been lessened by its proximity to the other.

In the fall of 1899, a site was agreed upon, and although there had been no new competition, a new design was accepted. The site was Riverside Drive at 83rd Street, and the design, at least, was the one that was finally built. The Stoughtons were the architects, but MacMonnies had been replaced by Paul E. Duboy. The terrace was similar to the original design, but the monument bore no resemblance to the lean column that had won the competition. In its place was a variation on the Choragic Monument of Lysicrates in Athens. Arthur Stoughton blithely based his right to redesign the monument on the fact that he and his brother had won the original competition fair and square over six competitors. He did not care that his winning submission had been for a different monument at a different site and that ethically a new competition should have been held. However, during the great site debate, a nine-story apartment house was built near the proposed site, which obstructed the "sought for" view, so once more the site was changed. The new site, and the monument's final resting place, was 89th Street, and on Memorial Day, 1902, Mayor Seth Low gave the keynote speech at the unveiling.

One disgruntled New Yorker wished that Low had succeeded Mayor Strong four years before, because then the "same judgement and artistic taste that selected the architects for a great library might be useful to Greater New York

in helping to provide it with a soldiers' monument that should be a dignified work of art." In this case, the city was lucky. Although the idea of reform and aesthetic standards does not appeal to all politicians, sometimes art muddles through.

274. The Stoughtons' final design for New York City's memorial to its Civil War dead was a variation on the Choragic Monument of Lysicrates in Athens. With its neoclassical landscaping, it was just the kind of architectural adornment that the City Beautiful movement advocated.

New-York Historical Society

New-York Historical Society
170 Central Park West, between 76th and 77th
Streets
1908
BUILDER: New-York Historical Society
ARCHITECTS: York & Sawyer

The New-York Historical Society, whose goal was to collect and preserve whatever related to the natural, civil, or ecclesiastical history of the nation in general and of the state in particular, was founded in 1804. By 1857, the society was occupying its seventh site, a two-story building on the southeast corner of Second Avenue and 11th Street, where it was suffering pains that are endemic to any institution that is successful in its quest for acquisitions—the building was capacious enough when it was first occupied, but its collection had grown until there was neither enough space to display it nor adequate room to store it. By 1890, the society had $250,000 in a site-acquisition fund but nothing in a building fund, and when a site on Central Park West was found in 1891 for $286,500, the society made the purchase. Corporation lawyer James W. Gerard said that not only was the price too high, so was the street, and members would seldom, if ever, venture that far north. The site's defenders said that when the society was looking for a new site in the 1850s, Union Square was deemed unacceptable because some members believed it was quite beyond the city's forseeable limits, so they settled on the neighborhood just south and east of it. Forty years later, fashionable New York had moved from the St. Marks area, and an immigrant population was moving in. The point was made.

The Panic of 1893 held up contributions to the building fund, and it was not until money men like J. Pierpont Morgan and George W. Vanderbilt were serving on the building committee in the late 1890s that funds began to be raised. In the meantime, some bizarre and unrealistic schemes were proposed. Mayor Thomas F. Gilroy offered City Hall, providing the society disassembled the building and moved it to the new site. The society's corresponding secretary, Edward F. DeLancey, politely informed the mayor that the society had "never proposed, asked for, or wished the removal of City Hall from City Hall Park, On the contrary," said DeLancey, "no doubt the voice of the membership would be to keep it where it is." Some members said that the society should turn a profit on its Central Park West site and buy the Lenox Library property. They assumed that the Central Park West site had appreciated at least $100,000 since its purchase, and the Second Avenue site was worth about $100,000, bringing the society's real-estate holdings to well over $450,000. The Lenox site, however, was out of sight at an estimated $1.75 million, and the

275

idea soon passed. By 1900, the society had determined to stay on the West Side and had raised enough money to begin the kind of building it wanted.

The architectural competition held in 1901 was won by York & Sawyer, a firm that had been created in 1898. Edward Palmer York and Philip Sawyer had been employed by McKim, Mead & White, until York was invited to enter a competition for a building at Vassar College. York had thought about the project but had not done his homework. The day before the deadline, he suggested that Sawyer should submit a drawing he had made for a high school in New Jersey to the Vassar competition. On a lark they changed the submission name, entered the drawing, and

275. The New-York Historical Society spurned the city's offer to disassemble City Hall and reassemble it on the society's property for its own uses, choosing instead to construct a new building to plans by York & Sawyer.

276. The reverential aura that stems from the cool classicism of the New-York Historical Society's reading room is mitigated by its ideal working conditions and the comfort of the furnishings.

won, which launched the firm on a long string of successful designs, many in a style dubbed "strong box" architecture.

Mayor Seth Low laid the cornerstone for the neoclassical building in 1903, but a year later construction came to a dead stop. The builder had learned that bedrock was 30 to 40 feet below the surface, which meant that caissons had to be sunk, and that meant that more money was required. As it was, the society had only set out to build the $400,000 central portion of the building, holding the flanking wings in abeyance until the full 200-by-100-foot lot was acquired and enough funds raised for the entire undertaking. Henry Dexter, who had consolidated news dealers into the American News Company, contributed $150,000 with the stipulation that the facade be pink granite. His gift was accepted and work proceeded.

The building was dedicated in 1906, but the central wing was not finished until 1908, when the great collection of Americana and New Yorkiana—the only library of its type in the city—opened its doors.

Memory

Straus Park, at the intersection of Broadway and West End Avenue at 106th Street
1915
BUILDER: Straus Memorial Committee
ARCHITECT: Evarts Tracy
SCULPTOR: Augustus Lukeman

The sinking of the *Titanic* on April 14, 1912, and the loss of 1,515 passengers and crew-members, sent shockwaves across the Atlantic. The impossible had happened, the unsinkable had sunk, a fact alone that staggered the imagination of even the least imaginative. When the truth was revealed that there had not been enough lifeboats even for some of the rich and famous, the *Titanic* would be remembered.

Throughout the sinking, the law of the sea and the pecking order of the day generally prevailed. The women and children traveling first-class, or those traveling with first-class passengers, were put into the lifeboats first. Mabel Bird, the maid to Ida Straus, was put into a lifeboat by her mistress, who then returned to her husband Isidor, the head of R. H. Macy & Co. The *Times* said that Isidor Straus, "ripe in years, with the consciousness of an honorable and useful career, . . . and for helpful work still undone," would not step into a lifeboat, or even try to save himself, until everyone else had been cared for. His wife, "obeying the impulse of long years of fidelity and that affection that unifies two souls, as calmly and resolutely

refusing to leave her husband. . . . 'Where you go, I shall go,' she said." With that, Ida and Isidor Straus went down together, hand in hand, on the *Titanic*.

Although more socially prominent names like Col. John Jacob Astor grabbed the headlines, the loss of Ida and Isidor Straus grabbed at the hearts and conscience of society. Andrew Carnegie said at the memorial service at Carnegie Hall that "time will not suffice to recount the various institutions founded, assisted, or supervised by them. Whenever a good cause languished, their sympathies were aroused, and both with head and heart they gave not only needed funds, but, what was more important and much more rare, they gave themselves to the work." On stage with Carnegie were the mayor of the City of New York, the president of the College of the City of New York, the president of the Chamber of Commerce of the State of New York, bishops, rabbis, the very leadership of society. The hall was filled to capacity, and hundreds were turned away.

By June 1912, a subscription was underway whose proceeds would turn the triangular plot of land at Broadway and 106th Street into a permanent memorial to the Strauses. The goal was to create a fountain and statue and to change the name from Bloomingdale Square to Straus Park. It was a propitious site. The Strauses had lived just around the corner on 105th Street between Broadway and West End Avenue in a three-story frame house whose porch and wisteria vines and lawns were reminiscent of the area when it was still the village of Bloomingdale.

The Straus Memorial Committee was chaired by Jacob Schiff. Serving with him were Isaac Seligman, Felix Warburg, and J. B. Greenhut, head of the Sixth Avenue department store. Even before the creation of the committee had been announced, these members had already raised about $10,000 from the likes of August Belmont II, Adolph Ochs, and Seth Low.

The committee held a competition in conjunction with the National Sculpture Society, who appointed Herbert Adams, Henry Bacon, and Karl Bitter as judges. The rules specified that the design should reflect the unostentatious and purposeful character of the Strauses, and represent an object of beauty without necessarily containing an allegorical expression of any particular theme or subject. The competitors were asked to landscape the park as part of the package, but anything monumental was undesirable because of the modest character of the Strauses, because it would reduce the available park space, and because an apartment house on 106th Street did not lend itself as a proper frame for anything rising high off the ground.

From 59 entries, the committee chose *Memory* by architect Evarts Tracy and sculptor Augustus Lukeman. It fitted the configuration of the plot and represented a "scheme of peaceful contemplation over a sheet of water, leaving it to the meditative public to muse over the sacrifice that the same element demanded of the *Titanic* disaster," said the jurors. Lukeman had been doing yeoman work, having already sculpted two pieces for the Brooklyn Museum under the aegis of McKim, Mead & White; *Manu, the Lawgiver* for the Appellate Division under James Brown Lord; and *Christopher Columbus* for Cass Gilbert's Custom House. He had studied with Daniel Chester French, and, to understand human form better, he had studied anatomy at Bellevue Hospital for two years.

For once there was no controversy over the appropriateness of the memorial or its site; however, the idea of changing the name from Bloomingdale Square to Straus Park created a small fuss. One letter to the *Times* said that "the entire region around there was known as Bloomingdale more than 150 years before the Revolution . . . [and] the present Broadway was called the Bloomingdale Road. . . . It is a beautiful and by far the most appropriate name for the precious little 'oasis,' which is the only souvenir left of the old Bloomingdale region. Let the proposed fountain be placed there by all means, and the grounds beautified. It will be a graceful reminder of the true-hearted man who lived nearby for many years. But let it be known as the Straus Memorial Fountain in 'Bloomingdale Square.'" Hopper Striker Mott, the neighborhood's historian, joined the cause in a conciliatory letter to Schiff, saying that "unfortunately the only geographic name in Manhattan that still bears the name Bloomingdale is the square." His idea was also to let the little park become Straus Park and to retain the open space surrounding it as Bloomingdale Square. Over the cry of these modest pleas, the Board of Aldermen approved the new name, and on April 15, 1915, almost three years to the day after the *Titanic* had gone down, Mayor John Purroy Mitchell accepted the statue on behalf of the city, with Seth Low and others looking on.

By the time *Memory* was in place, the Age of Elegance was beginning to slip into memory. Many of the period's greatest lights—Astor, White, Morgan, Hunt, McKim—were already dead. Taxes on inheritance and income were beginning to break up the great family fortunes. World War I was consuming the energies of the great nations just as it would consume a whole generation and create a lost one from what was left. And with the shipping lanes given over to holds full of war materiel instead of immigrants, the great source of cheap labor for the sweatshops and steel mills was shut off, as well as the seemingly endless stream of servants. It all conspires to make *Memory* a fitting end for those who created an elegant New York.

277. *Memory,* **the statue and fountain that was designed by architect Evarts Tracy and sculptor Augustus Lukeman to commemorate** *Titanic* **victims Ida and Isidor Straus, was intended to act as a place of contemplation. For elegant New York,** *Memory* **serves the same role.**

EVERY LAW NOT BASED ON **WISDOM** IS A MENACE TO THE STATE

Sources
Selected Bibliography
Acknowledgments
Index

The Michelangelo-like *Wisdom* is one of Frederic Ruckstill's two statues that flank the entrance to the Appellate Division Courthouse. Although the Bar Association acknowledged that there was an urgent need for municipal economy, architect Daniel Lord still convinced the power brokers that the arts ought to be incorporated in architecture.

Sources

CODE TO ABBREVIATIONS

Am Arch & Bldg News:
American Architecture and Building News
Arch: *Architecture*
Arch & Bldg: *Architecture and Building*
Arch & Builders: *Architecture and Builders*
Arch Rec: *Architectural Record*
JSAH: *Journal of the Society of
Architectural Historians*
NY Arch: *New York Architect*
NYT: *The New York Times*
Prog Arch: *Progressive Architecture*
RERec: *Real Estate Record and Guide*
Trib: *The New York Tribune*

(Reference titles below in italics indicate
entries in Bibliography)

1 / Corporate New York

Singer
NYT: F 22, '06; O 1, '06; Ag 30, '07; O 6, 8, '07;
N 10, '07; D 29, '07; F 4, '08; Mr 1, 7, '08; My 3, 10,
'08; Ag 7, '08; S 26, '09; Jl 16, '11; O 20, '12;
Ap 11, 47
Trib: F 22, '06; F 24, '06; Jl 7, '06
Am Arch & Bldg News: V 90, 1906
Arch Rec: V 10, O, '00; V 11, Ap, '02; V 22, S, '07
Prog Arch: V 48, S, '67
RERec: Jl 23, '98
Silver

Chamber of Commerce
NYT: F 7, '97; My 7, '97; F 16, '00; My 4, '00; D 16,
'00; Ja 9, '01; My 2, '01; N 9, '01; S 28, '02; N 12, '02
Trib: Ja 16, '01; N 14, '02
Arch Rec: V 13
Bishop

New York Stock Exchange
NYT: My 12, '95; O 19, '98; Ja 19, '99; Jl 21, '00; D 8,
'00; S 10, '01; Ap 19, '03
Trib: Ap 27, '01; My 2, '01; Jl 7, '01; Mr 30, '02; N 30,
'02

U.S. Trust
NYT: Ap 5, '96; Mr 25, '06; O 6, '07
Trib: Mr 24, '06; Jl 29, '06; D 28, '06
RERec: Ap 18, 96; Jn 8, 15, '01; Jn 7, '02

Trinity & U.S.
NYT: N 14, 23, '02; F 14, '03; My 1, '03; Ap 30, '04;
My 22, '04; D 18, '04; My 21, '05; My 27, '06; O 6,
'07; Mr 1, '08
Trib: N 24, '03
Arch & Bldg: V 37, 1907–8
RERec: Ja 2, '04

Morgan
NYT: N 10, '07; Jn 17, '10; Ja 1, '11; N 28, '11; Jl 7, '12;
Jl 27, '13
Arch Rec: V 15, F, '15
Allen

Woolworth
NYT: Jl 10, '10; N 13, '10; Ja 19, 20, 22, '11; Ap 20, '11;
My 7, 28, '11; Ag 2, '11; F 18, '12; Jn 30, '12; Jl 28,
'12; O 20, '12; Ap 25, '13; Mr 22, '14; Ap 10, '19
Arch & Bldg: V 45, 1913
Am Arch & Bldg News: Jl 10, '12
Arch Rec: V 33, F, '13
RERec: My 7, '10; Jn 11, '10; Ap 29, '11
Elmendorf (for a discussion of the building's
funding), *Nichols, Winkler*

2 / Political New York

Civic Center
NYT: Jl 21, '87; D 1, '87; Ja 29, 31, '88; My 22, '88;
Ja 22, '89; Ap 23, '89; Jl 11, '89; S 5, 19, '89; Jl 4,
23, '90; O 18, '90; Mr 26, '91; S 19, '91; F 19, 21, '92;
My 8, 9, '92; Ja 12, 19, 20, 26, '93; F 21, '93; Jl 19,
'93; S 2, '93; Ja 16, '94; Mr 28, '94; Ja 14, '95; O 14,
'94; My 4, '95; O 15, '95; D 4, '95; Ja 7, '96; F 18,
'96; F 20, '96; D 23, '96; Mr 21, '04
Trib: Jl 2, '03
Arch & Builders: V 6, 1904–5
Municipal Art Society, *Bulletin*: V 7, 1904

Engine Company 31
NYT: My 15, '95
RERec: N 24, '94
Arch Rec: V 27, Ap, '10
Fire Department, *Annual Reports*: '94, '95, '96
Board of Aldermen, *Proceedings*: Ag 21, '94

Hall of Records
NYT: Mr 21, '87; N 22, 25, '96; D 9, '96; Mr 27, '97;
Ap 3, '97; My 6, 30, '97; Jn 16, '97; N 27, '97; D 15,
17, '97; Mr 16, '98; D 15, '98; My 21, 26, '99; Jl 14,
15, '99; Ja 17, '00; Jl 20, '00; D 25, 26, '00; Ap 14, '01;
Jl 9, '01; S 12, 13, '01; N 15, '01; Mr 8, 21, '03; Jn 3,
'03; My 31, '05; Jn 24, '05; Ag 21, '06; D 16, '06;
Jn 17, '10
Trib: Ja 9, '01; Ag 29, '01; S 12, '01; Mr 6, '03
Arch & Builders: V 7, Ja, '07
Arch: Ja, '07
Municipal Art Society, *Bulletin*: No. 7, 1904

Custom House
NYT: F 1, 2, '87; O 5, 11, '88; N 2, '88; D 28, '88;
Ja 3, '92; Ap 8, 12, '92; Jn 8, '92; O 8, '92; Ja 13, '93;
F 9, '93; Mr 2, 8, '93; Ap 2, '93; My 13, '93; N 27,
'96; D 1, '96; F 13, 15, '98; F 3, '99; Mr 26, '99;
Ap 6, '99; My 3, 7, '99; Jn 23, '99; S 24, 26, '99;
O 25, '99; S 24, 26, '99; O 25, '99; N 2, 3, 4, '99;
F 11, '00; Jl 29, 31, '00; N 5, 8, 22, 23, '01; D 3, '01;
N 8, '03; N 23, '04; F 25, '05; Ja 14, '06; O 7, '06;
O 2, '07; Ja 9, '08; Mr 24, '08
RERec: Mr 7, '91
AIA Journal: V 2, 1914
Bishop, Richman

First Precinct
NYT: F 8, '84
RERec: Jn 13, '08
Am Arch & Bldg. News: V 93, F 12, '08; V 104,
S 24, '13
Police Commissioner, *Annual Reports*: 1907–8

Municipal Building
NYT: Jn 29, '02; Mr 6, '03; My 23, '03; Ap 29, '08;
My 3, '08; D 25, 29, '08; My 21, 27, '09; Jn 27, '09;

Jl 18, '09; D 21, '09; O 2, '10; F 16, '13; Ja 22, '14
Trib: Ja 17, '03; Mr 28, 30, '03
Stokes

3 / *Stanford White's Squares*

Madison Square Garden
Trib: Mr 22, '89; Ag 5, '89; Jn 10, 17, '90
Arch Rec: V 30, 1911
Am Arch & Bldg News: 100, 1911
Baldwin, DeKoven
Farragut
NYT: S 2, '80; O 5, '80; My 25, 26, '81
Trib: N 25, '80; My 26, '81
Tharp

Players
NYT: Ja 8, '88; Ap 29, '88; Ja 1, '89; Ja 7, '06
Baldwin, Frohman, Ruggles

Ascension
NYT: Jn 21, '78; S 27, '88; D 31, '88; Jn 12, '14
Arch Rec: V 13, 1903
Stewart, Brooklyn Museum, Upjohn

Washington Arch
NYT: My 7, '86; D 8, '87; Ja 12, '88; F 4, '88;
 Ap 13, '88; O 24, '88; N 9, '88; Ap 28, '89;
 My 4, 5, 13, '89; Jn 26, '89; S 6, '89; O 17,
 '89; N 2, '89; Ja 10, '90; F 11, '90; My 1, 28,
 31, '90; Mr 21, '91; Ap 30, '91; My 10, 20,
 '91; Mr 28, '92; Ap 6, '92; Jn 14, 17, '92;
 Mr 4, '93
Critic: Ap 27, '89; My 4, 11, 18, '89; Jn 1, '89
Am Arch & Bldg News: My 18, '89
Baldwin, Stewart

Judson Memorial
NYT: Jl 1, '90; F 7, '91; S 21, '91; O 31, '92; Ja 23, 27,
 30, '93
Baldwin, Stewart

Appellate
NYT: Mr 11, 12, '95; Jn 29, '95; Ag 6, '95; Ap 17, '96;
 My 22, '96; Jl 1, '96; F 17, '97; D 7, 21, 23, '97; Mr 5,
 '99; Jl 30, '99; D 21, 22, '99; Ja 3, 14, '00
Martin, Mowbray, Reed (Appellate)

Flatiron
NYT: Ap 13, '99; My 5, '99; N 27, '00; Mr 3, '01;
 Ja 23, '14
Trib: Mr 30, '01; Jl 19, '02
Arch Rec: V 12, O, '02
Arch & Builders: V 34, Ag, '02
Moore

Colony
NYT: D 5, 12, '97; F 26, '05; F 17, 18, '07; Ap 6, 17, '07;
 Ja 31, '08; S 18, '08; Jl 15, '10
Baldwin, Harriman

Prince George
NYT: Ap 2, 3, 4, '08; N 1, '47
Trib: My 19, '01; D 15, '01
Arch Rec: V 18, D, '05; V 101, Mr, '47
Arch & Builders: V 7, 1905–6
Mooney

4 / *The Murrays' Hill*

Waldorf-Astoria
NYT: O 19, '90; Mr 11, '91; Ja 1, '95; Jn 16, '96; S 4,
 '96; Ja 5, 31, '97; O 3, 16, '97; N 2, '97; O 10, '98;
 Ap 30, '99
Thirty-Fourth Street Midtown Association,
 Little Old New New York: Mr, '29
Murray Hill Covenant: F 15, 1847, Liber 485,
 Op 593
Hungerford, McCarthy

De Lamar
NYT: Ap 8, '04; D 2, '18; Jn 24, 25, '21; Jl 15, '22;
 D 16, '22; Jn 15, 16, '23
Am Arch & Bldg News: V 116, S 17, '19
Letter from Alice De Lamar to author, at Avery
 Library, Columbia University

Morgan
NYT: Ja 11, '00; F 28, '03; Ap 10, 29, '03; N 6, '03;
 S 24, '04; O 15, '04; N 23, '04; D 4, '08; My 4, '13
Allen, Moore (McKim), Mowbray

Altman
NYT: Ja 4, '89; Ja 13, '96; Mr 7, '00; Ag 4, '01; Ap 17,
 '02; Jl 9, '03; D 11, '04; Mr 4, 5, 7, '05; My 18, '05;
 Mr 25, '06; Ap 21, '06; O 16, '06; F 16, '09; Mr 4,
 '09; O 15, '09; D 7, '09; Ap 24, '10; O 5, '10; Jn 21,
 22, '11; Jl 17, '13; O 8, 15, '13; Jn 7, '14; Mr 18, '23
Arch: 1906
Behrman, Johnson, Tompkins

5 / *Vanderbilt's Grand Central Terminal*

Century Association
NYT: D 15, '89; F 11, '12
Gilder

New York Yacht Club
NYT: O 25, '96; Ja 30, '98; O 28, '98; D 15, '98;
 Ap 30, '99; D 9, '00; Ja 18, '01
Am Arch & Bldg News: V 66, D 30, '99; V 72,
 Ap 20, 27, '01
Arch Rec: V 10, Ap, '01
Parkinson

St. Bartholomew's
NYT: Jl 5, '90; O 26, '91; O 1, 23, '93; S 13, 14, 18, '99;
 O 27, '99; D 9, '00; Jn 6, 22, '02; Ap 18, 20, '14
Arch Rec: V 13, Jn, '03
Chorley, St. Bartholomew's

Home
NYT: Ja 25, '14
Arch: V 19, Ja 15, '09

Main Branch, NYPL
NYT: D 15, '85; D 1, '89; My 15, '92; Ag 24, '92;
 Mr 3, 14, 26, 29, '95; Ja 9, '96; Mr 25, 26, '96;
 My 20, 21, '96; Jn 9, 30, '96; My 24, '97; Jl 16, '97;
 Ag 5, 6, '97; N 12, '97; D 2, 5, '97; My 10, '00;
 D 30, '00; Ja 31, '01; O 1, '05; Ap 28, '07; O 21, 26,
 '08; Mr 27, '09; S 5, '09; My 2, '10; D 11, '10; My 24,
 28, '11
Am Arch: V 72
Arch Rec: V 12, N, '02
Antiques: V 109, My, '76
Lydenberg

Scribner's
NYT: My 25, '94; Mr 27, '97; My 13, '99; Jn 6, '05;
 F 18, '12; Mr 23, '13; My 18, '13
RERec: Ap 13, '12; Mr 9, 16, 23, '13
Evenson
Letter from Charles Scribner, Jr., to author, at
 Avery Library, Columbia University

Grand Central and Post Office
NYT: F 21, '92; Ja 22, '97; Ag 25, '97; F 5, '01; D 17,
 '04; Mr 7, '05; Ja 31, '09; N 5, '09; Mr 27, '10; Jl 10,
 '10; Ja 27, '11; Jn 16, '11; D 17, '11; My 7, '11; F 2, 9, '13;
 Jl 27, '13; Ja 25, '43
Trib: F 14, '03
RERec: Jl 5, '13
Am Arch & Bldg News: V 90, N 24, '06
Arch: V 13, 1906
*Droege, Fitch, Middleton, Nevins, New York
 Central*

6 / *The Times' Square*

Times Tower
NYT: Ag 4, '02; S 25, '02; N 23, '02; Jn 27, '03; N 24,
 29, '03; Ja 17, 19, 24, '04; Ap 9, 27, '04; N 6, 7, 15,
 '04; Ja 1, '05; My 14, '05; N 11, '06; N 11, '23
Trib: Ap 22, '02; S 25, '02
RERec: Mr 15, '94; F 1, '98; Ap 27, '98; My 7, '98;
 Jl 4, '03
Am Arch & Bldg News: 1905
Berger, Talese

Lyceum
NYT: F 6, '02; O 17, '02; S 27, '03; N 1, '03
RERec: F 22, '02
Arch: V 24, 1907
DeKoven, Frohman

Lyric
NYT: O 6, 11, 13, '03; Mr 14, '09; D 12, '37
RERec: My 31, '02; O 13, '03
DeKoven, Stagg

Belasco
NYT: N 19, '05; Jn 12, 23, 30, '06; Ap 29, '07; S 29, '07
Arch & Builders: V 40, N, '07
Winter

Algonquin
Trib: N 26, '01; N 23, '02; N 1, '03
RERec: Ja 4, '02; Mr 1, '02
Case, Harriman, Mayer

Knickerbocker
NYT: O 19, '92; D 21, '93; Jl 29, '94; N 28, '94; S 5,
'05; F 4, 18, '06; Ag 12, '06; O 21, 24, 28, '06; O 9,
'07; D 15, '08; S 17, 26, '09; D 16, '09; Ja 9, '10; Ja 8,
'11; Jl 14, '12; F 2, '13; N 12, '13
Arch Rec: V 24

7 / The Vanderbilts' Fifth Avenue

The Vanderbilt Mansions
NYT: Jl 14, '80; Ag 25, '81; Ja 16, '82; Mr 8, '82;
Jn 11, '82; O 3, '82; D 9, '85; Ja 10, '12; Ap 13, '52
Am Arch & Bldg News: V 9, My 21, '81
Reed (Golden City), *Tully, Van Pelt*

Villard
NYT: D 19, '83; My 4, '84; S 6, '84; F 3, '85; Ja 12,
'86; N 13, '09
Conveyances: Sec 5, Block 1286
Letter from Homes & Adams, Lawyers, to
MMW, Jn 17, '84, NYHS
Holbrook, Josephson

University Club
NYT: Ja 1, '80; Mr 15, '91; Ag 2, '91; S 6, '91; Jn 1, 2,
4, '93; N 27, '94; Mr 17, 24, '95
RERec: Ap 9, '98; Jl 23, '98
Am Arch & Bldg News: V 65, Ag 26, '99
Alexander, Moore (McKim), *Mowbray*

Stokes
NYT: Ja 4, '95; Ja 12, 15, 18, '23; My 20, '26
RERec: Jn 13, '98; Jl 9, '98; O 11, '02
Letter from Bishop Moore to author, at Avery
Library, Columbia University
Kirkland

St. Regis
NYT: My 19, '83; N 10, '92; Ja 16, 19, '96; Jl 19, '99;
D 30, '00; My 12, '04; S 4, '04; O 16, '04; N 6, '04;
F 4, '06; O 11, '08; N 1, '08; O 16, '11; D 12, 17, '11
Trib: My 13, '04; S 4, '04
Arch: Jn, '04

Gotham
NYT: Ap 19, '02; O 2, 4, '05; Jn 23, '07; Jl 3, 5, '08;
Ag 8, '08
Trib: Ap 19, '02
RERec: My 4, '01; Jn 28, '02
Arch & Builders: N, '05

Plant
NYT: N 29, '00; Jn 8, '01; Jl 11, '02; S 7, '02; D 16, '02;
My 2, '03; Jn 3, 25, '03; Ap 6, 8, '04; My 1, 27, '04;
Mr 30, '05; Ja 21, '07; F 7, '08; S 13, '08; Ja 10, '09;
Mr 14, '09; Ap 4, '09; N 5, 27, '09; D 31, '09; Jl 15,
18, '10; O 30, '10; Ja 29, '11; Mr 10, '11; My 7, '11; S 3,

'11; D 12, 17, '11; N 3, '12; F 2, '13; Mr 23, '13; S 14,
'13; O 4, 8, '16; N 5, '18
RERec: Ja 13, '00; O 7, '16

8 / The Plaza's Plaza

Carnegie Hall
NYT: D 15, '89; My 14, '90; F 22, '91; Ap 24, 27, 28,
29, '91; My 3, 6, 7, 8, 10, '91

American Fine Arts Society
NYT: Ja 4, '90; Jl 27, '90; O 15, '90; D 21, '90; D 28,
'90; D 31, '92
Critic: Jn 22, '89

Columbus Monument
NYT: Mr 23, '88; Jl 9, 11, 20, '90; My 3, '91; Jn 13,
'91; Ag 30, '91; My 17, '92; Mr 20, '92; My 24, '92;
Ap 26, '92; Jn 2, 13, '92; Jl 5, 26, '92; S 2, 3, 5, 6,
17, '92; O 10, 13, '92; N 28, '92; D 10, '92; Mr 31, '27

Sherman
NYT: Ap 30, '91; My 1, '01; Jl 31, '01; Mr 18, 25, '02;
My 31, '03; Jn 1, '03
Arch Rec: XII, N, '02
Bishop, Tharp

Plaza
NYT: S 30, '90; Ap 17, '99; My 1, 2, '02; Ag 16, '05;
S 12, 29, '07; O 1, '07; Ja 20, '08; Mr 1, '08; Ap 5,
'08; Jl 19, 26, '08; Jl 25, '09; My 22, '10
Brown

Alwyn Court
NYT: Ja 10, '09; Jn 11, '09; S 25, '10
RERec: N 6, '09

Maine Memorial
NYT: Ap 10, '04; Ap 4, '08; F 4, '10; Jl 9, '10; Jn 29,
'11; Jl 25, 27, 28, '11; Ag 3, 6, '11; N 9, '11; F 16, '12;
Jl 15, '12; My 25, 30, 31, '13; O 4, '14
Trib: F 21, '98; Mr 24, '98; F 16, '12
Arch & Bldg: V 45
Swanberg (Hearst)

Abundance
NYT: Mr 25, '02; N 14, '11; N 19, '12; D 22, '12; Ja 18,
21, 26, '13
Am Arch & Bldg News: F 2, '01
Dennis, Swanberg (Pulitzer)

9 / The Astors' Fifth Avenue

Astor
NYT: D 31, '92; Ja 23, 24, '94; Ap 6, '94; Ja 28, '96;
F 4, 9, '96; N 22, '96; O 15, '02; N 29, '02; O 15, '02;
N 29, '02; Ja 7, '06; S 6, '08; Ja 14, '09; Jn 17, '09;
Mr 4, '10
Trib: O 29, '93
Critic: Jl 8, '93
RERec: Ag 27, '91; Ja 14, '93
JSAH: V 11, My, '52
Arch Rec: V 27, Jn, '10; V 59, Ja, '26

Metropolitan
NYT: F 28, '91; Mr 8, 10, 15, '91; Ap 5, '91; My 20, 31,
'91; Ag 1, 2, 9, 16, 23, '91; S 20, '91; O 11, '91; F 12,
'92; F 25, 27, 28, '94; Mr 2, 22, '94; Ja 1, '95; F 6, 13,
'98
NYHerald: F 11, '92

Fabbri
NYT: Jl 4, '83; N 26, '91; S 27, '96; O 25, '96; D 19,
'09; N 10, '10; D 12, '11; S 30, '13; D 14, '13; Ap 25,
43; D 19, '54; O 2, '55
Trib: F 19, '98
Arch Rev: V 6, No. 2
RERec: Jl 23, '98; Jn 28, '99; O 8, '00
Am Arch & Bldg: Jn 2, '94

Schiefflin
NYT: F 6, '91; O 10, '97; Mr 4, '24; Ag 19, 48; My 1,
'55
RERec: Mr 7, '91; Jl 15, '91
Am Arch & Bldg News: F 23, '01

Studio Building
NYT: F 10, '07; Ap 25, '07; Jl 25, '09
RERec: 1904, 1905
Arch Rec: V 24, Jl, '08

Verona
NYT: O 2, '04; D 14, '13
RERec: N 6, '09
Arch Rec: V 24

Colony
NYT: S 18, '14; Ag 8, '15; D 12, '15
RERec: N 17, '15
Arch: V 33, 1916
Harriman

10 / James Lenox's Hill

Lenox
NYT: O 16, '11; My 29, '12; Jn 20, 21, '12; N 9, '13
Arch Rec: V 59, Ja, '26
Lenox Library

Hunt
NYT: Ag 1, 9, '95; F 15, '96; My 26, '96; Jn 12, '98;
O 23, '98; N 1, '98

Waldo
NYT: My 29, '09; D 24, '09; F 18, '12; My 28, 29, '14;
N 29, '14
Trib: My 19, '06
Arch Rec: V 7, Ap–Jn, '98

Fletcher
NYT: O 25, '05; Ja 28, '12; Ap 29, '17
RERec: N 13, '97
Metropolitan Museum of Art, *Bulletin*: N, '17
Arts & Decoration: S, '18
Craftsman: V 22, Jn, '12

Pulitzer
NYT: Ja 10, '00; Ap 13, '00
Seitz, Swanberg (Pulitzer)

Harkness
NYT: Ja 30, '40; O 2, '47; Jn 7, '50
Trib: Mr 1, '02
RERec: Ap 6, '06; Jn 1, '06
NY Arch: V 5, 1911

Pyne
NYT: S 18, '10; F 19, '11; Ap 23, '11; Jl 2, '11; Ag 23, '29
RERec: O 23, '09

Duke
NYT: N 30, '04; O 25, '05; S 3, '05; Ja 10, '09; Ag 29, '09; Ja 28, '12; O 11, '25; Ap 14, '62
RERec: F 20, '09; O 16, '09
Am Arch & Bldg News: V 107, Ap 7, '15
Arch: V 27, 1913

Frick
NYT: My 6, '99; Ap 16, '05; Jl 9, '05; Ja 6, 13, '06; D 13, 17, 18, 20, '06; Jn 2, '07; Ap 2, '11; D 5, '11; F 19, '12; My 26, 29, '12; Jn 20, 21, '12; Ja 5, '13; S 13, '13; D 7, '13; N 29, '14
Arch Rec: V 32, O, '12
Harvey, Bemelmans

11 / Carnegie's Hill

Metropolitan Museum
NYT: D 18, '88; O 24, '99; D 22, 23, 28, '02
Trib: Jn 17, '84; D 19, '88; Ja 13, '96; D 23, '02
Arch Rev: V 6
Metropolitan Museum of Art, *Annual Report:* 1895, 1899, 1901, 1902
Dennis

Carnegie
NYT: My 31, '96; D 3, '98; Ap 7, '99; My 27, '99; Jl 27, '99; O 14, '99; Ap 28, '01; F 21, '04; D 28, '05; Ag 12, '19; Jn 25, 46
Trib: D 2, 3, '98; Jl 4, '99; Ap 22, '01; My 31, '01; Jl 5, '01
RERec: D 17, '98
Am Arch: V 81, Jl 18, '03
Arch: 1903
Arch Rec: V 13, Ja, '03
Winkler

Burden/Hammond
NYT: My 7, '95; Jn 2, 7, '95; Mr 26, '99; Ap 5, 6, '99; F 28, '06; O 19, '06
Trib: O 21, '98; Ja 10, '01; N 17, '01; D 18, '02; Jl 13, '05; F 28, '06; Mr 23, '06
RERec: F 16, '01; N 23, '01; Ja 4, '02; Ap 5, '02
Antiques: V 110, Ag, '76
Conversation with John Hammond, O 27, '82, and *Hammond*

Yorkville Public Library
NYT: Jl 6, '88; Jn 12, 27, '97; Mr 16, '01; Jl 21, '01; O 17, '01; F 21, '02; Mr 2, 19, '02; Jn 2, '02; Jn 18, '06
Trib: Jn 2, '02

RERec: Ap 27, '01; My 11, '01
Municipal Art Society, *Bulletin:* No. 7

Warburg
NYT: O 21, '37; S 15, 23, '58
RERec: F 16, '07; Ag 3, '07
Birmingham, Warburg

998 Fifth
NYT: Mr 27, '10; S 25, '10; S 21, '13; O 29, '13; S 30, '58; Ja 4, '68
RERec: Jl 17, '09; Mr 26, '10; Ap 30, '10; Jl 30, '10; D 10, '10
NY Arch: Mr, '12

Kahn
NYT: Ag 7, '10; F 3, '12; S 26, '12; N 23, '12; Ag 13, '13; D 7, '13; Jl 9, '14
RERec: Jn, '13
Arch Rec: V 46, Ag, '19

12 / The Speculative West Side

Majestic
NYT: S 8, '94; D 28, '94; Ap 5, '11
Trib: D 27, '94
RERec: F 14, 21, '91; Mr 7, '91; Ap 4, '91; My 9, '91

Dakota
NYT: Ap 17, '81; O 17, '82; Mr 6, '93; Jn 7, '14
Am Arch & Bldg News: V 17, Jn 6, '85
Real Estate Record Association

True
NYT: S 18, '90; D 27, '91; Mr 10, '95; S 8, '95; S 28, '99
RERec: F 5, '98; F 7, '99; Ap 22, '99
True

Villa Julia
NYT: S 30, '02; Jn 30, '07; D 18, '07; Jn 4, '14; N 3, 15, 22, '15
Trib: S 30, '02
RERec: Jl 8, '99; N 11, '99; Mr 24, '00; Ag 4, '00
Arch Rec: V 15, Ja, '04
Hirsch, Viele

Ansonia
NYT: Mr 1, '86; Ap 13, '88; S 23, '04; My 1, '10
Trib: Ag 17, '02; F 14, '03
Letters from W.E.D. Stokes, Jr., to New York City Landmarks Preservation Commission, Ja 25, '71; F 9, '71; My 10, '80

St. Urban
Trib: Ag 23, '06
RERec: Jl 11, '03; N 7, 14, '03; Ja 9, '04; Mr 12, '04; Ag 20, '04; Jn 10, 24, '05; Mr 3, '06
St. Urban Prospectus, NYPL

Apthorp
NYT: Ap 21, '03; D 10, '05; S 25, '10
Trib: Ap 21, '03; Ja 21, '06
RERec: Jl 4, '08

Strathmore
NYT: S 11, '86; Ja 8, '88; Ag 30, '03; D 31, '05; F 8, '06; F 2, '08; S 19, '09; N 11, '09; Jn 23, '12; Ag 17, '13; F 15, '14; Jn 7, '14
RERec: Mr 28, '08; Jn 20, 27, '08
Hesselgram

13 / Seth Low's West Side

National Academy
NYT: Jn 22, '96; Jn 2, '99; S 18, '10
RERec: Mr 4, '99
Arch Rev: V 5, 1898

Grant Memorial
NYT: Jl 29, '85; Ag 21, '85; S 13, '85; N 10, '85; Mr 10, 24, '86; Ap 1, '86; D 3, 11, 26, '87; Ap 7, 9, '87; D 9, '87; Ja 27, '88; F 5, '88; Mr 16, '88; My 6, '88; Mr 5, 29, '89; F 21, '90; Mr 28, '90; Ap 1, '90; S 3, 6, 10, 11, 12, '90; My 5, '91; O 3, 30, '91; Ap 23, '92; Jn 1, 2, 9, '92; S 1, '95; Ag 11, '96; S 13, '96; F 12, 14, 21, '97; Mr 15, 22, '97; Ap 15, 24, 25, 26, 28, 29, '97; My 2, '97; S 10, '21

Columbia
NYT: Jl 8, '90; Ja 14, 21, '92; F 18, '92; My 22, '92; N 12, '92; Ja 15, '93; O 31, '94; Ja 8, '95; My 7, 12, '95; My 3, '96; Jn 5, '97; S 18, 19, '16
Trib: D 17, '91; F 27, '92; Ap 19, '96
Arch Rec: V 9, '99; V 27, '10
Arch & Bldrs: V 33, 1900–1901
Michigan Architect & Engineer: V 19, S, 41
JSAH: V 36, My, '77
Moore (McKim), *Ware & Olmsted*

Alma Mater
NYT: Jn 24, '97; S 24, '03; D 5, '12
Trib: S 22, '03
Richman

Shearith Israel
NYT: O 29, '93; N 1, '93; Ja 11, '95
Postal, Wischnitzer

Soldiers' and Sailors'
NYT: Jn 8, 9, '87; F 15, '88; D 14, '88; Mr 21, 24, '95; N 3, '95; D 11, 27, '95; Jn 11, '96; Jl 18, 19, 31, '97; O 2, 17, 20, '97; N 13, 24, 25, '97; D 15, 23, 29, '97; O 6, '99; N 1, '99; Ja 27, '00; Ap 1, '00; S 8, '00; My 31, '02; Mr 5, '09

New-York Historical
NYT: Ja 8, '90; Mr 11, '99; N 24, '00; D 6, '00; Jn 4, '02; N 21, '06; Ag 16, '08
Trib: O 2, 6, '01; S 13, '02; N 6, '02; My 17, '03; N 2, '04; N 21, '06
Arch Rec: V 16, 1909
AIA Journal: V 16, N, D, '51

Memory
NYT: Ap 16, 19, 20, 24, '12; My 13, 19, 26, '12; Jn 23, 30, '12; Jl 4, '12; Mr 21, '13; Ap 14, 16, '15
Am Arch & Bldg News: V 129, Ap 5, '26
Arch Rec: V 35, My, '14

Selected Bibliography

Alexander, James W. *A History of the University Club of New York*. New York: Charles Scribner's Sons, 1915.

Allen, Frederick Lewis. *The Great Pierpont Morgan*. New York: Harper & Brothers, 1949.

Alpern, Andrew. *Apartments for the Affluent*. New York: McGraw Hill Book Company, 1975.

Amory, Cleveland. *Who Killed Society?* New York: Harper & Brothers, 1960.

Andrews, Wayne. *Architecture and Americans: A Social History of American Architecture*. New York: Harper & Brothers, 1955.

Architectural League of New York City. *Catalog of the Twenty-third Annual Exhibition*. New York, 1908.

Art Students' League. *Catalog*. New York, 1979.

Ashton, Dore. *New York*. New York: Holt, Rinehart & Winston, 1972.

Baldwin, Charles C. *Stanford White*. New York: Dodd, Mead, 1931. Reprinted, New York: DaCapo Press, 1976.

Ballard, Robert F. *Directory of Manhattan Office Buildings*. New York: McGraw Hill Book Company, 1978.

Behrman, S. N. *Duveen*. Boston: Little, Brown & Company, 1972.

Bemelmans, Ludwig. *To the One I Love the Best*. New York: Viking Press, 1955.

Berger, Meyer. *The Story of The New York Times*. New York: Simon & Schuster, 1951.

Birmingham, Stephen. *Our Crowd: The Great Jewish Families in New York*. New York: Harper & Row, 1967.

Bishop, Joseph Bucklin. *A Chronicle of One Hundred & Fifty Years: The Chamber of Commerce of the State of New York*. New York: Charles Scribner's Sons, 1918.

Brooklyn Museum. *The American Renaissance, 1876–1917*. New York: Pantheon Books, 1979.

Brown, Eve. *The Plaza: Its Life and Times*. New York: Meredith Press, 1967.

Brown, Henry Collins. *In the Golden Nineties*. Hastings-on-Hudson: Valentine's Press, 1928.

Case, Frank. *Tales of a Wayward Inn*. New York: Frederick A. Stokes, 1938.

Chambers, Julius. *The Book of New York*. New York: The Book of New York Company, 1912.

Chorley, E. Clowes. *The Centennial History of St. Bartholomew's Church*. New York: St. Bartholomew's, 1935.

Churchill, Allen. *The Upper Crust: An Informal History of New York's Highest Society*. Englewood Cliffs: Prentice Hall, 1970.

DeKoven, Mrs. Reginald. *A Musician and His Wife*. New York: Harper & Brothers, 1926.

Dennis, James M. *Karl Bitter: Architectural Sculptor*. Madison: University of Wisconsin, 1967.

Droege, John A. *Passenger Terminals and Transportation*. New York: McGraw Hill Book Company, 1916.

Ellis, Edward Robb. *The Epic of New York City*. New York: Coward-McCann, 1966.

Elmendorf, Robert Holmes. *Evolution of Commercial Banking in New York City*. New York: Irving Trust, privately printed, 1951.

Evenson, Norma. *Paris: A Century of Change*. New Haven: Yale University Press, 1979.

Fitch, James Marston, and Waite, Diana S. *Grand Central Terminal and Rockefeller Center: A Historical–Critical Estimate of Their Significance*. New York: New York State Parks & Recreation Division for Historic Preservation, 1974.

Frohman, Daniel. *Daniel Frohman Presents: An Autobiography*. New York: Kendall & Sharp, 1935.

Gilder, Rodman, ed. *The Century: 1847–1946*. New York: The Century Association, 1947.

Goldberger, Paul. *The City Observed: A Guide to the Architecture of Manhattan*. New York: Vintage Books, 1979.

Goldstone, Harmon W., and Dalrymple, Martha. *History Preserved: A Guide to New York City Landmarks and Historic Districts*. New York: Simon & Schuster, 1974.

Hammond, John, with Townsend, Irving. *John Hammond on Record: An Autobiography*. New York: Penguin, 1977.

Harriman, Margaret Case. *Blessed Are the Debonair*. New York: Rinehart & Co., 1956.

Harriman, Mrs. J. Borden. *From Pianofortes to Politics*. New York: Henry Holt & Co., 1923.

Harvey, George. *Henry Clay Frick: The Man*. New York: Charles Scribner's Sons, 1928.

Henderson, Mary C. *The City and the Theatre, New York Playhouses from Bowling Green to Times Square*. Clifton, N.J.: James T. White & Co., 1973.

Hesselgren Publishing Company. *Apartment Houses of the Metropolis*. New York: 1909.

Hirsch, Mark D. *William C. Whitney, Modern Warwick*. New York: Dodd, Mead & Co., 1948.

Holbrook, Stewart H. *The Age of Moguls*. Garden City: Doubleday & Co., 1953.

Hoyt, Edwin P. *The Goulds: A Social History*. New York: Weybright & Talley, 1969.

Hungerford, Edward. *The Story of the Waldorf-Astoria*. New York: G. P. Putnam's Sons, 1925.

Johnson, E.W. *The Future of Murray Hill*. New York: E.W. Johnson, 1900.

Josephson, Matthew. *The Robber Barons: The Great American Capitalists*. New York: Harcourt, Brace & Co., 1934.

Kavaler, Lucy. *The Astors: A Family Chronicle of Pomp and Power*. New York: Dodd, Mead & Co., 1966.

Kidney, Walter C. *The Architecture of Choice: Eclecticism in America*. New York: George Braziller, 1974.

King, Moses. *Handbook of New York City*. New York: Moses King, 1892.

———. *King's Views of New York*. New York: Moses King, 1909.

———. *Notable New Yorkers, 1896–1899*. New York: Moses King, 1899.

Kirkland, Edward Chase. *Industry Comes of Age*. New York: Rinehart & Winston, 1961.

Kobbe, Gustav. *New York and Its Environs*. New York: Harper & Brothers, 1891.

Kouwenhoven, John A. *The Columbia Historical Portrait of New York*. Garden City: Doubleday & Co., 1953.

Lederer, Joseph. *All Around the Town: A Walking Tour to Outdoor Sculpture in New York City*. New York: Charles Scribner's Sons, 1975.

Lenox Library. *Annual Reports of the Trustees*. Albany: Weed, Parsons & Co., 1870–1878.

Lockwood, Charles. *Manhattan Moves Uptown*. New York: Houghton, Mifflin Company, 1976.

Lydenberg, Harry Miller. *History of the New York Public Library: Astor, Lenox and Tilden Foundations*. New York: New York Public Library, 1923.

Lynes, Russell. *The Art-Makers of Nineteenth-Century America*. New York: Atheneum, 1970.

McCarthy, James Remington. *Peacock Alley*. New York: Harper & Brothers, 1931.

McFadden, Elizabeth. *The Glitter and the Gold*. New York: The Dial Press, 1971.

McKim, Mead & White. *A Monograph on the Works of McKim, Mead & White*. New York: Architectural Book Publishing Company, 1915.

Marcuse, Maxwell F. *This Was New York*. New York: Carlton Press, 1965.

Marshall, David. *Grand Central*. New York: McGraw-Hill Book Company, 1946.

Martin, George. *Causes and Conflicts: The Centennial History of the Association of the Bar of the City of New York*. Boston: Houghton Mifflin Co., 1970.

Matz, Mary Jane. *The Many Lives of Otto Kahn*. New York: Macmillan Company, 1963.

Mayer, Grace. *Once Upon A City*. New York: Macmillan Company, 1957.

Metropolitan Museum of Art. *Annual Reports*. New York, various years.

Middleton, William D. *Grand Central Terminal, the World's Greatest Railroad Terminal*. San Marino: Golden West Books, 1977.

Mooney, Michael MacDonald. *Evelyn Nesbit and Stanford White: Love and Death in the Gilded Age*. New York: William Morrow & Co., 1976.

Moore, Charles. *Daniel Burnham: Architect, Planner of Cities*. Boston and New York: Houghton Mifflin Company, 1921.

———. *The Life and Times of Charles F. McKim*. New York: Houghton Mifflin Company, 1929.

Morris, Lloyd. *Incredible New York*. New York: Random House, 1951.

Mowbray, H. Siddons, and Sherwood, Herbert F., ed. *H. Siddons Mowbray, Mural Painter*. New York: privately printed, 1928.

Nevins, Deborah, and Stern, Robert A. M. *The Architect's Eye*. New York: Pantheon, 1979.

New York Central Railroad. *The Gateway to A Continent*. New York, 1938(?).

Nichols, John P. *Skyline Queen and the Merchant Prince*. New York: Trident Press, 1973.

O'Connor, Harvey. *The Astors*. New York: Alfred A. Knopf, 1941.

Parkinson, John, Jr. *The History of The New York Yacht Club*. New York: The New York Yacht Club, 1975.

Percy, Townsend. *Appleton's Dictionary of New York*. New York: D. Appleton & Co., 1879.

Platt, Frederick. *America's Gilded Age: Its Architecture and Decoration*. Cranbury, N. J.: A. S. Barnes & Co., 1976.

Postal, Bernard. *American Jewish Landmarks*. New York: Fleet Press, 1977.

Real Estate Record Association. *A History of Real Estate, Building and Architecture in New York City During the Last Quarter Century.* New York, 1898.

Reed, Henry Hope, Jr. *The Golden City.* New York: Norton & Company, 1971.

———. *Supreme Court, Appellate Division, First Department Courthouse: History and Guide.* New York: New York State Bar Association and Municipal Art Society, 1976.

Richman, Michael. *Daniel Chester French: An American Sculptor.* New York: Metropolitan Museum of Art, 1976.

Rider, Fremont. *Rider's Guide to New York City.* New York: Macmillan, 1924.

Roper, Laura Wood. *FLO: A Biography of Frederick Law Olmsted.* Baltimore: Johns Hopkins University Press, 1973.

Ruggles, Eleanor. *Prince of Players: Edwin Booth.* New York: Norton & Company, 1953.

St. Bartholomew's Church. *Architectural and Decorative Features of St. Bartholomew's Church.* New York: The Parish, 1949.

Seitz, Donald D. *Joseph Pulitzer: His Life and Letters.* New York: Simon & Schuster, 1924.

Silver, Nathan. *Lost New York.* New York: Houghton Mifflin Company, 1967.

Smith, Arthur D. Howden. *John Jacob Astor: Landlord of New York.* New York: Blue Ribbon Books, 1929.

Social Register Association. *New York Social Register.* New York, various years.

Stagg, Jerry. *The Brothers Shubert.* New York: Random House, 1969.

Stewart, William Rhinelander. *Grace Church and Old New York.* New York: E. P. Dutton & Co., 1924.

Still, Bayrd. *Mirror for Gotham: New York As Seen by Contemporaries.* New York: New York University Press, 1956.

Stokes, I. N. Phelps. *The Iconography of Manhattan Island.* New York: Robert H. Dodd, 1915.

Swanberg. W. A. *Citizen Hearst: A Biography of William Randolph Hearst.* New York: Charles Scribner's Sons, 1961.

———. *Pulitzer.* New York: Charles Scribner's Sons, 1967.

Talese, Gay. *The Kingdom and the Power.* New York: New American Library, 1969.

Tauranac, John. *Essential New York.* New York: Holt, Rinehart & Winston, 1979.

Tharp, Louise Hall. *Saint-Gaudens and the Gilded Era.* Boston: Little, Brown & Co., 1969.

Thomas, Dana L. *Lords of the Land.* New York: G. P. Putnam's Sons, 1977.

Tomkins, Calvin. *Merchants and Masterpieces: The Story of the Metropolitan Museum of Art.* New York: E. P. Dutton, 1970.

True, Clarence. *Riverside Drive.* New York: Press of UN2 & Co., 1899.

Tully, Andrew. *Era of Elegance.* New York: Funk & Wagnalls, 1947.

Upjohn, Everard M. *Richard Upjohn: Architect and Churchman.* New York: Columbia University Press, 1939.

Vail, R. W. G. *Knickerbocker Birthday: A Sesquicentennial History of the New-York Historical Society.* New York: New-York Historical Society, 1954.

Van Pelt, John Vredenburgh. *A Monograph on the William K. Vanderbilt House: Richard Morris Hunt, Architect.* New York: Van Pelt, 1925.

Viele, Egbert. *The West End Plateau of the City of New York.* New York: Viele, 1879.

Warburg, Edward. M. M. *As I Recall: Some Memoirs.* New York: privately printed, 1978.

Ware, William R., and Olmsted, Frederick Law. *Report of Ware and Olmsted on the Occupation of the New Site.* New York: Columbia University, 1893.

Wecter, Dixon. *The Saga of American Society.* New York: Charles Scribner's Sons, 1937.

White, Norval, and Willensky, Elliot. *AIA Guide to New York City.* New York: Macmillan Company, revised, 1978.

Who's Who in New York City and State. *Who's Who in New York.* New York: Who's Who, 1908, 1914.

Winkler, John F. *Five and Ten: The Fabulous Life of F. W. Woolworth.* New York: Robert M. McBride & Co., 1940.

———. *Incredible Carnegie: The Life of Andrew Carnegie.* New York: Vanguard Press, 1931.

Winter, William. *The Life of David Belasco.* New York: Moffat, Yard & Co., 1918.

Wischnitzer, Rachel. *Synagogue Architecture in the United States.* New York: The Jewish Publication Society of America, 1955.

Works Progress Administration. *New York City Guide.* New York: Guilds' Committee for Federal Writers' Publications, Inc., 1939.

Acknowledgments

We, the authors, are indebted to countless institutions and individuals and wish to acknowledge their contributions with thanks. First among the institutions is Columbia University, without whose libraries—especially Avery and its wonderful catalog and collection—this book could not have been written. The second great source—and another treasure—is the Main Branch of the New York Public Library. The third, a New Yorkophile's paradise regained, is the Print Department of the Museum of the City of New York. And the fourth is the New-York Historical Society. The lion's share of the floorplans and elevations used in this book comes from Avery Library, which not only furnished the material but a copy room as well; all but one of the McKim, Mead & White plans were supplied by Michael George; and the New-York Historical Society provided the elevation of the Stokes house.

Among the individuals who have contributed directly to this book are our friends Michael George, Elliot Willensky, Steve Miller, Sarah Zarmati and Christopher Gray, to whom we owe thanks for lots more than some of the stuff of this book; Joan Gers and Saul Katz, who provided unflagging encouragement; our editor Walton Rawls, who has guided the project gracefully, and Jim Wageman, who art directed with equal grace; the Right Reverend Paul Moore, Jr., Alice De Lamar, and Charles Scribner, Jr., who wrote thoughtful letters recounting childhood memories; Edward M. M. Warburg and John Hammond, who shared their reminiscences, and Mrs. Stuart C. Welch (née Edith Gilbert), from whom we learned that her grandfather's full, unabbreviated name is Charles Pierrepont Henry Gilbert. Among the many people who gladly opened their homes are Joan K. Davidson, Mary and Anthony Smith, Arthur Cantor, Emily Kimbrough, Doris Bry, Noah Caplan, and Philip Stehr. And we especially want to thank Betsy Kittredge for things too numerous to mention.

Institutions and individuals to whom we are indebted include Scope Associates, William Catherwood of the Lotos Club, New York University's Institute of Fine Arts, the Cooper-Hewitt Museum, Fran Friedman and Howard Rubenstein representing the Helmsley Palace Hotel, Joe Famolare of the Famolare Shoe Salon, Pam Paterson of the New York City Commission for the United Nations and Consular Corps, Consul General Kazmierera Cias, Consul Waldermar Lipka-Chudzik, Vice Consul Leszek Lampart, and Mr. Kondratowicz of the Consulate General of the Polish People's Republic, Cartier, the Commonwealth Fund, Margot Bloom and Joan Hartman of the Jewish Museum, Keith Greenberg of the Johnson O'Connor foundation, Beatrice Wolfe of the Center for Inter-American Relations, Charles Scribner III of Scribner's, the Convent of the Sacred Heart, the Church of the Ascension, Congregation Shearith Israel, the Century Association, the University Club, the New York Yacht Club, Francis Mason and Ronnie Boriskin of the Morgan Library, the Prince George Hotel, Andrew Anspach of the Algonquin Hotel, the St. Regis Hotel, Suzi Forbes of the Plaza Hotel, Carnegie Hall, Deborah Gardner of the New York Stock Exchange, Gerald Schoenfeld and Brooks McNamara of the Shubert Organization, Philippe de Montebello of the Metropolitan Museum of Art, Terence Murphy of the New York Public Library, Judith Leynse and Marion E. Jemmott of Columbia University, the Chamber of Commerce of the State of New York, the management of the Woolworth Building, Joe Lucchi, clerk of the court at the Appellate Division of the New York State Supreme Court, Susan Gilbert and Donna Evans of Metro-North, Mary Alice Kennedy and Edith Sackell of the New-York Historical Society, the superintendent at the Hall of Records/Surrogates Court, and the National Park Service at the General Grant National Memorial.

We are sure that there are people who have shown us kindness and generosity during the creation of this book whose names, for one reason or another, have been overlooked.

To all, our thanks.

Index